Practice *Pla*

Arthur E. Jong...

Practice*Planners*®

Homework Planners feature dozens of behaviorally based, ready-to-use assignments that are designed for use between sessions, as well as a disk or CD-ROM (Microsoft Word) containing all of the assignments—allowing you to customize them to suit your unique client needs.

- ❏ Brief Couples Therapy Homework Planner ....978-0-471-29511-2 / $55.00
- ❏ Child Psychotherapy Homework Planner, Second Edition....................978-0-471-78534-7 / $55.00
- ❏ Child Therapy Activity and Homework Planner.......................................978-0-471-25684-7 / $55.00
- ❏ Adolescent Psychotherapy Homework Planner, Second Edition ....978-0-471-78537-8 / $55.00
- ❏ Addiction Treatment Homework Planner, Third Edition..........................978-0-471-77461-7 / $55.00
- ❏ Brief Employee Assistance Homework Planner ....978-0-471-38088-7 / $55.00
- ❏ Brief Family Therapy Homework Planner..978-0-471-38512-7 / $55.00
- ❏ Grief Counseling Homework Planner ....978-0-471-43318-7 / $55.00
- ❏ Divorce Counseling Homework Planner..978-0-471-43319-4 / $55.00
- ❏ Group Therapy Homework Planner ....978-0-471-41822-1 / $55.00
- ❏ School Counseling and School Social Work Homework Planner ....978-0-471-09114-1 / $55.00
- ❏ Adolescent Psychotherapy Homework Planner II ....978-0-471-27493-3 / $55.00
- ❏ Adult Psychotherapy Homework Planner, Second Edition ....978-0-471-76343-7 / $55.00
- ❏ Parenting Skills Homework Planner..978-0-471-48182-9 / $55.00

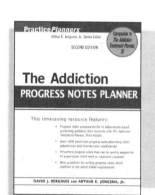

Progress Notes Planners contain complete prewritten progress notes for each presenting problem in the companion Treatment Planners.

- ❏ The Adult Psychotherapy Progress Notes Planner...................................978-0-471-76344-4 / $55.00
- ❏ The Adolescent Psychotherapy Progress Notes Planner ....978-0-471-78538-5 / $55.00
- ❏ The Severe and Persistent Mental Illness Progress Notes Planner..........978-0-471-21986-6 / $55.00
- ❏ The Child Psychotherapy Progress Notes Planner...................................978-0-471-78536-1 / $55.00
- ❏ The Addiction Progress Notes Planner..978-0-471-73253-2 / $55.00
- ❏ The Couples Psychotherapy Progress Notes Planner ....978-0-471-27460-5 / $55.00
- ❏ The Family Therapy Progress Notes Planner ....978-0-471-48443-1 / $55.00

Client Education Handout Planners contain elegantly designed handouts that can be printed out from the enclosed CD-ROM and provide information on a wide range of psychological and emotional disorders and life skills issues. Use as patient literature, handouts at presentations, and aids for promoting your mental health practice.

- ❏ Adult Client Education Handout Planner ....978-0-471-20232-5 / $55.00
- ❏ Child and Adolescent Client Education Handout Planner........................978-0-471-20233-2 / $55.00
- ❏ Couples and Family Client Education Handout Planner ....978-0-471-20234-9 / $55.00

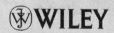

TheraScribe®

WILEY CONTINUING EDUCATION
FOR BEHAVIORAL HEALTH PROFESSIONALS
BOOK-BASED ONLINE LEARNING

Earn Accredited Continuing Education Online and On Time

NOW YOU CAN EARN CONTINUING EDUCATION CREDITS THROUGH OUR NEW BOOK-BASED, ONLINE EDUCATION PARTNERSHIP.

Our publications provide high quality continuing education to meet the licensing renewal needs of busy professionals like yourself. Best of all, you can complete this continuing education when and where you choose! Simply read the book, take the online test associated with the book and as soon as you have passed the test and completed the evaluation, you can print out your CE credit certificate— a valuable benefit for those facing imminent license renewal deadlines.

Clinical book content and the associated assessments meet the requirements of many state licensing boards and national accreditation bodies such as:

- American Psychological Association
- Association of Social Work Boards
- National Board of Certified Counselors
- National Association of Alcohol and Drug Abuse Counselors
- American Nurses Credentialing Center

Topics covered include:

- Addiction and Recovery
- Forensic Psychology
- Psychological Assessment
- School Psychology
- Therapy and Counseling

Each available book has a companion online course that consists of the Learning Objectives, post-test and course evaluation, so you can take them from anywhere you have Internet access. Likewise, you can take these courses at your own pace, any time of the day or night—whenever you have the time.

IT'S EASY TO GET STARTED!
Visit us online today at www.wiley.com/go/ceuLearn to find out how.

WILEY
Now you know.
wiley.com

The School Counseling and School Social Work Treatment Planner

PRACTICE*PLANNERS*® SERIES

Treatment Planners

The Complete Adult Psychotherapy Treatment Planner, 2e
The Child Psychotherapy Treatment Planner, 2e
The Adolescent Psychotherapy Treatment Planner, 2e
The Continuum of Care Treatment Planner
The Couples Psychotherapy Treatment Planner
The Employee Assistance Treatment Planner
The Pastoral Counseling Treatment Planner
The Older Adult Psychotherapy Treatment Planner
The Behavioral Medicine Treatment Planner
The Group Therapy Treatment Planner
The Gay and Lesbian Psychotherapy Treatment Planner
The Family Therapy Treatment Planner
The Severe and Persistent Mental Illness Treatment Planner
The Mental Retardation and Developmental Disability Treatment Planner
The Social Work and Human Services Treatment Planner
The Crisis Counseling and Traumatic Events Treatment Planner
The Personality Disorders Treatment Planner
The Rehabilitation Psychology Treatment Planner
The Addiction Treatment Planner, 2e
The Special Education Treatment Planner
The Juvenile Justice and Residential Care Treatment Planner
The School Counseling and School Social Work Treatment Planner

Progress Notes Planners

The Child Psychotherapy Progress Notes Planner
The Adolescent Psychotherapy Progress Notes Planner
The Adult Psychotherapy Progress Notes Planner
The Addiction Progress Notes Planner
The Severe and Persistent Mental Illness Progress Notes Planner

Homework Planners

Brief Therapy Homework Planner
Brief Couples Therapy Homework Planner
Chemical Dependence Treatment Homework Planner
Brief Child Therapy Homework Planner
Brief Adolescent Therapy Homework Planner
Brief Employee Assistance Homework Planner
Brief Family Therapy Homework Planner
Grief Counseling Homework Planner
Group Therapy Homework Planner
Divorce Counseling Homework Planner
School Counseling and School Social Work Homework Planner

Documentation Sourcebooks

The Clinical Documentation Sourcebook
The Forensic Documentation Sourcebook
The Psychotherapy Documentation Primer
The Chemical Dependence Treatment Documentation Sourcebook
The Clinical Child Documentation Sourcebook
The Couple and Family Clinical Documentation Sourcebook
The Clinical Documentation Sourcebook, 2e
The Continuum of Care Clinical Documentation Sourcebook

Practice*Planners*®

Arthur E. Jongsma, Jr., Series Editor

The School Counseling and School Social Work Treatment Planner

Sarah Edison Knapp

Arthur E. Jongsma, Jr.

JOHN WILEY & SONS, INC.

ISBN 0-471-08496-4

Printed in the United States of America.

10 9 8 7 6 5

I dedicate this book to the many students, educators, and parents with whom I have worked, during my 25 years as a school social worker, who taught me so many lessons about coping with the joys and challenges of childhood and adolescence, and to my mother, Marion Edison, who taught me that life is a mystery to be experienced and enjoyed even when not fully understood.

—Sarah Edison Knapp

To my wife, Judy, who has consistently kept her promise to always love me. I am blessed and grateful.

—Arthur E. Jongsma, Jr.

CONTENTS

SERIES PREFACE

The practice of psychotherapy has a dimension that did not exist 30, 20, or even 15 years ago—accountability. Treatment programs, public agencies, clinics, and even group and solo practitioners must now justify the treatment of patients to outside review entities that control the payment of fees. This development has resulted in an explosion of paperwork.

Clinicians must now document what has been done in treatment, what is planned for the future, and what the anticipated outcomes of the interventions are. The books and software in this Practice Planner series are designed to help practitioners fulfill these documentation requirements efficiently and professionally.

The Practice Planner series is growing rapidly. It now includes not only the original *Complete Adult Psychotherapy Treatment Planner,* second edition, the *Child Psychotherapy Treatment Planner,* second edition, and the *Adolescent Psychotherapy Treatment Planner,* second edition, but also Treatment Planners targeted to specialty areas of practice, including: addictions, juvenile justice/residential care, couples therapy, employee assistance, behavioral medicine, therapy with older adults, pastoral counseling, family therapy, group therapy, neuropsychological, therapy with gays and lesbians, special education, and more.

Several of the Treatment Planner books now have companion Progress Notes Planners (e.g., Adult, Adolescent, Child, Addictions, Severe and Persistent Mental Illness). More of these planners that provide a menu of progress statements that elaborate on the client's symptom presentation and the provider's therapeutic intervention are in production. Each Progress Notes Planner statement is directly integrated with "Behavioral Definitions" and "Therapeutic Interventions" items from the companion Treatment Planner.

The list of therapeutic Homework Planners is also growing from the original Brief Therapy Homework for adults to Adolescent, Child, Couples, Group, Family, Chemical Dependence, Divorce, Grief, Employee Assistance, and School Counseling/School Social Work Homework Planners. Each of these books can be used alone or in conjunction with their companion Treatment Planner. Homework assignments are designed around each presenting problem (e.g., Anxiety, Depression, Chemical Dependence, Anger Management, Panic, Eating Disorders) that is the focus of a chapter in its corresponding Treatment Planner).

In addition, the series also includes TheraScribe®, the latest version of the popular treatment planning, clinical record-keeping software. TheraScribe allows the user to import the data from any of the Treatment Planner, Progress Notes Planner, or Homework Planner books into the software's expandable database. Then the point-and-click method can create a detailed, neatly organized, individualized, and customized treatment plan along with optional integrated progress notes and homework assignments.

Adjunctive books, such as *The Psychotherapy Documentation Primer*, and *Clinical, Forensic, Child, Couples and Family, Continuum of Care*, and *Chemical Dependence Documentation Sourcebook* contain forms and resources to aid the mental health practice management. The goal of the series is to provide practitioners with the resources they need in order to provide high-quality care in the era of accountability—or, to put it simply, we seek to help you spend more time on patients, and less time on paperwork.

ARTHUR E. JONGSMA, JR.
Grand Rapids, Michigan

ACKNOWLEDGMENTS

I was so pleased when I received a phone call from Art Jongsma, the editor of the Practice Planners® Series, asking me to coauthor a planner for school social workers and counselors. I was aware of the need for such a treatment planner as I worked with students experiencing diverse problems and challenges, supervised several social work student interns in the schools, and worked on numerous committees trying to define the role of the counselor and social worker in the schools. The job description of the school counselor or school social worker involves a vast series of expectations, which includes providing therapeutic services to students who experience social/emotional difficulties, their parents, and teachers. This Planner will help the affective educator deal with these problems in an organized and goal-directed manner, freeing up time for the many other tasks these professionals are asked to assume.

I was fortunate during my 25 years as a school social worker to collaborate with so many skilled, gifted, and loving professionals, including school social workers and counselors, school psychologists, teacher consultants, special education service providers and teachers, administrators, secretarial staff, paraprofessionals, and regular education teachers. The work being done by these dedicated professionals allows students who are coping with social/emotional challenges to address their difficulties with encouragement, support, and guidance, and to thus benefit more fully from their school experience.

I would like to recognize some very special educators who greatly expanded my knowledge in this field: Jean Kamps Ettesvold, my first school social work field supervisor, who taught me how to manage a caseload; Dorothy Laufer, who gave me insight into learning disabilities; Case DeKryger, who gave me my first job as a school social worker; and Diane Pinard, a masterful teacher of the emotionally impaired and an educational soul mate. Family members who have offered their full support and encouragement include my sisters, Judith Forker and Ann Walz; my son, Michael Knapp, Jr.; my daughter, Heather Werkema; her

husband, Tim; their daughter, Lyndsay; and my late mother, Marion
Edison.

Writing this Planner has been the greatest challenge and the most
rewarding experience I have ever undertaken. Its completion would not
have been possible without the inspiration, patience, and guidance of
Art Jongsma, who envisioned this project and has worked diligently
with me on it ever since our first meeting. Further special thanks go to
Jennifer Byrne, who applied her transcription gifts to make this Planner consistent, well organized, and user-friendly. Peggy Alexander, Cris
Wojdylo, and the rest of the staff at John Wiley & Sons are the final link
in a collaborative chain that produced this book in its final form.

SARAH EDISON KNAPP

INTRODUCTION

PLANNER FOCUS

The School Counseling and School Social Work Treatment Planner is designed for all counselors, social workers, psychologists, and other mental health professionals working in the school setting who provide guidance, counseling, and therapeutic support to students with needs in the affective domain. It incorporates an extensive representation of the social/emotional, behavioral, academic, and interpersonal challenges with which students struggle as they matriculate through the educational system.

Interventions have been designed to offer the school-based mental health specialist a variety of workable, constructive, and meaningful strategies to improve the quality of the student's educational and social/emotional experience in a collaborative model involving the student, parents, and other school professionals. The emphasis is always on enhancing the independence and personal competency of the student, regardless of the type or intensity of the treatment issue. The interventions target the student's functioning in the classroom, family, social settings, and the community. Reality-based therapeutic interventions are offered to encourage the student's growth in social skills development, personal responsibility, self-esteem, self-control, academic achievement, and preparation for future independence.

The writing of quality therapeutic treatment plans for students with social/emotional challenges based on specific, targeted areas of need can offer the school mental health professional an essential tool in identifying meaningful and effective interventions. Further, it is our belief that, in creating and following an individualized treatment plan, this process can enhance and, in many situations, increase the overall functioning and performance of the student in the school setting.

HISTORY AND BACKGROUND

Counselors and social workers along with psychologists, nurses, student assistance workers, substance abuse and family education specialists, and other school-based mental health professionals have for decades provided therapeutic and counseling services to both special education and general education students in the school setting. Among the services provided are schoolwide affective or educational programs, classroom presentations, small-group counseling, individual counseling, assessment for special services, staff development, teacher and parent consultation, parent education, home-school liaison, community and agency intermediary, and school-to-work or -college transition. The essential role of the school mental health professional is to assist students who are unable to benefit fully from their educational experience due to social, emotional, or behavioral difficulties.

School counseling services began to be offered in the early 1900s and were performed by visiting teachers who coordinated services between the school and the student's family. In the 1960s and 1970s, school social workers and school counselors assumed the role of meeting the affective needs of students and their families in the school setting. Although school-based mental health services have increased greatly since that time, there seems to be an ever-expanding need for social/emotional support. Up until the early 1970s, there were limited services available for children with special needs. However, with the inception of mandatory special education [e.g., PL-142 (in 1975), PL-99-457 (in 1986), and the Individuals with Disabilities Education Act (IDEA) (in 1990)], services for students with identified disabilities, including emotional impairment, were designated by federal and state laws. School social workers were assigned the task of providing therapeutic support for special education students with social/emotional disabilities. In addition, many schools recognized the ongoing pressing demand of numerous regular education students to receive counseling services in the school setting. Both school counselors and school social workers along with other mental health specialists address this challenge today.

The School Counseling and School Social Work Treatment Planner can assist the mental health specialist to meet the ever-expanding demand for affective education in the school. By creating and following an individually tailored intervention plan, the service provider can assist the student in achieving specific goals by using a range of eclectic and research-based therapeutic interventions designed to treat specific problems, concerns, and challenges. The range of issues addressed in *The School Counseling and School Social Work Treatment Planner* includes personal challenges (e.g., self-esteem, anxiety, attention-seeking behavior), family concerns (e.g., divorce, blended family, sibling rivalry), social adjustment issues (e.g., conflict management, social skills, sexual responsibility), academic problems (e.g., learning difficulties, academic motivation, career planning), and community issues (e.g., poverty, parenting skills, diversity). The interventions can be applied effectively in many treatment modalities, including individual therapy, group counseling, classroom presentations, parent education, and in schoolwide initiatives. This Planner is a guide designed to supplement the skills training, education, and good judgment of the school mental health professional.

TREATMENT PLAN UTILITY

Detailed, written treatment plans can benefit not only the student, the teacher(s), the social worker or counselor, or other service provider, but also the parents, the school, and the greater community. The student is served by a written plan because it stipulates the issues that are the focus of the treatment process. In attempting to meet the student's goals stipulated in an individualized education plan, his/her needs as identified on a Section 504 plan or directly developed with the student, parents, and teachers, the focus can be lost in the day-to-day logistics of the hectic and frequently interrupted school day. The treatment plan is a guide that structures the focus of the therapeutic interventions, which are essential for the student to progress. Since issues can change as the student's circumstances or needs change, the treatment plan must be viewed as a dynamic document that can, and must be, updated to reflect any major change of problem, definition, goal, objective, or intervention.

The student, parents, teachers, and the therapeutic service provider for that student benefit from the treatment plan, which forces all to think carefully and directly about the desired treatment outcomes. Behaviorally stated, observable objectives clearly focus the treatment endeavor. The student and parents no longer have to wonder what the goals of counseling are. Clear objectives also allow the student to channel effort into specific changes that will lead to the long-term goal of problem resolution and/or improved functioning. Both the student and the social worker or counselor are concentrating on specifically stated objectives using specific interventions.

The process of developing an affective and behavioral treatment plan assists the mental health specialist to consider analytically and critically which therapeutic interventions are best suited for objective attainment of the student's goal. Goals are developed and interventions are implemented based on the professional service provider's advance attention to the unique abilities, qualities, and circumstances of each student.

A well-crafted treatment plan that clearly stipulates presenting problems and intervention strategies facilitates the treatment process carried out by the mental health specialist during individual or group counseling sessions, in the classroom, or in the community. Good communication with the parents and among the school staff team members about what approaches are being implemented and who is responsible for which intervention is important. A thorough treatment plan stipulates in *writing* the details of the established objectives and the varied interventions, and can identify who will implement them.

School counselors and school social workers along with other educational consultants will benefit from the use of more precise, observable objectives to evaluate success in school-based therapy and counseling. With the advent of detailed treatment plans, outcome data can be more easily collected for interventions that are effective in achieving specific goals.

HOW TO DEVELOP A TREATMENT PLAN

The process of developing a treatment plan involves a logical series of steps that build on each other, much like constructing a house. The foundation of any effective treatment plan is the data gathered in a comprehensive evaluation. As part of the process prior to developing the treatment plan, the social worker or counselor must sensitively listen to and understand what the student struggles with in terms of emotional status, learning deficits, current stressors, social network, physical health and physical challenges, coping skills, self-esteem, family issues, and so on. It is imperative that assessment data be drawn from a variety of sources, which could include developmental and social history, physical exam, clinical interview, psychoeducational testing, psychiatric evaluation/consultation, and assessment of the student's school history and records. The integration of the data by the mental health professional or team is critical for understanding the student and his/her needs. We have identified five specific steps for developing an effective treatment plan based on assessment data.

Step One: Problem Selection

Although the student, teachers, or parents may discuss a variety of issues during the assessment, the school social worker or counselor must ferret out the most significant problems on which to focus the treatment process. Usually a primary problem will surface, and secondary problems may also be evident. Some other problems may have to be set aside as not urgent enough to require treatment at this time. An effective treatment plan can only deal with a few selected problems; otherwise, treatment will lose its direction. A variety of problems are presented as chapter titles, representing specific social/emotional issues within *The School Counseling and School Social Work Treatment Planner*. The mental health professional may select those that most accurately represent the student's current needs.

As the problems to be selected become clear to the social worker, counselor, or team, it is important to consider opinions from the student (as appropriate, dependent upon the student's age and maturity level), the parents, and the teachers as to the prioritization of social/emotional concerns. The student's motivation to participate in and cooperate with the treatment process depends, to some extent, on the degree to which treatment addresses his/her greatest needs, particularly in circumstances with secondary students who may have strong feelings as to what should be emphasized.

Step Two: Problem Definition

Each student presents with unique nuances as to how a problem behaviorally reveals itself in his/her life. Therefore, each problem that is selected for treatment focus requires a specific definition about how it is evidenced in the particular student. The symptom pattern is associated with diagnostic criteria similar to those found in the *Diagnostic and Statistical Manual of Mental Disorders,* fourth edition (*DSM-IV*™). The Planner offers behaviorally specific definition statements to choose from or to serve as a model for your own personally crafted statements. You will find several behavior symptoms or syndromes listed that may characterize one of the 30 presenting problems identified in the Planner. Turn to the chapter that identifies the presenting problem being experienced by the student. Select from the listed behavioral definitions the statements that best describe the observable behavior directly interfering with the student's social/emotional adjustment.

Step Three: Goal Development

The next step in treatment plan development is that of setting broad goals for the resolution of the target educational problem. These statements need not be crafted in measurable terms but can be global, long-term goals that indicate a desired positive outcome to the treatment procedures. The Planner suggests several possible goal statements for each problem, but one statement is all that is required in a treatment plan.

Step Four: Objective Construction

In contrast to long-term goals, educational objectives must be stated in behaviorally observable language. It must be clear when the student has achieved the objectives; therefore, vague, subjective objectives are not acceptable. Various alternatives are presented to allow construction of a variety of treatment plan possibilities for the same presenting problem. The social worker or counselor must exercise professional judgment as to which objectives are most appropriate for a given student.

Each objective should be developed as a step toward attaining the broad instructional goal. In essence, objectives can be thought of as a series of steps that, when completed, will result in the achievement of the long-term goal. There should be at least two objectives for each problem, but the mental health professional may construct as many as are necessary for goal achievement. Target attainment dates may be listed for each objective. New objectives should be added to the plan as the student's treatment progresses. When all the necessary objectives have been achieved, the student should have resolved the target educational problem successfully.

Step Five: Intervention Creation

Interventions are the therapeutic actions of the counselor designed to help the student complete the objectives. There should be at least one intervention for every objective. If the student does not accomplish the objective after the initial intervention has been implemented, new interventions should be added to the plan.

Interventions should be selected on the basis of the student's affective needs and the mental health specialist's full instructional and/or therapeutic repertoire. *The School Counseling and School Social Work Treatment Planner* contains interventions from a broad range of approaches, including cognitive, behavioral, academic, dynamic, medical, and family-based. Other interventions may be written by the provider to reflect his/her own training and experience. The addition of new problems, definitions, goals, objectives, and interventions to those found in the Planner is encouraged because doing so adds to the database for future reference and use.

Some suggested interventions listed in the Planner refer to specific books or journals where specific methodologies can be located for the affective educator to look for a more lengthy explanation or discussion of the intervention. Appendix A offers a bibliotherapy reference for students and parents, suggesting reading material that may be helpful to families, referenced by disability or disorder. A bibliographic reference for the professional is also included in Appendix B.

HOW TO USE THIS PLANNER

The School Counseling and School Social Work Treatment Planner was developed as a tool to aid school mental health professionals in writing a treatment plan in a rapid manner that is clear, specific, and highly individualized according to the following progression:

1. Choose one presenting problem/disability (Step One) that you have identified through your assessment process. Locate the corresponding page number for that problem/disability in the Planner's table of contents.

2. Select two or three of the listed behavioral definitions (Step Two) and record them in the appropriate section on your treatment plan form. Feel free to add your own defining statement if you determine that your student's behavioral manifestation of the identified problem is not listed.

3. Select one or more long-term goals (Step Three) and again write the selection, exactly as it is written in the Planner or in some appropriately modified form, in the corresponding area of your own form.

4. Review the listed objectives for this problem and select the ones that you judge to be clinically indicated for your student (Step Four). Remember, it is recommended that you select at least two objectives for each problem. Add a target date for the attainment of each objective, if necessary.

5. Choose relevant interventions (Step Five). The Planner offers suggested interventions that are related to each objective in the parentheses following the objective statement. However, do not limit yourself to those interventions. Just as with definitions, goals, and objectives, there is space allowed for you to enter your own interventions into the Planner. This allows you to refer to these entries when you create a plan around this problem in the future. You may have to assign responsibility to a specific person for implementation of each intervention if the treatment is being carried out by a team.

Congratulations! You should now have a complete, individualized, treatment plan that is ready for immediate implementation and presentation to the student. It should resemble the format of the sample plan presented on the next page.

A FINAL NOTE

One important aspect of effective treatment planning is that each plan should be tailored to the individual student's problems and needs. The student's strengths and weaknesses, unique stressors, social network, family circumstances, and symptom patterns *must* be considered in developing a treatment strategy. Drawing upon our own years of educational and clinical experiences, we have put together a variety of treatment choices. These statements can be combined in thousands of permutations to develop detailed treatment plans. Relying on their own good judgment, school mental health professionals can easily select the statements that are appropriate for the students on their caseload. In addition, we encourage readers to add their own definitions, goals, objectives, and interventions to the existing samples. It is our hope that *The School Counseling and School Social Work Treatment Planner* will promote effective, creative treatment planning—a process that will ultimately benefit the student, the mental health professionals working with that student, the parents, and the greater school community.

SAMPLE TREATMENT PLAN

PROBLEM: DIVORCE

Definitions: Parents' marital separation has led to fear of abandonment, feelings of insecurity, shock, deep loss, and vulnerability.

Mood swings, weariness, depression, and a tendency to withdraw since parental divorce.

Declining grades and a lack of interest in school and social activities.

Aggressive, acting-out behaviors, impulsivity, and oppositional reactions.

Goals: Accept parents' decision to separate or divorce without feelings of rage, guilt, or depression.

Stabilize mood swings and reduce regressive, oppositional, or aggressive behavior.

Reestablish interest and involvement in school and social activities.

Short-Term Objectives

1. Discuss the parents' decision to separate, and verbalize areas of personal fear and feelings of loss.

2. Parents discuss their current separation or divorce with a counselor and indicate its effect on the student and the family.

Therapeutic Interventions

1. Ask the student to share the effect of his/her parents' divorce on his/her life by describing family life before, during, and after the divorce.

2. Assist the student in listing all fears and personal feelings of loss related to his/her parents' divorce.

1. Meet with both parents jointly, or separately (if necessary), to discuss the current family situation and the effects of the separation or divorce on the student (e.g., daily routines, emotional stability, custody, visitation, possible moves).

2. Assign the parents to read a book that describes the effects of divorce on children (e.g., *Helping Children Cope with Divorce* by Teyber).

3. Explore divorce-related feelings, and identify appropriate methods for expressing these feelings.

1. Ask the student to identify five divorce-related feelings, and then brainstorm an appropriate method of expressing each of these feelings (e.g., anger: talk it out with a caring adult; jealousy: invite a parent to play a game; sadness: draw a picture expressing personal feelings.

4. Parents express acceptance of the student's feelings and encourage him/her to continue appropriate expression of feelings.

1. Meet with the parents to prepare them for actively listening to the student's feelings and to reinforce the importance of providing time for emotional expression.

5. Outline methods of seeking support from extended family members.

1. Assist the student in writing a letter or sending a card to an extended family member that shares feelings and expresses a need to spend time together.

6. Identify constructive ways to express underlying feelings and fears that trigger self-defeating behaviors.

1. Explore the student's emotional reactions (e.g., screaming, hitting, withdrawing, or destroying property), and suggest a more rational method of expressing his/her feelings (e.g., using an "I" statement, writing in a personal journal, drawing a feelings picture, or taking a walk).

2. Brainstorm with the student methods of reducing underlying fears and

7. Participate in several organized and informal extracurricular events or activities per month.

frustrations (e.g., sharing feelings with his/her parents, counselor, empathetic friend, or supportive adult).

1. Encourage the student to join an athletic team, school club, church, or interest group. Monitor his/her subsequent participation.

2. Devise a plan with the student for inviting a friend to participate in a social activity.

ACADEMIC MOTIVATION/STUDY AND ORGANIZATIONAL SKILLS

BEHAVIORAL DEFINITIONS

1. A significant difference between ability as measured by a standardized IQ or achievement test and lower-than-expected academic performance.
2. Poor study habits and disorganization (e.g., loses assignments, forgets homework, doesn't take notes, wastes time in school, doesn't complete tasks).
3. Manipulative and blames poor work effort on others or on the curriculum.
4. Low self-esteem and high level of anxiety, especially in the academic environment.
5. Gives up easily in the face of struggle (e.g., a difficult assignment or a challenging task).
6. Avoids competition unless success is guaranteed.
7. Procrastinates and works slowly, often not completing the task or rushes through an assignment without regard to the quality of work.
8. Family's value system does not place a high priority on education.
9. Family instability (e.g., frequent moves, unemployment, lack of financial resources and parental supervision) interferes with the student's focus on school and the demands of learning.

__. _____
   _____
__. _____
   _____
__. _____
   _____

LONG-TERM GOALS

1. Academic achievement in school is comparable to ability level.
2. Exhibit intrinsic motivation and positive attitudes toward learning and academic achievement.
3. Develop a positive self-concept and reduce anxiety associated with academic accomplishment.
4. Develop effective study habits and an organizational structure for academic accomplishment.
5. Demonstrate a personal responsibility toward learning, and acknowledge the relationship between personal effort and positive results in school.
6. Parents and school staff establish reasonable academic expectations for the student and reinforce his/her efforts to achieve success in school.

—. _____
   _____
—. _____
   _____
—. _____
   _____

SHORT-TERM OBJECTIVES

1. Cooperate with providing biopsychosocial information to assist in determining the causes for the underachievement. (1, 2)

THERAPEUTIC INTERVENTIONS

1. Gather information about the student's academic performance and his/her social, medical, family, or behavioral difficulties from discussions with the student, parents, referring teacher, or special educator.

2. Collaborate with the school or a private psychologist to complete a psychological evaluation of the student if deemed appropriate by the parents and school child study team.

2. Parents and teachers verbalize an understanding of the causes of underachievement and implement management strategies and interventions to help the student become academically motivated. (3, 4, 5)

3. Assign the parents to read *Smart Parenting: How to Raise a Happy, Achieving Child* (Rimm); *SOS: Help for Parents,* 2nd edition (Clark); or other literature to prepare for subsequent discussions with the student and teachers concerning the student's underachievement.

4. Refer the parents to a support group addressing underachievement, academic motivation, or giftedness in children [e.g., Council for Exceptional Children (703-620-3660 or www.cec.sped.org) or The National Association for Gifted Children (202-785-4268 or www.nacg.org)].

5. Meet with the teacher regularly to review strategies from *Underachievement Syndrome, Causes and Cures* (Rimm); *Guidebook for Implementing the TRI-FOCAL Underachievement Program for Schools* (Rimm, Cornale, Manos, and Behrend); or other best-practice literature offering classroom techniques for teaching and encouraging students who are underachieving.

3. Participate in a functional analysis to determine specific academic and behavioral goals and to design strategies to support goal achievement. (6, 7)

6. Complete a functional analysis of the student to define learning and behavior patterns, analyze the probable causes for underachievement, and develop

reinforcement interventions to correct the problems and provide intrinsic motivation.

7. Collaborate with the student and his/her parents and teachers to complete the "Record of Behavioral Progress" from the *School Counseling and School Social Work Homework Planner* (Knapp) to analyze the student's behavior and plan specific intervention strategies to help him/her develop positive approaches to learning and academic motivation.

4. Verbalize the awareness that all people are unique, learn differently, and have various strengths and weaknesses. (8, 9, 10, 11)

8. Explain the theory of multiple intelligences (see *Frames of Mind: The Theory of Multiple Intelligences* by Gardner), which stipulates that people are smart in different ways, and ask the student to identify his/her personal areas of greater and lesser intelligences. Have the student add to his/her personal ability list by soliciting input from others.

9. Ask the student to complete the "Skill Assessment" activity from the *School Counseling and Social Work Homework Planner* (Knapp) to evaluate existing abilities in terms of multiple intelligences. (See *Frames of Mind: The Theory of Multiple Intelligences* by Gardner.)

10. Assign the student to determine his/her personal

learning styles (e.g., visual or seeing what is being learned; auditory, hearing, or saying what is being learned; kinesthetic or needing motion to learn) through self-observation and observations from his/her parents and teachers.

11. Ask the student to complete the "Building on Strengths" activity from the *School Counseling and School Social Work Homework Planner* (Knapp) to identify personal strengths and discover how these strengths can be used to reach goals.

5. Apply unique learning style to academic assignments and process the results. (12)

12. Instruct the student to use his/her primary learning style while preparing for the next quiz or test and to report the results during a subsequent counseling session.

6. Increase the rate of completion of in-class assignments and homework. (13, 14, 15)

13. Assign the student to use a study planner to list all assignments, record working time, and check off when completed.

14. Play Study Smart (ADHD Warehouse) with the student to assist him/her in the development of study skills, comprehension, test taking, and memory.

15. Ask the parents and teachers to monitor the student's assignment planner daily and to give encouragement and direction as needed.

7. Establish a routine or schedule to prioritize and organize key daily activities. (13, 16, 17)

13. Assign the student to use a study planner to list all assignments, record working time, and check off when completed.

16. Assist the student in listing and prioritizing key daily activities at home, school, and in the community; assign times for completion and record these in a personal journal or an assignment planner.

17. Instruct the student to complete the "Growing and Changing" activity from the *School Counseling and School Social Work Homework Planner* (Knapp) to encourage him/her to view learning as a lifelong process that begins at birth.

8. Verbalize an awareness of the long- and short-term effects of underachievement upon the quality of life and goal attainment. (18, 19)

18. Have the student begin a personal journal, entitled *My Learning Adventures,* which contains thoughts, feelings, successes, and challenges related to academic accomplishment.

19. Read with the student children's literature that explains underachievement, explores feelings, and suggests management strategies (e.g., *The Gifted Kid Survival Guide: Ages 10 and Under* or *The Gifted Kid Survival Guide: A Teen Handbook* by Galbraith).

9. Disclose feelings to parents, teachers, and other significant adults. (20, 21)

20. Use puppets or role playing to help the student prepare for appropriate sharing of

personal feelings about academics with significant adults.

21. Assign the student to discuss a personal concern or academic problem with a parent, teacher, or friend and to process the results during the next counseling session.

10. Participate in programs designed for gifted or underachieving students in lieu of mainstream classes. (22, 23)

22. Consult with the student and his/her teacher(s) and parents regarding necessary accommodations to encourage academic success (e.g., mentorships or apprenticeships, ability grouping for class projects, provision for continuous progress, accelerated classes, appropriate challenge in curriculum delivery).

23. Involve the student in a community service project with other students, allowing the group to choose the project and plan for its implementation; encourage the teacher to allow the student to earn class credit for his/her efforts.

11. Implement problem-solving strategies to improve social interaction, school performance, and personal satisfaction. (24, 25)

24. Assist the student in completing the "Personal Problem-Solving Worksheet" from the *School Counseling and School Social Work Homework Planner* (Knapp) to outline strategies for solving personal problems and academic concerns.

25. Introduce activities from the program *I Can Problem*

Solve (Shure) to teach problem solving and predicting the result of specific actions.

12. Participate in a study skills group. (26, 27, 28)

26. Refer the student to a school-sponsored study skills instructional group.

27. Teach the student to use academic coping skills (e.g., take notes, plan assignments, design a home study area, choose creative or meaningful homework projects).

28. Explore feelings about academic achievement with the student in a study skills group. Brainstorm the pluses and minuses of underachievement versus successful academic participation (or assign "The Good News and Bad News of Making It in School" activity from the *School Counseling and Social Work Homework Planner* by Knapp).

13. Parents and teachers empower the student by emphasizing personal responsibility and the benefits of considering the consequences before acting. (29, 30)

29. Encourage the teacher(s) and parents to use positive discipline strategies to help the student to develop responsibility (e.g., chores, assignments and tasks, learning from mistakes, consequences, choices, and a chance to try again next time). (See the Responsible Behavior Training chapter in this Planner.)

30. The parents discuss their own learning and work-related challenges and joys with the student,

emphasizing that choices and the struggle to achieve are essential components of any successful endeavor.

14. Verbalize an increased awareness of how personal choices and behavior create specific results. (31, 32)

31. Have the student complete the "Decision Making" activity from the *School Counseling and Social Work Homework Planner* (Knapp) either individually or in a small group session to increase his/her awareness of the connection between personal choices and specific results.

32. Instruct the student to list 10 positive academic choices he/she made during the school year and 10 inappropriate or irresponsible choices and to record the results of each decision (e.g., decided to study for science test and received an A, or didn't turn in homework assignment and received a 0).

15. Implement communication techniques to build social relationships. (33, 34)

33. Teach the student to use "I" messages and reflective listening (see *Teaching Children Self-Discipline* by Gordon, or the Bug-Wish Technique: "It bugs me when you . . . I wish you would. . . .").

34. Use the *Peacemaking Skills for Little Kids Student Activity Book* (Schmidt, Friedmann, Brunt, and Solotoff) to develop social assertiveness and conflict management skills.

16. Actively seek friendships among peer group. (34, 35, 36)

34. Use the *Peacemaking Skills for Little Kids Student Activity Book* (Schmidt, Friedmann, Brunt, and Solotoff) to develop social assertiveness and conflict management skills.

35. Encourage the student's teacher(s) to involve him/her in cooperative learning groups.

36. Support the student in joining an extracurricular social group sponsored by the school, church, or community.

17. Verbalize pride in schoolwork. (37, 38)

37. Ask the student to bring completed assignments to each session and discuss his/her positive efforts.

38. Review teacher assessments or report cards with the student, and have him/her relate what personal strengths are being reflected.

18. Chart progress in academic areas. (39)

39. Reinforce the idea that academic progress should be measured in terms of personal progress and not by competing against other students. Ask the student to chart his/her progress in several academic areas by establishing a baseline and recording his/her growth throughout the school year in a personal journal (or assign the "Personal Best" activity from the *School Counseling and School Social Work Homework Planner* by Knapp).

19. Verbalize confidence in own test-taking ability and reduced fear of testing event. (40, 41)

40. Assist the student in identifying and recording several self-talk statements that can be used during test taking to ward off worry (e.g., "I am prepared for this test"; "I can handle this subject"; "I practiced for this at home"; or "I've done well on tests like this before").

41. Encourage the student's use of muscle relaxation and deep breathing techniques during test taking to reduce stress.

20. Demonstrate success in test-taking performance. (40, 41, 42)

40. Assist the student in identifying and recording several self-talk statements that can be used during test taking to ward off worry (e.g., "I am prepared for this test"; "I can handle this subject"; "I practiced for this at home"; or "I've done well on tests like this before").

41. Encourage the student's use of muscle relaxation and deep breathing techniques during test taking to reduce stress.

42. Process with the student methods used to prepare for a test (e.g., set a study schedule, outline the material, read, write, verbalize, study smaller sections, use flash cards for key ideas, or pneumonic devices); assess their effectiveness and revise the preparation routine to prepare for the next test.

21. Parents, teachers, and counselor affirm the student for progress in assuming responsibility and acquiring independence. (43, 44)

43. Encourage the student's teachers and parents to give frequent affirmations to him/her for progress noted in a private, low-key manner.

44. Allow time during the counseling sessions to affirm the student for progress in school, home, and social adjustment, and to encourage him/her to share personal successes with his/her parents, teacher(s), counselor, and group members.

22. Mentor other students who are coping with underachievement and academic motivation. (45, 46)

45. Arrange with the teacher to have the student assist classmates or younger students who are coping with underachievement or lack of academic motivation.

46. Invite the student to share personal strategies and successes with students of a newly formed study skills group.

__. _____
   _____

__. _____
   _____

__. _____
   _____

__. _____
   _____

__. _____
   _____

__. _____
   _____

DIAGNOSTIC SUGGESTIONS

Axis I: 315.00   Reading Disorder
                315.1   Mathematics Disorder
                315.2   Disorder of Written Expression
                V62   Academic Problem
                314.01   Attention-Deficit/Hyperactivity Disorder,
                           Combined Type
                314.00   Attention-Deficit/Hyperactivity Disorder,
                           Predominantly Inattentive Type
                300.4   Dysthymic Disorder
                313.81   Oppositional Defiant Disorder
                312.9   Disruptive Behavior Disorder, NOS

                _____   _____

                _____   _____

Axis II: 799.9   Diagnosis Deferred
                V71.09   No Diagnosis on Axis II

                _____   _____

                _____   _____

                _____   _____

                _____   _____

ANGER MANAGEMENT/AGGRESSION

BEHAVIORAL DEFINITIONS

1. Anger is used as an immediate and default reaction to a perceived loss of control or inability to cope with an event or situation.
2. Anger is relied upon as the first approach to solve problems.
3. Lack of prosocial, nonaggressive strategies to deal with anger.
4. View of self as a victim even though behavior emulates that of a bully.
5. Perception that anger results in control and power.
6. The fight-or-flight response is used to respond to all conflict.
7. Lack of empathy for another person's point of view.
8. An inability or refusal to consider the consequences of angry reactions before they occur.
9. Lack of accountability for angry reactions and a tendency to blame others for resulting inappropriate behavior.
10. Pervasive, destructive entitlement beliefs that people and situations should conform to personal wishes and perception.
11. Internalized anger causes chronic physical and emotional symptoms (e.g., excessive anxiety, stomach and bowel distress, headaches, muscle tightness).
12. Chronic anger interferes with family, social, and academic functioning.

__. _____
   _____

__. _____
   _____

__. _____
   _____

LONG-TERM GOALS

1. Find constructive, healthy ways to release and/or express anger, frustration, and hostility.
2. Recognize the early warning signs of the onset of anger and antecedents or triggers to anger that are experienced on a daily basis.
3. Learn to express a variety of emotions, including hurt and fear, which are often manifested as anger or rage.
4. Develop empathy and understanding for another person's point of view.
5. Terminate underlying expectations and entitlement beliefs that can lead to anger and social isolation.
6. Seek win/win solutions instead of anger and revenge.

—. _____
   _____
—. _____
   _____
—. _____
   _____

SHORT-TERM OBJECTIVES

1. Participate in a counseling group that focuses on developing personal anger management skills. (1, 2)

2. Define and demonstrate empathy. (3, 4, 24)

THERAPEUTIC INTERVENTIONS

1. Facilitate an anger management group for students having difficulty with expression of anger and aggressive interactions either at home or at school.

2. Implement a program designed to teach the student effective means of dealing with chronic anger (e.g., *Anger Management Developing Options to Anger* by Crumbley, Aarons, and Fraser).

3. Define empathy during a group session (e.g., understanding another's feelings

and perceptions versus focusing only on one's own thoughts and feelings); discuss with the student the role of empathy in the effective and productive expression of anger.

4. Use role playing to demonstrate the calming effects of predicting the thoughts, feelings, and actions of self and others prior to the outbreak of a conflict; ask the student to share anticipatory thoughts and feelings and to indicate how this process reduces angry reactions.

24. Read a story involving entitlement beliefs (e.g., *Nothing's Fair in Fifth Grade* by DeClement), and discuss with the student how empathy, communication, and awareness of another's point of view can prevent or reduce conflicts.

3. Define potential antecedents or triggers that spark or intensify anger. (5, 6)

5. Brainstorm with the student a list of conflicts that typically occur in his/her life at home, school, or in the community; identify possible conditions or triggers that preceded the actual conflict (e.g., shoving in the hallway, competition for grades or friends, vying for a parking spot).

6. Ask the student to identify actions and reactions that cause anger to intensify (e.g., physical contact,

verbal aggression, threats, facial expressions, body language); have him/her describe a scenario from a TV program, movie, or book illustrating how a small negative reaction can escalate into an angry reaction.

4. Verbalize the steps in a positive approach to conflict resolution. (7)

7. Teach the student the "Rules for Fighting Fair" (from *Mediation: Getting to Win/Win* by Schmidt): Identify the problem; focus on the problem; attack the problem, not the person; listen with an open mind; treat the person's feelings with respect; take responsibility for your actions.

5. Identify a range of emotions commonly experienced that often lead into or become interpreted as anger or rage. (8, 9, 10)

8. Introduce a list of words that express feelings, and have the student select feelings that are commonly confused or associated with anger (or assign the "Feelings Vocabulary" activity from the *School Counseling and School Social Work Homework Planner* by Knapp).

9. Ask the student to list methods of supporting someone who is experiencing excessive anger (e.g., empathic listening; staying with them; asking, "How can I help?"; seeking assistance from an adult).

10. Assign the student to identify the underlying initial personal feelings experienced in situations that can

develop into anger (e.g., teacher confronts him/her with late homework: fear, guilt, confusion, humiliation; friend uses a put-down: rejection, hurt, resentment; peers exclude him/her from a game: lonely, valueless, degraded; sibling takes a personal possession: challenged, used, offended).

6. List the underlying causes of personal anger. (11, 12)

11. Ask the student to brainstorm some preexisting conditions that contribute to angry reactions (e.g., friendship cliques, feelings of exclusion, excessive competition, lack of cooperation, blaming problems on others, parental conflict, boy/girl jealousy); instruct the student to record five personal triggers in his/her anger management journal.

12. Read *The Cybil War* (Byars), and discuss with the student the underlying causes of the conflict between friends, as well as interventions and strategies that could have prevented it.

7. Verbalize the importance of listening to another's point of view and understanding both sides of a conflict. (13, 14, 15)

13. Introduce the concept of *point of view* (individual perception) versus factual information (concrete data). Brainstorm with the student various situations where differing points of view can lead to conflict (e.g., who won the game,

the grass needs cutting, it's my turn).

14.   List for the student the steps that are necessary for understanding both points of view in a conflict (e.g., allow each person to state his/her point of view without interruption, repeat back each statement to check for understanding).

15.   Have the student role-play several scenarios to portray one point of view, check for understanding, and then reverse roles in order to advocate and recognize both points of view.

8.   Demonstrate techniques necessary for becoming an active listener. (16, 17, 18)

16.   Define active listening (see *Teacher Effectiveness Training* by Gordon) for the student during an anger management group session (e.g., listening without interruption, decoding the other person's message, and reflecting back both the perceived message and the underlying feelings to check for understanding); demonstrate the process in role playing with the student, and then have him/her practice this technique by describing events of his/her day to an active listener and then reversing roles.

17.   Teach the student the effective questioning technique of communication and conflict resolution (from *Mediation: Getting to Win/Win* by

Schmidt) in which he/she uses open-ended, nonjudgmental questions to help clarify another's point of view (e.g., "I need more information, help me understand, tell me how it happened").

18. Ask the student to complete the "Listening Skills" activity from the *School Counseling and School Social Work Homework Planner* (Knapp) to practice the skill of active listening and reflecting the feeling.

9. Verbalize an understanding of the impact of nonverbal communication on inciting or resolving personal anger and interpersonal conflict. (19, 20, 21)

19. Define nonverbal communication for the student, and teach how facial expressions and body language can either encourage or discourage a peaceful solution to a conflict.

20. Brainstorm examples of encouraging nonverbal communication cues (e.g., smiling, establishing eye contact, leaning toward a speaker, nodding the head) versus discouraging cues (e.g., rolling eyes, finger-pointing, raising eyebrows, folding arms); have the student demonstrate and react to both types of nonverbal cues.

21. Ask the student to role-play scenarios that involve the expression of angry feelings, first using encouraging nonverbal communication, then using

discouraging nonverbal cues. Record reactions in an anger management journal (or see the "Cases of Conflict" activity from the *School Counseling and School Social Work Homework Planner* by Knapp).

10. Identify and verbalize destructive entitlement beliefs that lead to chronic or excessive anger and social isolation. (22, 23, 24)

22. Define entitlement beliefs for the student (e.g., "The world owes me"; "I deserve to get what I want"; "Pay up or I will blow up"); ask him/her to brainstorm more examples and to list five personal entitlement beliefs in an anger management journal.

23. Assign the student to rephrase several personal entitlement beliefs to reflect more realistic and productive thinking (e.g., "I will start saving for a new car" versus "I deserve a new car").

24. Read a story involving entitlement beliefs (e.g., *Nothing's Fair in Fifth Grade* by DeClement), and discuss with the student how empathy, communication, and awareness of another's point of view can prevent or reduce conflicts.

11. Demonstrate interpersonal skills that develop social awareness and promote appropriate social interaction. (25)

25. Assign the student to participate in a volunteer effort designed to help others, which requires cooperation and team playing (e.g., school food drive, tutoring a younger student, becoming

a conflict manager, working with Habitat for Humanity).

12. Designate a time and place for resolving angry conflicts in a constructive manner. (26, 27)

26. Establish with the student and staff a designated place in the classroom or school where negotiation or mediation of conflicts can occur. This should be a private area where the student can concentrate on conflict resolution and confidentiality can be maintained.

27. Brainstorm with the student appropriate places to resolve conflict in the home (e.g., kitchen table, bedroom, office or den, outside, or another area conducive to focusing on the problem away from the interference of activities or unnecessary input from uninvolved family members).

13. Implement a time-out procedure to reduce the intensity of feelings. (28)

28. Review with the student the concept of taking a time-out to gain control of anger and returning later to problem-solve once calmness has been established; brainstorm ways to take a personal time-out (e.g., leave the room or area, change seats, put on headphones, visualize a peaceful scene).

14. Implement the brainstorming process for seeking potential solutions. (29, 30, 31)

29. Introduce the concept of brainstorming to the student, and identify the steps (e.g., state any idea or possible solution and write it down; no idea is laughed at

or discarded; consider the ideas on their merits; choose a solution that everyone agrees upon).

30. Ask the student to use the brainstorming process to resolve several mock conflicts; act as an observer and guide the process to develop authenticity and teach the value of this technique.

31. Assign the student to use brainstorming during the following week to resolve personal conflicts encountered at home or school; process the results at the next session.

15. Make amends to people hurt by personal overreactions and angry behavior. (32, 33)

32. Instruct the student to list each person hurt by his/her angry outbursts in the previous month, and brainstorm methods of apologizing to as many as possible (e.g., write a letter, compose a poem, say "I'm sorry" in person, send flowers, repay with a favor, assign the "Problem Solving Worksheet" activity from the *School Counseling and School Social Work Homework Planner* by Knapp).

33. Instruct the student to role-play the process of making amends, which involves stating the damage done, apologizing, and pledging to correct the hurtful behavior.

16. Focus on one anger-producing situation and develop problem-solving

34. Discuss areas of personal anger with the student and begin the reframing process

and decision-making skills for that situation. (34, 35, 36)

by suggesting alternative methods of interpreting and coping with each situation that creates angry outbursts (e.g., listening to and trying to understand the other person's point of view, listing several positive options for dealing with the situation, recording the situation in a personal journal, deciding to delay any corrective action until after having a discussion with a trusted adult).

35. Ask the student to draw a picture or cartoon entitled "Positive Ways to Manage My Anger"; interpret the drawing during a counseling session and suggest actions for productive expression of angry feelings.

36. Ask the student to identify one source of anger to work on during the following week; brainstorm possible remedies to the troubling situation, choose an option that is most likely to reduce the chances of an angry reaction, and report the outcome of implementation during the next counseling session.

17. Differentiate between disturbing situations that can be dealt with and those that are beyond personal control. (37, 38)

37. Ask the student to review techniques that reduce impulsive reactions to conflict and promote measured, thoughtful responses to a disturbing event (e.g., relaxation techniques,

visualization, time-out, brainstorming responsive options, seeking advice or counseling).

38. Assign the student to create a list of disturbing events and to differentiate those that have potential solutions within his/her immediate control (e.g., an unfair grade, an argument with a friend, parental displeasure, billing dispute) from those that are beyond his/her personal control (e.g., air flight delay, national election dispute, required class for graduation, cost of gas for car). Discuss the value of spending time and energy on both sets of circumstances.

18. Develop assertive strategies for self-expression. (39, 40, 41)

39. Define "I" messages (see *Teacher Effectiveness Training* by Gordon) for the student: State your concern in a nonblaming, nonjudgmental description; state the concrete effect; state your feeling. Ask him/her to practice giving and receiving "I" messages using the format "I feel . . . when you . . . because. . . ."

40. Have the student complete the "Speaking Skills" activity from the *School Counseling and School Social Work Homework Planner* (Knapp) to develop the skill of using "I" messages to state feelings, concerns, or frustrations.

41. Assign the student to complete the "Communication with Others" activity from the *School Counseling and School Social Work Homework Planner* (Knapp) to increase his/her awareness of appropriate times for talking and appropriate times for listening.

19. List methods of resolving personal conflict fairly and positively. (42, 43)

42. Identify a simple process for a younger student to use in resolving conflicts in his/her life (e.g., state the problem; listen to the other's point of view; share feelings about the problem; brainstorm ideas for solving the problem; agree to a solution and work it out).

43. Teach a conflict resolution process for the older elementary and secondary students to use in resolving personal disputes and in mediating the disputes of their peers (e.g., find a private place to talk; discuss the problem without judging; brainstorm possible solutions; agree on a solution that works for both; try the solution and agree to renegotiate if it is not effective). (See the Conflict Management chapter in this Planner.)

20. Demonstrate the ability to work toward a mutually acceptable (win/win) solution. (44, 45, 46)

44. Discuss win/win (both parties are satisfied with the outcome) versus win/lose (one person agrees with the outcome and the other person disagrees) with the

student, and have him/her identify situations reflecting each outcome.

45. Brainstorm with the student a list of win/lose situations (e.g., Jimmy gets to go first and Janice doesn't; Jamaul gets to play with the ball and Derrick doesn't; Cynthia invites Shirley to play and ignores Latricia) and win/win scenarios (e.g., Jimmy and Janice take turns; Jamaul and Derrick play ball together; Cynthia asks both Shirley and Latricia to play). Ask him/her to identify the feelings resulting from a win/lose outcome versus feelings resulting from a win/win solution.

46. Assist the student in creating a conflict resolution chart that lists various ways to solve a dispute (e.g., share, take turns, listen, talk it over, apologize, get help, use humor, start over, flip a coin) on different segments of the chart. Instruct him/her to use this chart when trying to determine alternatives to using anger to problem-solve.

21. List the benefits of using anger management versus engaging in power struggles, internalizing rage, aggression, or arguments to solve interpersonal conflict. (46, 47, 48)

46. Assist the student in creating a conflict resolution chart that lists various ways to solve a dispute (e.g., share, take turns, listen, talk it over, apologize, get help, use humor, start over, flip a coin) on different

segments of the chart. Instruct him/her to use this chart when trying to determine alternatives to using anger to problem-solve.

47. Brainstorm with the student the benefits of peaceful negotiations and problem-solving (e.g., respect and dignity are maintained; problems are resolved rather than intensified; friendships continue or develop; social skills are learned) versus the results of conflict and power struggles (e.g., broken friendships, hostile school environment, suspicion, aggression).

48. Request that the student's parents and teachers affirm him/her verbally and in writing for his/her efforts in managing personal anger and using positive and effective alternatives to angry outbursts, retaliation, and aggression. Ask the student to read the positive comments during a session.

___. _____
_____

___. _____
_____

___. _____
_____

___. _____
_____

___. _____
_____

___. _____
_____

DIAGNOSTIC SUGGESTIONS

Axis I:	313.81	Oppositional Defiant Disorder
	312.34	Intermittent Explosive Disorder
	312.30	Impulse Control Disorder, NOS
	312.8	Conduct Disorder
	312.9	Disruptive Behavior Disorder, NOS
	314.01	Attention-Deficit/Hyperactivity Disorder, Predominantly Hyperactive-Impulsive Type
	314.9	Attention-Deficit/Hyperactivity Disorder, NOS
	V71.02	Child Antisocial Behavior
	V61.20	Parent-Child Relational Problem
	300.02	Generalized Anxiety Disorder
	V62.81	Relational Problem, NOS
	_____	_____
	_____	_____
Axis II:	799.9	Diagnosis Deferred
	V71.09	No Diagnosis on Axis II
	_____	_____
	_____	_____

ANXIETY REDUCTION

BEHAVIORAL DEFINITIONS

1. A pervasive feeling of unease, hypervigilance, or tension.
2. Restless agitation, muscle tension, and increased heart rate.
3. Fear of failure in any situation that is challenging (e.g., academic tasks, athletic skills, social encounters).
4. Persistent worrying about the future.
5. Excessive concern or awareness of somatic symptoms.
6. Difficulty getting to or remaining asleep.
7. Lack of confidence in social abilities or acceptance, leading to social withdrawal.
8. Either exaggerated or deficient expression of emotions and feelings.
9. Lack of confidence in test-taking ability, leading to debilitating anxiety that significantly reduces academic performance.

—. _____
   _____

—. _____
   _____

—. _____
   _____

LONG-TERM GOALS

1. Reduce the overall level of worry and fear.
2. Learn techniques to reframe and redirect anxiety-producing stressors.
3. Reduce somatic symptoms.
4. Reduce the impact of anxiety on restful sleep.

5. Develop confidence in social skills.
6. Express emotions in an open, age-appropriate manner.
7. Develop resilience in facing stressful situations and participate in various activities.
8. Improve test-taking performance.

___. _____

  _____

___. _____

  _____

___. _____

  _____

SHORT-TERM OBJECTIVES

1. Identify areas of elevated anxiety. (1, 2, 3)

THERAPEUTIC INTERVENTIONS

1. Develop a positive, trusting relationship with the student through supportive, clinical discussions of current worries and concerns and their underlying causes.

2. Assess the student's current level and areas of anxiety by administering an objective inventory (e.g., The Revised Children's Manifest Anxiety by Reynolds and Richmond, available from Western Psychological Services).

3. Use a therapeutic game (e.g., The Talking, Feeling, Doing Game, available from Creative Therapeutics or The Ungame, available from the Ungame Company) to expand the student's awareness of his/her own feelings and the triggers for these feelings.

2. Prioritize and reduce the number of generalized worries. (4)

3. Verbalize how personal stressors interfere with daily functioning. (5, 6)

4. Focus on one anxiety-producing situation and develop problem-solving and decision-making skills for that situation. (6, 7, 8, 9)

4. Brainstorm with the student an extensive list of personal worries, and ask him/her to prioritize them from the greatest to least troubling, eliminating duplications and consolidating overlapping items.

5. Explore how the student's anxiety reaction interferes with his/her daily functioning.

6. Ask the student to draw a picture entitled *What Stress or Fear Looks Like to Me;* interpret the drawing during a counseling session, and suggest coping skills.

6. Ask the student to draw a picture entitled *What Stress or Fear Looks Like to Me;* interpret the drawing during a counseling session, and suggest coping skills.

7. Discuss areas of personal anxiety with the student, and begin the reframing process by suggesting alternative methods of interpreting and coping with each situation that creates stress (e.g., listing several positive options for dealing with the situation, recording the situation in a personal journal, deciding to delay any corrective action until after a discussion with a trusted adult).

8. Ask the student to draw a picture entitled *What Serenity and Calm Look*

Like to Me; interpret the drawing during a counseling session, and suggest actions to achieve serenity.

9. Ask the student to identify one source of anxiety to work on during the week; brainstorm possible remedies to the troubling situation, choose an option most likely to reduce his/her level of concern, and report the outcome of implementation during the next counseling session.

5. Verbalize an understanding that mistakes are a natural part of learning and can strengthen and enrich life. (10, 11, 12)

10. Assign the student to list at least 10 mistakes that he/she has made and then to identify how these mistakes have contributed to personal wisdom (or assign the "Mistake or Learning Opportunity" activity from *The School Counseling and School Social Work Homework Planner* by Knapp).

11. Relate to the student stories of how numerous successful people have overcome significant personal problems and challenges and become successful and famous (e.g., Bill Gates, Thomas Edison, Theodore Roosevelt, Wilma Rudolph).

12. Ask the student to record in a journal some mistakes made by people he/she admires along with observations of how they have

corrected or managed these mistakes.

6. Reframe situations that have triggered feelings of fear concerning self, parents, family, school, friends, and others. (10, 13, 14)

10. Assign the student to list at least 10 mistakes that he/she has made and then to identify how these mistakes have contributed to personal wisdom (or assign the "Mistake or Learning Opportunity" activity from the *School Counseling and School Social Work Homework Planner* by Knapp).

13. Council the parents to help the student to reframe situations that trigger feelings of fear by discussing events rationally and logically with their child.

14. Use rational emotive techniques [e.g., the "Reframing Your Worries" activity from the *School Counseling and School Social Work Homework Planner* (Knapp)] to help the student to identify situations that have contributed to fearful feelings and to reevaluate these events in a more realistic and positive manner. (See *A New Guide to Rational Living* by Ellis.)

7. Identify how stress is manifested in physical symptoms. (15, 16, 17)

15. Ask the student to note in a journal several incidents of elevated stress and related physical symptoms (e.g., rapid heartbeat, headache, stomach distress, sweaty palms).

16. Help the student to heighten his/her awareness of anxious

moments by wearing a bio dot (biofeedback stress patch available from the Biodot Company), and record times of stress and accompanying physical reactions in a journal.

17. Ask the student to identify areas on an image of the human body where personal stress is most commonly reflected (or assign the "Physical Receptors of Stress" activity from the *School Counseling and School Social Work Homework Planner* by Knapp).

8. Implement relaxation techniques during periods of stress. (18, 19, 20, 21)

18. Teach the student how to relax different areas of the body by first tightening and then relaxing muscles, paying particular attention to areas where stress is typically manifested (e.g., jaw, neck, shoulders, stomach).

19. Ask the student to hold a stress ball and practice squeezing and relaxing his/her arm and fist while breathing in and out at an even pace.

20. Have the student record in a journal several occasions during the week when he/she feels calm and his/her muscles are relaxed and breathing is even.

21. Assign the student to practice deep, even breathing and muscle relaxation during daily stressful situations.

9. Participate in aerobic exercise on a regular basis to reduce tension. (22)

22. Encourage the student to participate in an aerobic exercise for one-half hour, three to four times per week.

10. Implement a routine nightly sleep pattern. (23, 24)

23. Help the student to develop a bedtime routine that reduces anxiety and encourages sleep (e.g., taking a bath or shower, playing soft music, reading a story, repeating a positive self-talk phrase, or counting backward until sleep occurs).

24. Counsel the parents to provide the student with an environment that is conducive to peaceful nighttime sleep and to support and/or enforce a bedtime routine.

11. Use relaxation and deep breathing techniques to fall asleep easily. (18, 23, 25)

18. Teach the student how to relax different areas of the body by first tightening and then relaxing muscles, paying particular attention to areas where stress is typically manifested (e.g., jaw, neck, shoulders, stomach).

23. Help the student to develop a bedtime routine that reduces anxiety and encourages sleep (e.g., taking a bath or shower, playing soft music, reading a story, repeating a positive self-talk phrase, or counting backward until sleep occurs).

25. Encourage the student to implement the use of relaxation and deep breathing techniques to facilitate falling asleep; review and

process success, redirecting for failure.

12. Report being less disturbed by dreams, and remain in bed throughout the night. (23, 24, 26)

23. Help the student to develop a bedtime routine that reduces anxiety and encourages sleep (e.g., taking a bath or shower, playing soft music, reading a story, repeating a positive self-talk phrase, or counting backward until sleep occurs).

24. Counsel the parents to provide the student with an environment that is conducive to peaceful nighttime sleep and to support and/or enforce a bedtime routine.

26. Assist the student in dealing with distressful dreams and periods of wakefulness during the night by encouraging him/her to listen to quiet music, read, repeat positive self-talk, or record the dream in a dream journal and discuss it later with a counselor.

13. Reduce excessive daytime sleep and increase daily activity. (22, 27)

22. Encourage the student to participate in an aerobic exercise for one-half hour, three to four times per week.

27. Plan with the student and/or his/her parents to reduce daytime sleep in order to promote normal nighttime sleep.

14. Increase appropriate social interaction with others to at least three encounters per day. (28, 29, 30, 31)

28. Refer the student to or conduct a social skills therapeutic group.

29. Encourage the student's teacher(s) to involve the student in cooperative learning groups.

30. Ask the teacher(s) to recognize the student for successful participation in class.

31. Support the student in joining an extracurricular group sponsored by the school, church, or community.

15. Implement conflict management skills in daily social interaction. (32, 33, 34)

32. Teach the student techniques of conflict management (e.g., sharing, taking turns, listening, talking the problem over, apologizing, getting help).

33. Teach the student to use "I" messages and reflective listening. [See *Teaching Children Self-Discipline* by Gordon or the Bug-Wish Technique (e.g., "It bugs me when you . . . I wish you would. . . .").]

34. Use the *Peacemaking Skills for Little Kids Student Activity Book* (Schmidt, Friedmann, Brunt, and Solotoff) to develop social assertiveness and conflict management skills.

16. List the benefits of sharing feelings with others. (35)

35. Brainstorm with the student the personal and social benefits of sharing one's thoughts and feelings with others (e.g., increases understanding and empathy, reduces stress, builds trust, strengthens friendships).

17. Risk expressing feelings with parents, teachers, and peers three times per week. (36, 37)

36. Use puppets or role playing to help the student to prepare for appropriate sharing of his/her feelings with others.

37. Assign the student to share his/her feelings with his/her parents, teachers, or peers three times per week; review and process the experience.

18. Implement coping strategies to reduce daydreaming and other symptoms of stress. (38, 39)

38. Use brainstorming to develop a list of stress reducers, and ask the student to select several approaches that could reduce personal stress (e.g., playing with a pet, wearing comfortable clothing, or reminding himself/herself that stress is an attitude) (or assign the "101 Ways to Cope with Stress" activity from the *School Counseling and School Social Work Homework Planner* by Knapp).

39. Help the student to develop techniques to refocus and halt excessive, inappropriate daydreaming (e.g., snapping a rubber band on the wrist, rotating feet, reestablishing eye contact, or changing expression).

19. Verbalize pride in schoolwork. (40, 41)

40. Ask the student to bring completed academic assignments to each counseling session, and discuss his/her positive efforts.

41. Review teacher assessments or report cards with the student, and have

him/her relate what personal strengths are being reflected.

20. Verbalize confidence in own test-taking ability and reduced fear of testing event. (42, 43)

42. Assist the student in identifying and recording several self-talk statements that can be used during test taking to ward off worry (e.g., I am prepared for this test; I can handle this subject; I practiced for this at home; I've done well on tests like this before).

43. Assist the student in recording in a personal journal the steps that are necessary to prepare for an upcoming academic test or classroom presentation. Prioritize the steps, and assign a time for their completion.

21. Demonstrate success in test-taking performance. (42, 43, 44, 45)

42. Assist the student in identifying and recording several self-talk statements that can be used during test taking to ward off worry (e.g., I am prepared for this test; I can handle this subject; I practiced for this at home; I've done well on tests like this before).

43. Assist the student in recording in a personal journal the steps that are necessary to prepare for an upcoming academic test or classroom presentation. Prioritize the steps, and assign a time for their completion.

44. Encourage the student's use of muscle relaxation and deep breathing techniques

during test taking to reduce stress.

45. Process with the student methods used to prepare for a test (e.g., set a study schedule, outline the material, read, write, verbalize, study smaller sections, flash cards for key ideas or pneumonia devices); assess their effectiveness and revise the preparation routine to prepare for the next test.

22. Verbalize optimism toward the present and future. (38, 46, 47, 48)

38. Use brainstorming to develop a list of stress reducers, and ask the student to select several approaches that could reduce personal stress (e.g., playing with a pet, wearing comfortable clothing, or reminding himself/herself that stress is an attitude) (or assign the "101 Ways to Cope with Stress" activity from *The School Counseling and School Social Work Homework Planner* by Knapp).

46. Use cartooning (see "Cartooning as a Counseling Approach to a Socially Isolated Child" by Sonntag in *The School Counselor* (1985, vol. 32, pp. 307–312) by having the student begin a cartoon story that is completed with the counselor in progressive cartoon frames and that eventually concludes with a potential solution.

47. Ask the student to record in a personal journal successful methods that he/she has used in dealing with anxiety.

48. Discuss with the student his/her personal plans for the future and methods of achieving these goals.

—. _____   —. _____
   _____   _____

—. _____   —. _____
   _____   _____

—. _____   —. _____
   _____   _____

DIAGNOSTIC SUGGESTIONS

Axis I:	300.02	Generalized Anxiety Disorder
	300.00	Anxiety Disorder NOS
	300.02	Attention-Deficit/Hyperactivity Disorder, Combined Type
	309.21	Separation Anxiety Disorder
	_____	_____
	_____	_____
Axis II:	799.0	Diagnosis Deferred
	V71.09	No Diagnosis on Axis II
	_____	_____
	_____	_____

ASSESSMENT FOR SPECIAL SERVICES

BEHAVIORAL DEFINITIONS

1. Difficulty with behavioral self-control in the school setting.
2. Refusal to follow school rules or respond appropriately to authority.
3. Serious conflicts within adult and peer relationships.
4. Unusually high level of anxiety.
5. Negative emotional and behavioral reaction to situational stress (e.g., divorce, family move, death, abuse, neglect).
6. Low academic performance.
7. Physical problems or disabilities that interfere with school performance.
8. Lack of personal responsibility and ability to function at an age-appropriate level of independence.
9. Low self-esteem, which interferes with academic progress and social adjustment.
10. Feelings of inadequacy resulting from learning disabilities or mental impairment.

—. _____
   _____
—. _____
   _____
—. _____
   _____

LONG-TERM GOALS

1. Educators follow the school's prereferral process to identify social and/or academic adjustment difficulties.

2. Parents agree to a school evaluation to determine the underlying nature of the student's presenting behavioral, social/emotional, or academic difficulties.
3. Participate in an assessment of speech/language, social/emotional, behavioral, cognitive, and academic functioning.
4. Participate in an independent medical evaluation.
5. Parents, educators, and student, if appropriate, participate in a multidisciplinary evaluation team (MET) review.
6. Parents, educators, and student, if appropriate, participate in an individualized education planning and placement committee (IEPC) meeting or a Section 504 plan (Federal Disabilities Act) meeting.
7. IEPC or Section 504 recommendations are implemented at school.

__. _____

_____

__. _____

_____

__. _____

_____

SHORT-TERM OBJECTIVES

1. School social worker/counselor coordinates a prereferral assessment for the teacher and other involved school staff and the parents. (1, 2, 3, 4)

THERAPEUTIC INTERVENTIONS

1. Discuss concerns about the student's school adjustment difficulties with his/her parents, referring teacher, administrator, and other involved educators and schedule for review by the school's child study team (e.g., administrator, school psychologist, school social worker, school counselor, special education representative, presenting teacher).

2. Gather relevant school information (e.g., cumulative record perusal, participation in counseling, discipline reports) for presentation to the child study team.

3. The teacher completes a list of educational strategies that have been implemented to aid the student's academic and social/emotional progress (e.g., individualized instruction, modification of assignments, motivational techniques, study buddy, oral testing).

4. The teacher completes a prereferral informational form (e.g., Prereferral Evaluation Form by McCarney) to assess behavioral symptoms that may indicate the need for a special education or Section 504 evaluation.

2. Teacher and counselor present the prereferral information to the school child study team. (5, 6)

5. The teacher presents the prereferral information to the child study team where educational history, strategies already attempted, and further recommendations are discussed.

6. The child study team determines the appropriateness of a referral for further evaluation to be completed and assigns specific MET responsibilities.

3. The school child study team makes recommendations for immediate accommodation or further evaluation of the student. (6, 7)

6. The child study team determines the appropriateness of a referral for further evaluation to be completed and assigns specific MET responsibilities.

7. Complete a referral for defining specific evaluations requested, reason for referral, student's personal data (e.g., name, date of birth),

and a request for the parents' permission.

4. A designated school representative (e.g., school counselor, social worker, teacher, or administrator) contacts the parents to gain permission for implementation of the recommended accommodations or for signed permission to conduct an assessment or special education evaluation of the student. (8, 9)

8. Contact the parents to discuss the child study team's recommendations and to obtain their signed permission to proceed with the evaluation.

9. Discuss with the parents the nature of the evaluation process, the specific assessments being proposed, and give written information available that explains special education and Section 504 accommodations [e.g., parents' rights booklets or tips for writing IEPC and Section 504 plans, available from Children with Attention Deficit Disorders (CHADD) (1-301-306-7070 or www.chadd.org)]

5. Parents provide background information and developmental history. (10, 11)

10. Gather background information about the student from his/her parents, including pertinent medical, vision, hearing, and developmental history.

11. Ask the parents to complete a student's personal history form (or assign the "Student and Family History Form" from the *School Counseling and School Social Work Homework Planner* by Knapp).

6. Parents provide the school with information from existing independent evaluations. (12, 13)

12. Request that the parents sign a release of information form to allow for obtaining any existing diagnostic information from

mental health agencies, physicians, private therapists, or previous schools.

13. Send for written reports or gather information verbally from any schools, agencies, therapists, or physicians who have worked with the student.

7. Complete diagnostic social/emotional testing. (14, 15, 16, 17, 18)

14. Assign the parents to complete a normed behavior scale, describing the student from their perspective (e.g., the Child Behavior Checklist by Achenbach).

15. Complete a clinical interview that assesses the student's social and emotional adjustment (or assign the "Student Interview Outline" from the *School Counseling and School Social Work Homework Planner* by Knapp).

16. Administer a normed, self-reporting emotional assessment scale to the student [e.g., The Coopersmith Self-Esteem Inventory, The Children's Manifest Anxiety Scale, The Youth Self-Report (by Achenbach), or the Piers-Harris Self-Concept Scale].

17. Complete at least one systematic observation of the student in the classroom setting, noting his/her behavior patterns, frequency, duration, and intensity of any inappropriate behavior as compared with other students of similar age and gender.

18. Ask the student to complete several figure drawings for assessment purposes (e.g., House, Tree, Person, Kinetic Family Drawing, Draw-a-Person, or the Kinetic School Drawing).

8. Participate in intelligence testing. (19)

19. The school psychologist administers intelligence and ability tests to the student [e.g., Kaufman Assessment Battery for Children (AGS), McCarthy Scales for Children's Abilities (The Psychological Corporation), Stanford-Binet (Houghton-Mifflin), Wechsler Intelligence Scale for Children—III (The Psychological Corporation), Woodcock-Johnson Psycho-Educational Battery Part I (DLM)].

9. Complete various tests of academic achievement and recent learning. (20, 21)

20. The teacher, teacher consultant, or school psychologist administers academic achievement tests [Woodcock-Johnson Psycho-Educational Battery Part II (DLM), Kaufman Test of Educational Achievement (AGS), Basic Achievement Skills Individual Screener (The Psychological Corporation), Peabody Individual Achievement Test (AGS), Wide Range Achievement Test (Jastek)].

21. The teacher, teacher consultant, or school psychologist evaluates informal data from quizzes, tests, class and homework assignments, and report cards.

10. Participate in a perceptual motor skills evaluation. (18, 22)

11. Provide information for an assessment of attention deficit disorder (ADD) and attention deficit/hyperactivity disorder (ADHD). (23, 24)

18. Ask the student to complete several figure drawings for assessment purposes (e.g., House, Tree, Person, Kinetic Family Drawing, Draw-a-Person, or the Kinetic School Drawing).

22. The teacher, teacher consultant, or school psychologist administers a perceptual motor skills test [e.g., Keith Beery Test of Visual Motor Integration (Modern Curriculum Press), the Bender Visual Motor Gestalt Test, or Ruthers Drawing Test].

23. Ask the student's parents and teachers to complete several ADHD assessment scales or surveys [e.g., *Conners' Teacher and Parent Rating Scales, ACTeRS* (Ullmann et al.), *ADHD: A Handbook for Diagnosis and Treatment* (Barkley), available from ADD Warehouse or Western Psychological Services].

24. Gain the parents' permission to prepare a summary of the home/school ADHD assessment for the student's doctor to use for possible diagnosis of ADHD and prescription medication. Attach a cover letter to describe the school and parent's concerns (or assign the "ADHD Assessment Summary Sheet" from the *School Counseling and School Social Work Homework Planner* by Knapp).

12. Participate in speech and language, physical therapy, and occupational therapy evaluations. (10, 11, 25)

10. Gather background information about the student from his/her parents, including pertinent medical, vision, hearing, and developmental history.

11. Ask the parents to complete a student's personal history form (or assign the "Student and Family History Form" from the *School Counseling and School Social Work Homework Planner* by Knapp).

25. The speech and language therapist assesses the student's linguistic abilities and determines the need for services in this area.

13. Engage in a complete medical evaluation to determine or rule out physical or health problems that interfere with academic performance or social/behavioral adjustment. (10, 11, 26)

10. Gather background information about the student from his/her parents, including pertinent medical, vision, hearing, and developmental history.

11. Ask the parents to complete a student's personal history form (or assign the "Student and Family History Form" from the *School Counseling and School Social Work Homework Planner* by Knapp).

26. Request that the student's parents provide recent medical information and reports, or schedule a complete medical examination for him/her to determine his/her current health status.

14. Consult specialists as recommended by a personal physician or school evaluators. (27, 28)

27. Consider with the parents and MET members the necessity of obtaining further specialized diagnostic information from a psychologist, psychiatrist, or other evaluation specialists (e.g., neurological, psychiatric, psychomotor).

28. Request that the student's parents discuss further medical testing with his/her physician, or refer them to a community mental health facility for further diagnostic psychological assessment.

15. Parents, teachers, and MET members collaborate to develop a plan for a functional behavioral analysis of the student. (29, 30)

29. Collaborate with MET members to formalize an analysis of the student's behavior and plan for specific intervention strategies that help the child to develop positive alternative behaviors (or assign the "Record of Behavioral Progress" from the *School Counseling and School Social Work Homework Planner* by Knapp).

30. Formulate a behavior intervention plan with the student and his/her teachers, parents, and other MET members that addresses student target behaviors and outlines intervention strategies for modification of problematic behavior, skill development, and reinforcement of positive behavior.

16. Parents and the student attend an MET meeting to review all assessments and discuss the student's eligibility for special services or accommodations.
    (31, 32, 33)

31. Schedule an MET meeting with all evaluators, parents, and student, if appropriate, to review the results of the evaluation and make recommendations.

32. Meet with MET members and the student's parents to present the comprehensive written reports submitted from the school social worker, school psychologist, speech, occupational, and/or physical therapist, as well as detailed information regarding the student's performance from the teacher, principal, counselor, and other educators.

33. Gather any additional information from the parents and the student at the MET meeting, discuss eligibility factors based on state and federal special education and Section 504 guidelines, and formulate a recommendation to the IEPC.

17. Parents and the student attend an IEPC or Section 504 meeting to determine his/her eligibility for special education services and designate services or accommodations to be implemented.
    (34, 35)

34. Conduct a Section 504 meeting to determine the student's eligibility for accommodations, and participate in the selection of services to assist academic, behavioral, and social/emotional adjustment.

35. Members of the IEPC, including the parents, student, teacher, evaluators, and school administrator consider the MET recom-

mendations and write the specific individualized special education program or Section 504 services or accommodations to be implemented.

18. Cooperate with the implementation of accommodations and services recommended by the IEPC or Section 504 plan. (36, 37)

36. The IEPC members assign responsibility for the implementation of services for the student to specific team members who submit specific written student goals and objectives to be accomplished during the school year.

37. The teacher, special educators, and other educational personnel implement the written plan for special services and accommodations in the school setting as designated by the IEPC.

19. Meet with the teacher, school social worker, or counselor to discuss the impact of the IEPC or Section 504 plan on personal and school adjustment. (38, 39)

38. Meet with the student on a regular basis to discuss the IEPC or Section 504 plan and to determine its effectiveness in assisting his/her educational and social/emotional progress.

39. Meet with the parents and teachers each marking period or on some other predetermined schedule to review the student's school performance and to determine any indicated modifications.

20. Parents and the student, if appropriate, attend the annual IEPC or Section 504

40. Attend the annual IEPC review meeting to reflect on the student's progress and

meeting to review progress, evaluate the accommodations and services, and make any recommended changes. (40, 41)

discuss appropriate future programming.

41. Participate in a three-year reevaluation of the student's status and subsequent MET meeting to review his/her eligibility for special services and to formulate recommendations to the IEPC.

__. _____
   _____

__. _____
   _____

__. _____
   _____

__. _____
   _____

__. _____
   _____

__. _____
   _____

DIAGNOSTIC SUGGESTIONS

Axis I:	300.4	Dysthymic Disorder
	300.23	Social Phobia
	296.3x	Major Depressive Disorder
	307.1	Anorexia Nervosa
	300.02	Generalized Anxiety Disorder
	300.00	Anxiety Disorder NOS
	300.02	Attention-Deficit/Hyperactivity Disorder, Combined Type
	314.00	Attention-Deficit/Hyperactivity Disorder, Predominately Inattentive Type
	314.01	Attention-Deficit/Hyperactivity Disorder, Predominantly Hyperactive-Impulsive Type
	314.9	Attention-Deficit/Hyperactivity Disorder NOS
	312.8	Conduct Disorder/Childhood-Onset Type
	313.81	Oppositional Defiant Disorder
	312.9	Disruptive Behavior Disorder NOS

	296.xx	Bipolar I Disorder
	_____	_____
	_____	_____
Axis II:	799.9	Diagnosis Deferred
	V71.09	No Diagnosis on Axis II
	_____	_____
	_____	_____

ATTACHMENT/BONDING DEFICITS

BEHAVIORAL DEFINITIONS

1. Severe breaks in the initial bonding process with the primary care-taker during the first two years of life due to abuse, neglect, illness, separation, or adoption.
2. Inability to form close, loving relationships with family members, teachers, or peers.
3. Indiscriminately affectionate with strangers.
4. Demonstrates an extreme need to be in control and a lack of trust in others.
5. Absence of normal, age-appropriate conscience development and lack of remorse for pain caused to others.
6. Superficially engaging, charming, phony, and manipulative.
7. Chronic lying and stealing for no apparent reason or need.
8. Cruel to animals; destructive to self, others, and material things.
9. Lack of cause-and-effect thinking and poor impulse control.
10. Preoccupation with fire, gore, blood, and/or identification with evil or satanic representations.
11. Gorging on and hoarding of food.
12. Parents appear unreasonably angry and frustrated with the student.
13. Abnormal speech patterns, frequent use of nonsense questions, and nonstop chatter.

—. _____
_____

—. _____
_____

—. _____
_____

LONG-TERM GOALS

1. Form close, loving relationships with family members, teachers, and friends.
2. Learn to trust others and reduce the need to be in constant control.
3. Reduce internal rage and develop healthy self-esteem.
4. Establish a normal level of conscience development, empathy, and ability to experience remorse.
5. Eliminate cruel, destructive, and antisocial behavior.
6. Parents and teachers combine affection, nurturing, and highly structured discipline to set limits and help the student establish self-control and develop responsible behavior.
7. Parents and teachers understand the underlying causes and options for treating attachment disorder.

—. _____
_____

—. _____
_____

—. _____
_____

SHORT-TERM OBJECTIVES

1. Parents provide background information, developmental history, and current functioning information regarding their child. (1, 2, 3, 4)

THERAPEUTIC INTERVENTIONS

1. Elicit the parents' signed permission to proceed with a school-based evaluation of the student and/or to refer him/her to a private agency or psychotherapist for an independent evaluation.

2. Gather background information from the parents about the student's past and present functioning, including pertinent medical, vision, hearing, and developmental history.

3. Ask the parents to complete a developmental history

2. Parents sign release of information forms, allowing school staff to request evaluation information regarding their child from professional resources. (5)

3. Parents seek information about attachment disorder from literature or an attachment or adoption support group or organization. (6, 7)

4. Parents, teachers, and counselor give support, nurturance, and unconditional positive regard to the student. (8, 9, 10)

form for their child (or assign the "Student and Family History Form" from the *School Counseling and School Social Work Homework Planner* by Knapp).

4. Assign the parents to complete a normed behavior scale, describing the student from their perspective (e.g., the Child Behavior Checklist by Achenbach).

5. After obtaining a signed release of information form to allow for obtaining any existing diagnostic information from mental health agencies, physicians, private therapists, or previous schools, send for reports.

6. Refer the parents to an organization that educates and supports families who are dealing with attachment disorder {e.g., The Attachment Center at Evergreen [(303) 674-1910 or www.attachmentcenter.org]}.

7. Assign the parents to read a book that focuses on parenting children with attachment disorder (e.g., *When Love Is Not Enough* by Thomas or *The Whole Life Adoption Book* by Schooler).

8. Discuss bonding essentials with the parents and teachers (e.g., eye contact, rocking, smiles, active listening, reciprocal activities, sharing meals, playtime, and

promoting continuity with the child's past).

9. Suggest that the parents meet alone with the student at a designated time each week to review progress, give encouragement, note continuing concerns, and keep a written progress report to share with the counselor or private therapist.

10. Provide the parents and teachers with therapeutic support to remain positive and loving despite chronic and frequent challenges and frustrations with the student.

5. Parents and teachers formulate a structured system of discipline, which enables them to set firm limits and promote responsible behavior. (11, 12, 13, 14)

11. Refer the parents to a structured parenting class [e.g., *Systematic Training for Effective Parenting (STEP)* by Dinkmeyer and McKay, *Becoming a Love and Logic Parent* by Fay, Cline, and Fay, or *The Parent Talk System* by Moorman and Knapp] to acquire techniques of positive discipline to use with the student.

12. Meet with the parents to discuss and help them initiate parenting strategies of positive discipline learned in parenting classes or from recommended parenting books or tapes (e.g., *Your Defiant Child: Eight Steps to Better Behavior* by Barkley; *Parent Talk* by Moorman; or *It's Nobody's Fault: New Hope and Help*

for Difficult Children by Koplewicz).

13. Encourage the teacher(s) to establish a structured and positive form of classroom discipline that uses firm limits, logical consequences, and recognition for positive behavior.

14. Discuss attachment disorder with the teacher and its ramifications for managing the student (e.g., establish a highly structured environment, insist all privileges be earned, keep teacher in control at all times, establish trust slowly, use encouragement rather than praise, use unconditional positive regard despite extreme challenges, seek support for teacher burnout).

6. Engage in daily activities that promote bonding with members of the family unit. (15, 16, 17)

15. Encourage the parents and the student to participate in bonding activities that promote attachment for a designated period of time each day (e.g., snuggle time, playing games that require interaction, back or foot rubs, nightly prayers, reciprocal reading, singing together, cooking, cleaning, or any work or play activity that requires cooperation and interaction).

16. Assign the parents to read *Holding Time* (Welch) to understand the technique of

personal touch in promoting the bonding process with the student. Discuss the implementation of this concept in subsequent sessions.

17. Ask the parents to promote feelings of continuity with the student's past by sharing baby and family pictures, telling early childhood stories, recounting the student's first few years of life, and connecting with significant others from the past if appropriate.

7. Engage in daily activities that promote a sense of belonging in the classroom. (18, 19)

18. Encourage the teacher and other school personnel to involve the student in reciprocal activities that enhance a feeling of belonging and self-worth (e.g., one-to-one chats, high-fives, daily greetings, reciprocal smiles, interactive tasks or activities, caught being good, low-key personal affirmations).

19. Include the student in a counseling group at school that identifies his/her negative, self-defeating behaviors and teaches him/her how to replace them with positive and productive actions. (See the *Red Light, Green Light* technique in *Parent Talk* by Moorman.)

8. Use appropriate social interaction skills with peers at school and in the community. (20)

20. Brainstorm with the student about strategies for initiating friendships at school or in the community (e.g., invite a classmate to

9. Participate in special programming at school that establishes firm limits and teaches self-control. (21, 22, 23)

10. Attend family counseling sessions to work on compliance and behavior issues.

play at recess, share a game, invite a friend home for after-school play) and list in a personal journal; ask him/her to choose one strategy to implement during the following week and discuss the results during the next counseling session.

21. Advise the teachers and administrators to establish a time-out area or student responsibility center where the student can go when he/she is disruptive or uncooperative to cool off and plan for more appropriate behavior before participating in routine classroom activities.

22. Recommend special education or Section 504 accommodations to help the student participate successfully in the academic environment (e.g., smaller classroom, assistance from an instructional or behavioral paraprofessional, reduced school day, one-to-one instruction, social work services).

23. Encourage the teachers to attend workshops or seminars defining attachment disorder and teaching strategies for working with students who are affected by attachment difficulties.

24. Meet with the parents and the student on a monthly

(24, 25)

basis to discuss the challenges of attachment disorder for him/her in the school setting.

25. Refer the parents to a private therapist or to an agency for family counseling to work on strategies for coping with noncompliant behavior and relationship issues at home. Stress to the parents the importance of ongoing therapy and personal effort by all family members to rectify this serious emotional disorder.

11. Keep a daily journal to record thoughts, feelings, and significant incidents of fear, anger, and distrust. (26, 27)

26. Have the student begin a personal journal entitled *Learning to Trust* to record thoughts, feelings, successes, and the challenges of living with attachment issues.

27. Have the student begin a list in a personal journal of daily, weekly, and monthly situations that cause anger or rage, and brainstorm appropriate alternative methods of coping with these frustrations (e.g., take a walk, plan an alternative activity, take a time-out, read a book, plan ahead).

12. Express remorse to the family, counselor, teacher, or friends when actions or words create problems or pain for others. (28, 29)

28. Review with the student any poor decisions that may have caused distress for others, and brainstorm appropriate expressions of remorse. Assign the student to apologize for any problems that his/her actions

have caused and to offer appropriate restitution. Record the results in the student's personal journal.

13. Improve articulation and language patterns. (30, 31)

29. Play the Talking, Feeling, and Doing Game (Gardner) during a group counseling session to help the student identify and express feelings related to empathy and remorse.

30. Request a speech and language assessment of the student's linguistic abilities, and determine his/her need for services in this area.

31. Instruct the parents and teachers to "establish respect through speech patterns" (see *When Love Is Not Enough* by Thomas) by maintaining eye contact, engaging in listening exercises, using firm directions, and insisting on a polite, calm response.

14. Participate in a counseling group that focuses on communication skills. (32)

32. Include the student in a school social skills group that focuses on social interaction and communication skills, or refer him/her to a similar group offered by a mental health agency or private therapist.

15. Increase the frequency of compliance with the parents' requests, and demonstrate respect for their role as head of the household. (33, 34, 35)

33. Include the student in a counseling group at school that identifies negative, self-defeating behaviors and teaches how to replace them with positive and productive actions. (See the *Red Light, Green Light* tech-

nique in *Parent Talk* by
Moorman.)

34. Review the family rules
with the parents and the
student to help them formulate a plan for compliance;
instruct the student to
chart his/her progress.

35. Ask the student to draw the
cycle of negative behavior
and the resulting conse-
quences (e.g., event, student
reacts negatively, adult criticizes the student, student
escalates the negative reaction), and then list strategies for breaking the cycle
(e.g., count to 10, engage in
positive self-talk, write instead of verbalize reaction,
take a short mental time-
out).

16. Verbalize responsibility for
own behavior and positive
alternatives to anger outbursts. (36, 37, 38, 39)

36. Ask the student to create
self-monitoring charts that
are kept on his/her classroom desk or in a personal
planner to track emotional
reactions, behaviors, and
social interactions (or assign the "Student Self-
Report" activity from *The
School Counseling and
School Social Work Home-
work Planner* by Knapp).

37. Brainstorm with the student appropriate, socially
acceptable methods of dealing with the triggers and
targets of his/her anger and
rage (e.g., use an "I" statement, walk away, use

humor, take a personal time-out).

38. Instruct the student to complete the "Problem-Solving Worksheet" from *The School Counseling and School Social Work Homework Planner* (Knapp) to analyze an inappropriate behavior and plan for an appropriate response.

39. Read and discuss *Everything I Do You Blame on Me* (Aborn) with the student to help him/her understand the importance of taking responsibility for personal actions.

17. Reduce the number of incidents of dishonesty to the teacher, counselor, and parents. (40, 41)

40. Help the parents and teachers understand that appropriate skepticism is essential when dealing with children experiencing an attachment disorder and that chronic lying is often the norm. Advise them to reserve judgment when lying is suspected and to express appreciation when honesty is shown by the student.

41. Advise the parents and teachers to place the burden of proof on the student when lying, stealing, or personal dishonesty is in question and to require restitution for damages caused (e.g., additional tasks or chores, repayment in the form of personal possessions or money, personal time spent helping the injured party).

18. Eliminate stealing from family, school, and community. (41, 42)

41. Advise the parents and teachers to place the burden of proof on the student when lying, stealing, or personal dishonesty is in question and to require restitution for damages caused (e.g., additional tasks or chores, repayment in the form of personal possessions or money, personal time spent helping the injured party).

42. Discuss with the student, in either an individual or a group session, the underlying unmet needs that lead to stealing and lying (e.g., the need for control and feeling unloved, unvalued, or unfairly treated), and help him/her to develop a list of positive alternatives for meeting these needs. Ask the student to record ideas in a personal journal and to continue to enter additional ideas during future counseling sessions.

19. Develop healthy eating habits and eliminate hoarding of food at home and at school. (43, 44)

43. Advise the teachers and parents to establish food and food-free zones and to require that eating take place in designated areas only, using appropriate manners.

44. Ask the parents to establish regular family meal times, where a variety of food is served, table manners are observed, conversation is enjoyed, and the student is required to remain until the

meal is completed. Caution the parents to avoid entering into control battles over food issues by insisting that the student eat everything that is served.

20. List those people whose love is given unconditionally. (45)

45. Define unconditional love (e.g., complete and constant love given regardless of personal attributes, attitude, behavior, or performance). Have the student write the definition in a personal journal and list significant others who give him/her unconditional love on a regular basis.

21. Identify positive goals for the future in the areas of occupation, family, friends, leisure activities, lifelong learning, and spiritual and character development. (46, 47, 48)

46. Discuss with the student his/her personal plans for the future and methods of achieving these goals.

47. Assign the student to complete the "Growing and Changing Activity" from the *School Counseling and School Social Work Homework Planner* (Knapp), which is designed to create an awareness that learning, changing, and self-improvement are a lifelong process.

48. Assign the student to complete the "My Predictions for the Future" activity from the *School Counseling and School Social Work Homework Planner* (Knapp) to help him/her establish positive goals for the future.

__. _____   __. _____

_____   _____

__. _____   __. _____

_____   _____

__. _____   __. _____

_____   _____

DIAGNOSTIC SUGGESTIONS

Axis I:	313.89	Reactive Attachment Disorder of Infancy and Early Childhood
	314.9	Attention-Deficit/Hyperactivity Disorder, NOS
	296.3x	Major Depressive Disorder, Recurrent
	300.4	Dysthymic Disorder
	309.4	Adjustment Disorder With Mixed Disturbance of Emotions and Conduct
	309.81	Posttraumatic Stress Disorder
	300.3	Obsessive-Compulsive Disorder
	313.81	Oppositional Defiant Disorder
	_____	_____
Axis II:	799.9	Diagnosis Deferred
	V71.09	No Diagnosis on Axis II
	_____	_____
	_____	_____

ATTENTION-DEFICIT/HYPERACTIVITY DISORDER (ADHD)

BEHAVIORAL DEFINITIONS

1. Physically overactive, difficulty sitting still, fidgety and squirmy.
2. Easily distracted by external or internal stimuli and frequent movement from one activity to another.
3. Social impulsivity and lack of polite, expected social behavior.
4. Difficulty remembering and following rules.
5. Poor listening skills and difficulty processing information and directions.
6. Failure to complete games, tasks, or activities due to diverted attention or loss of interest.
7. Lack of age-appropriate organizational skills, poor study habits, and a deficit in the ability to function independently.
8. Inappropriate risk taking, proneness to accidents, and lack of cause-and-effect thinking.
9. Failure to monitor volume of voice and excessive, often rambling monologues.
10. Low self-esteem due to difficulty with social interaction and lack of responsible behavior.

—. _____

_____

—. _____

_____

—. _____

_____

LONG-TERM GOALS

1. Reduce physical overactivity and become more attentive.
2. Acquire and use appropriate social interaction skills.
3. Develop study and organizational skills.
4. Acquire an understanding of the attention-deficit/hyperactivity disorder (ADHD) syndrome along with parents and teachers.
5. Parents use consistent and supportive disciplinary strategies to help the student manage his/her symptoms and develop responsibility.
6. Teachers implement strategies to assist the student with academic and social requirements.

—. _____

_____

—. _____

_____

—. _____

_____

SHORT-TERM OBJECTIVES

1. Participate in an ADHD assessment to be completed at home and school.
   (1, 2, 3, 4, 5)

THERAPEUTIC INTERVENTIONS

1. Assess concerns about the student's inattention, distractability, impulsivity, and hyperactive behavior as described by the parents, referring teacher, or other educator.

2. Complete a cumulative record perusal and note any information relevant to the student's ADHD symptomatology and how this affects his/her school adjustment.

3. Contact the student's parents to gain permission for an ADHD assessment by a psychologist, and allow time for them to express their

concerns and give some background information.

4. Ask the parents and teachers to complete ADHD assessment scales [e.g., the *Conners' Teacher and Parent Rating Scales, ACTeRS,* by Ullmann et al., or surveys from *Attention-Deficit Hyperactivity Disorder: A Handbook for Diagnosis and Treatment* by Barkley (available from ADD Warehouse or Western Psychological Services)].

5. Meet with the parents to gather a developmental history and to review the results of the ADHD assessment, which has been completed and scored.

2. Participate in a medical evaluation to determine a diagnosis of symptoms of ADHD. (6, 7)

6. Discuss treatment options with the parents (e.g., medical intervention as prescribed by a physician, counseling for the student, behavioral interventions, structuring the environment, or a combination of the aforementioned strategies); refer the student to a physician for evaluation, if necessary.

7. Gain the parents' permission to prepare a summary of the home/school ADHD assessment for the student's doctor to use for possible diagnoses of ADHD and prescription medication. Attach a cover letter to describe the school and parents' concerns

(or assign the "ADHD Assessment Summary Sheet" from the *School Counseling and School Social Work Homework Planner* by Knapp).

3. Complete psychological, social/emotional, and medical testing to rule out alternative causes for symptomatology. (3, 5, 8)

3. Contact the student's parents to gain permission for an ADHD assessment by school evaluators, and allow time for them to express their concerns and give some background information.

5. Meet with the parents to gather a developmental history and to review the results of the ADHD assessment, which has been completed and scored.

8. Collaborate with the school or a private psychologist to complete a social-emotional and psychological evaluation of the student if deemed necessary by the parents or physician.

4. Take medication as prescribed by a physician to treat symptoms. (9, 10, 11)

9. Discuss the medication schedule with the parents and the student, and plan for an effective delivery at home and/or school.

10. Monitor the medication schedule, dosage, and positive and negative behavioral changes, and communicate regularly with the student, parents, teacher, and physician (or assign the "Medication Monitoring Form" in the *School Counseling and School Social Work Homework Planner* by Knapp).

11. Advise the parents to ask the doctor to explain ADHD and medication to them and the student and to answer any resulting questions.

5. Parents verbalize an understanding of the effects of ADHD upon the student and possible management strategies. (11, 12, 13, 14)

11. Advise the parents to ask the doctor to explain ADHD and medication to them and the student and to answer any resulting questions.

12. Assign the parents to read literature explaining ADHD to prepare them for subsequent discussions with the student concerning the nature of ADHD. (See *About Attention Deficit Disorder* by Channing and *Attention Deficit Hyperactivity Disorder: Questions and Answers for Parents* by Greenberg and Horn.)

13. Meet with the parents on a monthly basis to discuss the challenges of ADHD for the student and family, review medication, and develop strategies to help the student and family adjust, or refer to a private therapist for family counseling.

14. Refer the parents to an ADHD parent support group [e.g., Children with Attention Deficit Disorders (CHADD) (301-306-7070 or www.chadd.org), The Attention Deficit Disorder Association (ADDA) (P.O. Box 488, W. Newbury, MA 01985), The Attention Deficit Information Network (AD-IN)

6. Parents attend a support group for families with ADHD. (14)

7. Verbalize a clear understanding of ADHD and its causes, effects, and treatments. (15, 16, 17)

(508-747-5180), The Learning Disabilities Association (412-341-1515 or www .ldanatl.org), or The National Attention Deficit Disorder Association (400-350-9595 or www.add.org)].

14. Refer the parents to an ADHD parent support group [e.g., CHADD (301-306-7070 or www.chadd .org), ADDA (P.O. Box 488, W. Newbury, MA 01985), AD-IN (508-747-5180), The Learning Disabilities Association (412-341-1515 or www.ldanatl.org), or The National Attention Deficit Disorder Association (400-350-9595 or www.add.org)].

15. Meet with the student to explore his/her feelings, answer questions, and plan for the management of the medication schedule.

16. Have the student begin a personal journal, entitled *Coping with ADHD,* which contains thoughts, feelings, successes, and challenges of living with this syndrome.

17. Read children's literature with the student that explains ADHD, explores feelings, and suggests management strategies (e.g., *Jumpin' Johnnie Get Back to Work!* by Gordon or *Putting on the Brakes* by Quinn and Stern).

8. Participate in group counseling to acquire more general and personal awareness of ADHD, its management strategies, and social/emotional effects. (18)

9. Implement the use of relaxation or stress reduction techniques to control physical activity. (19, 20, 21, 22)

10. Increase the frequency of aerobic exercise to reduce energy and tension. (23)

18. Include the student in an ADHD counseling group at school that discusses the nature of ADHD, associated problems, and strategies for coping successfully.

19. Ask the student to identify areas on an image of the human body where excessive body movement is most commonly reflected (or assign the "Physical Receptors of Stress" activity from the *School Counseling and School Social Work Homework Planner* by Knapp).

20. Teach the student how to relax different areas of the body by first tightening and then relaxing muscles, paying particular attention to areas where hyperactivity is typically manifested (e.g., jaw, neck, shoulders, stomach).

21. Ask the student to hold a soft rubber ball and practice squeezing and relaxing his/her arm and fist while breathing in and out at an even pace and to use this technique during times of hyperactivity.

22. Assign the student to practice deep, even breathing and muscle relaxation during daily times of physical overactivity.

23. Encourage the student to participate in an aerobic exercise for one-half hour,

11. Use self-monitoring charts to record improvement in the ability to remain calm and relaxed, stay in a designated location, or maintain focus of attention. (24, 25, 26)

12. Participate in an extracurricular activity group, team, or church/synagogue group for a designated period of time and chart progress. (26, 27)

three to four times per week.

24. Have the student record in a journal several occasions during the week when he/she feels calm and his/her muscles are relaxed and breathing is even.

25. Work with the student, in either an individual or a group session, to create a chart that tracks improved ability to remain physically in a specific location (e.g., study desk, group activity, dinner table, car seat) and discuss the results of this self-monitoring during weekly sessions.

26. Assign the student to graph the length of his/her attention span during classroom activities (e.g., teacher instruction, independent seat work, cooperative groups, and large group activities) (or assign the "Sustained Attention Span Graph" from the *School Counseling and School Social Work Homework Planner* by Knapp).

26. Assign the student to graph the length of his/her attention span during classroom activities (e.g., teacher instruction, independent seat work, cooperative groups, and large group activities) (or assign the "Sustained Attention Span Graph" from the *School Counseling and*

School Social Work Home-work Planner by Knapp).

27. Explore with the student various interest groups (e.g., sports, hobby, syna-gogue/church, exercise). Se-lect one to join, determine a reasonable time duration, and chart his/her participa-tion.

13. Actively seek friendships with peers from school, church/synagogue, or the community. (27, 28, 29)

27. Explore with the student various interest groups (e.g., sports, hobby, syna-gogue/church, exercise). Se-lect one to join, determine a reasonable time duration, and chart his/her participa-tion.

28. Assist the student in identi-fying, individually or in a group session, the positive aspects and challenges of sustained involvement in a friendship or activity group, and record ideas in a per-sonal ADHD journal either in written or picture form.

29. Brainstorm with the stu-dent, alone or in an ADHD group session, strategies for initiating friendships at school or in the community (e.g., invite to play at re-cess, share a game, invite home for after-school play), and list in a personal ADHD journal. Have the student choose one strategy to implement during the fol-lowing week, and discuss the results during the next counseling session.

14. Complete assigned chores at home. (30, 31, 42)

30. Create and instruct the student to use a chore chart, which monitors the student's weekly chores, time spent on a task, and a grade given by both the parents and the student (or assign the "Chore Report Card" from the *School Counseling and School Social Work Homework Planner* by Knapp).

31. Brainstorm strategies with the student, in either an individual or a group session, that encourage sustained effort and task completion (e.g., self-monitoring, taking a short break, scheduling a specific time, prioritizing jobs, stretching muscles, standing while working); process his/her personal successes or challenges with implementation of these strategies.

42. Meet with the parents to make recommendations for assisting the student in gaining independence, completing chores and homework, engaging in cooperative behavior, and gaining independence (e.g., maintain eye contact when delivering instructions, encourage questions, offer guidance on an as-needed basis, simplify directions, ask the student to describe what type of assistance is needed).

15. Verbalize an understanding of cause-and-effect thinking

32. Use children's literature to explore the causes of the

as applied to own behavior. (32, 33, 34)

student's behavior and the resulting consequences (e.g., *Don't Pop Your Cork on Mondays* or *Don't Feed the Monster on Tuesdays* by Moser).

33. Introduce activities from the program *I Can Problem-Solve* (Shure, available from ADD Warehouse) to teach problem solving and predicting the result of specific actions.

34. Assign the student to record several problematic experiences in an ADHD personal journal and to analyze in terms of A = antecedent or prior circumstances, B = the student's behavior, C = the resulting consequences. Process these journal entries in either a group or an individual counseling session.

16. Describe alternative positive behavioral choices that will increase the probability of positive consequences. (35, 36)

35. Have the student review, in either an individual or an ADHD group session, an experience in which an impulsive choice created a negative result. Then describe a more appropriate action and predict the probable result (or assign the "Rewind Game" from *The School Counseling and School Social Work Homework Planner* by Knapp).

36. Ask the student to describe a recent problematic situation at home, at school, or with friends. Ask him/her

to create a positive ending using a storytelling approach, which involves a beginning (situation), middle (behavior or choice), and end (result or consequence), or use this activity in an ADHD group session and allow the student to take turns with others, describing the three parts of the story in a round-robin fashion.

17. Parents and teacher empower the student by emphasizing personal responsibility and the benefits of considering the consequences before acting. (37)

37. Encourage the teacher(s) and parents to use positive discipline strategies for helping the student to develop responsibility by (1) assigning tasks and chores, (2) viewing mistakes as learning opportunities, (3) using consequences to teach appropriate behavior, (4) giving another chance to try again after the consequence has been experienced.

18. Increase completion of in-class assignments and homework. (38, 39, 40)

38. Play *Study Smart* (available from ADD Warehouse) with the student to assist in the development of study skills, comprehension, test taking, and memory.

39. Ask the parents and teachers to monitor the student's assignment completion through the use of a planner daily, and give encouragement and direction as needed.

40. Consult with the teacher(s) and parents regarding necessary accommodations to encourage the student's suc-

cess (e.g., give one task at a time, monitor frequently, use an affirming attitude, modify assignments as needed, allow extra time if necessary).

19. Establish a routine or schedule to prioritize and organize key daily activities. (41)

41. Assist the student in listing and prioritizing key daily activities at home, school, and in the community; assign times for completion, and record in the personal ADHD journal or an assignment planner using a star, sticker, or smiley face next to each chore, task, or assignment that is completed.

20. Parents implement recommended strategies for helping the student manage ADHD symptoms. (42)

42. Meet with the parents to make recommendations for assisting the student in gaining independence, complete chores and homework, engage in cooperative behavior, and gain independence (e.g., maintain eye contact when delivering instructions, encourage questions, offer guidance on an as-needed basis, simplify directions, ask the student to describe what type of assistance is needed).

21. Teacher(s), counselor, student, and parents collaborate to devise a plan for helping the student become more successful in the classroom. (43, 44)

43. Arrange a meeting with the teacher(s), parents, and the student to determine accommodations that encourage successful participation by the student in classroom activities (e.g., close supervision during times of transition, sit near the teacher's desk, sit in an area of low distractions, or sit near a good role model; involve the

student in lesson discussions; give simple, clear instructions; affirm progress quickly and frequently).

44. Meet with the teacher regularly to review strategies for classroom management techniques (e.g., *The ADHD Hyperactivity Handbook for Schools* by Parker).

22. Parents, teachers, and counselor affirm the student for progress in assuming responsibility and acquiring independence. (45, 46)

45. Discuss with the teachers and parents the importance of giving frequent affirmations to the student for progress noted in a private, low-key manner.

46. Assign the student to affirm himself/herself for progress in school, home, and social adjustment and to share these successes with his/her parents, teacher(s), and counselor.

23. Mentor other students who are coping with ADHD symptoms. (47, 48)

47. Arrange with the teacher to have the student assist classmates or younger students who are coping with various aspects of ADHD.

48. Invite the student to share personal strategies and successes with students of a newly formed ADHD group.

—. _____

_____

—. _____

_____

—. _____

_____

—. _____

_____

—. _____

_____

—. _____

_____

DIAGNOSTIC SUGGESTIONS

Axis I: 314.01   Attention-Deficit/Hyperactivity Disorder,
Combined Type

314.00   Attention-Deficit/Hyperactivity Disorder,
Predominantly Inattentive Type

314.01   Attention-Deficit/Hyperactivity Disorder,
Predominantly Hyperactive-Impulsive Type

314.9   Attention-Deficit/Hyperactivity Disorder, NOS

312.81   Conduct Disorder-Childhood Onset Type

313.81   Oppositional Defiant Disorder

312.9   Disruptive Behavior Disorder, NOS

296.xx   Bipolar I Disorder

_____   _____

_____   _____

Axis II: 799.9   Diagnosis Deferred

V71.09   No Diagnosis on Axis II

_____   _____

_____   _____

ATTENTION-SEEKING BEHAVIOR

BEHAVIORAL DEFINITIONS

1. Engagement in frequent attention-seeking behaviors (e.g., showing off, calling out, requesting unnecessary help, asking nonsense or irrelevant questions).
2. Continually demanding that others do more for him/her.
3. Escalation of negative behaviors if initial attempts to be recognized are not met with sufficient attention.
4. Makes frequent statements that indicate that the primary focus is on self rather than on the needs of another person or group.
5. Seeks approval and recognition based in an overwhelming desire to feel special or better than others in family, class, or peer group.
6. Verbalizes a mistaken internal belief that he/she is worthy only when he/she is the center of attention.
7. Pervasive feeling or fear of not belonging or fitting in.
8. Low self-esteem and lack of confidence in the ability to be independently successful as evidenced by self-disparaging statements and a refusal to try new experiences.

—. _____
   _____
—. _____
   _____
—. _____
   _____

LONG-TERM GOALS

1. Verbalize a belief in self as being lovable and capable.
2. Demonstrate appropriate interpersonal skills, assertiveness, confi-

dence in self, and empathy for the needs and feelings of other people and groups.

3. Gain necessary recognition using positive and appropriate strategies.

4. Eliminate the frequent attempts to acquire extrinsic recognition, and learn to use intrinsic gratification.

5. View self as an essential member of the family, classroom, and peer group.

6. Parents and teachers work to extinguish the student's maladaptive behavioral attempts to gain recognition and give positive attention when the student behaves appropriately.

—. _____

_____

—. _____

_____

—. _____

_____

SHORT-TERM OBJECTIVES

1. Cooperate with an assessment of social, emotional, and behavioral adjustment. (1, 2, 3)

THERAPEUTIC INTERVENTIONS

1. Administer a normed, self-reporting assessment scale to the student [e.g., the Coopersmith Self-Esteem Inventory, the Children's Manifest Anxiety Scale (Reynolds and Richmond), the Youth Self-Report (Achenbach) or the Piers-Harris Self-Concept Scale] to determine specific areas of social/emotional concern.

2. Administer to the student the Goals of Misbehavior Inventory (Manly) or another index to identify his/her current misperceptions, which may be motivating inappropriate

behavior, according to Dreikurs's theory of misbehavior. (See *Children: The Challenge* by Dreikurs and Soltz.)

2. Acknowledge lovable/likable personal qualities to self. (4, 5)

3. Have the student complete an information sheet that details pertinent personal data (or assign the "Personal Profile" activity from the *School Counseling and School Social Work Homework Planner* by Knapp).

4. Create a counseling journal with the student that will contain his/her therapeutic worksheets and serve as a record of progress.

5. Assist the student in developing a written list of his/her positive personal attributes; ask him/her to save the list in his/her counseling journal and post the list prominently at home.

3. Identify causes for low self-esteem. (6, 7, 8)

6. Process questions and answers from the self-assessment scales and the Goals of Misbehavior Inventory (Manly) to begin the process of reframing and building a more positive self-image. Have the student explain responses in more detail to identify and clarify possible causes of low self-esteem and/or relationship difficulties.

7. Explore with the student the family situation and the relationship with his/her parents that may be

contributing to the need to gain attention in desperate ways (e.g., parents preoccupied with conflict between themselves, parents preoccupied with a special-needs child, substance abuse occurring within the family, predominantly negative and critical parenting style).

8. Meet with the family and the student to observe and assess the family dynamics that may contribute to the student's attention-seeking behavior (e.g., parents preoccupied with conflict between themselves, parents preoccupied with a special-needs child, substance abuse occurring within the family, predominantly negative and critical parenting style).

4. Identify significant others who communicate love and care. (9, 10)

9. Ask the student to make a list of significant others in his/her life, including family members, friends, teachers, mentors, and role models, and rate the degree of support given, closeness felt, or positive influence that person has (or assign the "Important People in My Life" activity from the *School Counseling and School Social Work Homework Planner* by Knapp).

10. Assist the student in writing a definition of unconditional love (e.g., complete and constant love given, regardless of personal at-

tributes, attitude, behavior, or performance) in a counseling journal, and list significant others who show him/her unconditional love.

5. Parents and teacher(s) attend workshops and read literature focusing on teaching children to become more self-confident and responsible. (11, 12, 13)

11. Refer the parents to a class that focuses on helping children develop self-confidence and responsible behavior [e.g., *Systematic Training for Effective Parenting (STEP)* by Dinkmeyer and McKay, *Becoming a Love and Logic Parent* by Fay, Cline and Fay, and *The Parent Talk System* by Moorman and Knapp].

12. Refer the teachers to workshops or books that are designed to promote independence and responsible behavior in children (e.g., *Teaching with Love and Logic Resource Guide* by Fay and Funk, *Teacher Talk* by Moorman and Moorman, *"Positive Discipline, What Does and Does Not Work"* by Knapp).

13. Assign the teachers and parents to read child development literature that addresses promoting self-assurance in children (e.g., *Children: The Challenge* by Dreikurs and Soltz, *The Underachievement Syndrome* by Rimm, *Parent Talk* by Moorman, or *Teaching with Love and Logic* by Fay and Funk).

6. Teacher(s) implements classroom interventions that encourage the student

14. Ask teachers to substitute the phrase "next time" for "don't" in order to shape

to be self-reliant, organized, and self-confident. (14, 15)

positive future efforts from the student (e.g., "Next time you turn in a paper, make sure your name is at the top," versus "Don't turn in a paper without your name at the top"). (See *Teacher Talk* by Moorman and Moorman).

15. Request that teachers use "Act as if" to encourage the student to make an effort despite fear of failure (e.g., "Act as if you know how to draw that tree"; "Pretend you can jump rope"; "Play like you've done this before"; or "Fake it till you make it"). (See *Teacher Talk* by Moorman and Moorman).

7. Implement positive self-talk to encourage confidence and build self-esteem. (16, 25)

16. Brainstorm positive statements of encouragement that the student could apply to himself/herself. Ask him/her to record these affirmations in a counseling journal in addition to actual encouraging statements received from others during the course of the week.

25. Assist the student in identifying his/her propensity for negative self-talk by reviewing situations in which the student felt anxious, inferior, or rejected; reframe his/her thinking into more positive, realistic self-talk.

8. Recognize and acknowledge encouraging comments from others. (16, 17)

16. Brainstorm positive statements of encouragement that the student could

apply to himself/herself. Ask him/her to record these affirmations in a counseling journal in addition to actual encouraging statements received from others during the course of the week.

17. Role-play social encounters in which the student receives compliments or encouragement from others; emphasize the need to accept rather than discount such praise, thank the giver, and integrate the message into his/her self-concept.

9. Increase social interaction with classmates and friends. (18, 19)

18. Help the student plan for an after-school or weekend activity with a friend. Record the event in his/her counseling journal with a photo, paragraph description, or drawing.

19. Encourage the student to join a social group or club. Brainstorm options and help him/her make a selection.

10. Use appropriate social interaction skills with peers at school and in the community. (20, 21, 22)

20. Have the student review, in either an individual or a group session, an experience in which an inappropriate action created a negative interpersonal problem. Then select a more appropriate action and predict the probable result (or assign the "Rewind Game" from the *School Counseling and School Social Work Homework Planner* by Knapp).

21. Ask the student to describe a recent problematic situation with friends and create a positive ending using a storytelling approach that involves a beginning (situation), middle (behavior or choice), and end (result or consequence); use this activity in a group session and allow students to take turns describing the three parts of the story in a round-robin fashion.

22. Include the student in a social skills training group to explore and practice appropriate peer interaction.

11. Identify strengths in the area of multiple intelligences. (23, 24)

23. Perform an aptitude assessment with the student listing skills that are currently mastered, skills being learned, and skills needed in the future in each area of multiple intelligences (from *Intelligence Reframed: Multiple Intelligences for the 21st Century* by Gardner). Discuss the concept that skill acquisition is a lifelong process that requires effort and persistence.

24. Ask the student to draw a picture of a skill that he/she now has, one that is being learned, and one that will be necessary in the future; discuss the importance of these skills during the counseling session (or assign the "Skill Assessment" activity from the *School Counseling and School So-*

cial Work Homework Planner by Knapp).

12. Reframe negative self-talk into positive, realistic messages. (25, 26)

25. Assist the student in identifying his/her propensity for negative self-talk by reviewing situations in which he/she felt anxious, inferior, or rejected; reframe his/her thinking into more positive, realistic self-talk.

26. Ask the student to describe a disappointing event in his/her life in a personal journal and then use the reframing process to rewrite the scenario to reflect a healthier interpretation.

13. Express feelings directly and assertively. (27, 28)

27. Role-play with the student a discussion with his/her parents and/or a teacher concerning his/her attention needs or feelings of inadequacy.

28. Teach the student about "I" messages (see *Teacher Effectiveness Training* by Gordon) and the Bug-Wish Technique (e.g., "It bugs me when you . . . I wish you would. . . ."). Role-play the use of these techniques to respond to distressing behavior from others or to clarify personal feelings or concerns.

14. Demonstrate persistence and systematic problem solving in resolving academic, social, and personal challenges. (29, 30)

29. Use a problem-solving outline to guide the student to identify a problem, brainstorm potential solutions, list the pros and cons of each solution, implement a

solution, and assess the outcome. Assign him/her to use this process when resolving personal problems, either alone or with help from appropriate others.

30. Assign the student to complete the "Personal Problem Solving" activity from the *School Counseling and School Social Work Homework Planner* (Knapp) to analyze a personal problem and develop strategies for a solution.

15. Monitor personal behavior and interactions with adults and peers using a chart to record improvement in ability to remain appropriate. (31, 32)

31. Work with the student, in either an individual or a group session, to create self-monitoring charts that are kept on his/her classroom desk or in a personal planner to track emotional reactions, behaviors, and social interactions (or assign the the "Student Self-Report" from the *School Counseling and School Social Work Homework Planner* by Knapp).

32. Review the student's self-monitoring charts during weekly counseling sessions, giving affirmations for progress that is made and guidance in those areas of no or little progress.

16. Increase the frequency of positive interactions with parents and educators. (33, 34, 35)

33. Have the student complete, in either an individual or group session, the "Criticism, Praise, and Encouragement" activity from the *School Counseling and*

School Social Work Homework Planner (Knapp) to gain insight regarding the effects of positive and negative attention-seeking behavior.

34. Assist the student in creating a list of positive and negative attention-seeking behaviors, compare the length of the lists, and discuss how to engage more frequently in the positive behaviors (or assign the "Positive Versus Negative Attention-Seeking Behavior" activity from the *School Counseling and School Social Work Homework Planner* by Knapp).

35. Read *Everything I Do You Blame on Me* (Aborn) during an individual group session to help the student to understand the importance of taking responsibility for personal actions.

17. Parents and teachers use strategies to enhance the student's ability to seek recognition using appropriate behaviors. (36, 37, 38, 39)

36. Meet with the parents to discuss strategies that will encourage the student to gain independence, complete chores and homework, engage in cooperative behavior, and gain independence (e.g., maintain eye contact with the student when delivering instructions, encourage questions, offer guidance on an as-needed basis, simplify directions, and ask him/her to describe what type of assistance is needed).

37. Encourage the parents and teachers to allow the student to seek his/her own solutions with guidance, even if it requires some struggling and learning from mistakes. Recommend that the parents and teachers listen to his/her problems with empathy and give guidance or assistance only when requested.

38. Advise the parents and teachers to use the empowering statement, "I think you can handle it," when the student is becoming overly dependent and asking for too much assistance.

39. Ask the parents to use the "Check Yourself" technique (e.g., "This is sharing day at school, check yourself to make sure you have what you need when it's your turn to share") to help the student develop the ability to prepare successfully for upcoming events and personal experiences. (See *Parent Talk* by Moorman).

18. Work productively in a cooperative effort at school, and report progress to the counselor. (40, 41)

40. Encourage the teacher to use activities from *TRIBES: A New Way of Learning and Being Together* (Gibbs) to foster a cohesive spirit of community and shared responsibility in the classroom. Ask the student to discuss his/her feelings of connectedness during a counseling session.

41. Engage the student in activities during a group counseling session that require cooperation and shared responsibility (e.g., mutual storytelling, putting together a puzzle, creating a structure using Tinkertoys, panning a community project); analyze and discuss his/her cooperative efforts.

19. Work with the counselor, teacher, and parents to plan for leadership roles in the classroom and at home. (42, 43)

42. Meet with the student, parents, and teachers to brainstorm areas where the student could practice leadership and responsibility (e.g., babysitting, teaching a classroom lesson, caring for the class pet or a pet at home, getting a job); ask the student to select an area for participation and enlist the parents' and teachers' support.

43. Assign the student to assume one new responsibility each month, record his/her progress in a counseling journal, and share this with a counselor in either individual or group sessions.

20. Identify the rewards and challenges of developing responsible behavior. (44, 45)

44. Explore with the student, in either an individual or a group session, the personal joys and challenges of developing responsible behavior (e.g., a more organized daily routine, respect of family and friends, increased personal freedom).

45. Ask the student to write a story or draw a picture in his/her counseling journal, depicting himself/herself demonstrating self-reliance and responsibility. Discuss the story or picture in a group or individual counseling session.

21. Parents, teachers, and counselor affirm the student for progress in assuming responsibility and acquiring independence. (46, 47)

46. Assign the student to affirm himself/herself for progress made in developing personal responsibility and self-confidence at home, school, and in the community and to share his/her successes with his/her parents, teachers, and counselor.

47. Discuss with the teachers and parents the importance of giving frequent affirmations to the student for appropriate behavior and independent functioning in a private, low-key manner.

—. _____

—. _____

—. _____

—. _____

—. _____

—. _____

DIAGNOSTIC SUGGESTIONS

Axis I: 300.4   Dysthymic Disorder
              300.23   Social Phobia
              300.00   Anxiety Disorder NOS

314.01	Attention-Deficit/Hyperactivity Disorder, Combined Type
300.02	Generalized Anxiety Disorder
309.21	Separation Anxiety Disorder
312.9	Disruptive Behavior Disorder NOS
313.81	Oppositional Defiant Disorder
995.52	Neglect of Child (Victim)
V62.81	Relational Problem NOS
_____	_____
_____	_____

Axis II:

799.0	Diagnosis Deferred
V71.09	No Diagnosis on Axis II
_____	_____
_____	_____

BLENDED FAMILY

BEHAVIORAL DEFINITIONS

1. Breakup of former family has resulted in sadness, grief, guilt, fear, confusion, and fragile self-esteem.
2. Poorly defined roles in newly created family leads to confusion, anger, and insecurity.
3. Resistance, distrust, and opposition toward new stepparent.
4. Conflict or inappropriate relationships among stepsiblings living together in the blended family.
5. Legal issues between the parents regarding custody and visitation create feelings of divided loyalty.
6. Difficulty adjusting to the new household rules and customs and a longing to return to previous family rituals.
7. Compares blended family with an idealized former family.
8. Stepparents and stepchildren view one another as obstacles or competition to intimate relationships with their spouse or natural parents.
9. Parents' denial of and failure to respond to the student's feelings of being excluded or displaced, jealousy, resentment, and lack of trust.
10. Parents trying to force bonding prematurely.

—. _____

_____

—. _____

_____

—. _____

_____

LONG-TERM GOALS

1. Accept the need to mourn the loss of the primary family entity.
2. Develop a positive working relationship with parents and stepparents.
3. Establish appropriate sibling relationships with stepbrothers and stepsisters.
4. New roles of family members are accepted over time.
5. View the blended family as a necessary and positive unit that is not in competition with the former family entity.
6. Family members agree to work out inevitable family conflicts and to seek professional help if necessary.
7. Parents and stepparents work together to help the children adjust.

—. _____
   _____
—. _____
   _____
—. _____
   _____

SHORT-TERM OBJECTIVES

1. Verbalize feelings of grief related to the former family. (1, 2, 3)

THERAPEUTIC INTERVENTIONS

1. Ask the student to describe his/her life before and after death or divorce of the parent(s), and current life in a blended family.

2. Brainstorm with the student all fears and feelings (e.g., grief, guilt, anger, confusion) related to the loss of the original family entity using the format of "I feel _____ because _____."

3. View the video *Sarah Plain and Tall Trilogy* (Sargent), and discuss the feelings of the children and adults when Sarah came to live

2. Verbalize an understanding
   and acceptance of the fact
   that adjusting to a new
   family takes time after the
   death or divorce of
   parent(s). (4, 5)

3. State positive feelings for
   original and blended family
   members. (6, 7)

4. Share feelings of insecurity,
   fear, or loss with the par-
   ent(s), and seek reassur-

with the family after the
death of the mother and the
length of time it took to adjust to one another.

4. Ask the student to list several worthwhile endeavors
   that take time (e.g., growing a tree, learning to read,
   riding a bike, growing up),
   and then estimate how long
   it will take to accept and
   eventually care for each
   stepfamily member.

5. Assign the student to interview several peers who live
   in blended families, to determine how long it took for
   them to establish a positive
   relationship with their stepparents, and to report the
   findings in a counseling session.

6. Have the student make a
   collage of pictures and
   memorabilia of original
   family members and trea-
   sured moments.

7. Assist the student in drawing a heart and filling in
   the names of original family
   members. Then add the
   names of blended family
   members to illustrate that
   the heart's capacity to love
   is great (or assign the
   "Many Rooms in My Heart"
   activity from the *School
   Counseling and School Social Work Homework Planner* by Knapp.)

8. Help the student to write a
   note to his/her parent(s) requesting a meeting to dis-

ance of the continuation of a strong relationship between the parent and child. (8, 9)

5. Parents and stepparents agree to be honest with the student about family arrangements and to solicit his/her feelings. (10, 11, 12)

6. Verbalize gradually increasing positive feelings toward stepparent. (13, 14, 15)

cuss his/her feelings related to the new family situation.

9. Brainstorm with the student a list of fears and feelings to share with his/her parents, along with assurances that are being sought from them.

10. Meet with both parents jointly, or separately (if necessary), to discuss the current family situation and how the student is adjusting to the blended family.

11. Ask the parents to detail immediate plans for the student (e.g., custody, visitation, possible moves).

12. Encourage the parents to reassure the student about his/her personal security and to express awareness and empathy for his/her fears and feelings.

13. Assist the student in entering personal thoughts, feelings, and fears in a personal journal that will reflect through activities, writing, and drawing the process of adjustment to the blended family.

14. Assign parents to read *How to Talk So Kids Will Listen and Listen So Kids Will Talk* (Faber and Mazlish) to develop additional positive communication skills with their children.

15. Brainstorm with the student possible names to call

stepparents (e.g., Papa, Mum, first name), and seek a mutually agreeable title to use through a discussion with both parents and stepparents.

7. Define how own role in the family has changed from original to blended family. (16, 17)

16. Assist the student in defining a desired role in the newly blended family, and prepare to discuss these ideas with blended parents or in a family meeting.

17. Ask the student to list the similarities and differences in his/her role in the original and blended family and to record his/her ideas in a personal journal.

8. Parents and stepparents verbalize empathy for children's emotional reaction to their relationship and the formation of a blended family. (10, 12, 18, 19)

10. Meet with both parents jointly, or separately (if necessary), to discuss the current family situation and how the student is adjusting to the blended family.

12. Encourage the parents to reassure the student about his/her personal security and to express awareness and empathy for his/her fears and feelings.

18. Meet with the blended parents to discuss the negative impact of overly romantic or sexualized interactions in the student's presence (e.g., jealousy, questioning of own sexual development, and future sexual relationships), and agree to respect his/her and other siblings' sensitivity to this behavior.

9. Parents and stepparents work together to resolve custody, visitation, and other legal issues affecting the family. (20)

10. Parents and stepparents agree to remove the child from adult conflicts and eliminate triangulation. (21, 22, 23)

11. Parents agree to support each other in child manage-

19. Assign the parents and stepparents to read *Living in Step* (Roosevelt and Lofas) for an understanding of how various family members react to the formation of a blended family, and discuss with the counselor.

20. Parents and stepparents agree to arrange custody and visitation to emphasize the needs of the student rather than the adults.

21. Solicit an agreement from all family members to eliminate put-downs and disrespectful comments about the parents, stepparents, children, and other extended family members and to discuss any incidences of hurt feelings openly, either one-to-one or in a family forum.

22. Discuss with the blended family members the predominant role of the natural parent in the student's life, and recognize that this primary relationship should not be challenged or replaced.

23. Encourage the biological parents to express their acceptance of and encouragement to the student (verbally and nonverbally) regarding his/her desire to form a positive relationship with the new stepparent.

24. Teach the parents the importance of reinforcing

ment issues and to work together to eliminate resistance, manipulation, and
competition from children
and former spouse(s).
(24, 25)

12. Parents agree to encourage
their parents to form and
maintain a positive rela-
tionship with the step-
grandchildren. (26)

13. Parents and stepparents
list behavioral/emotional
signs that indicate that professional help may be
needed for the student.
(27, 28)

14. Attend a support group for
children in blended fami-
lies. (29)

positive behavior from all of
the children, administering
discipline to all of the children in an even-handed and
logical manner, and remov-
ing the influence of the former spouse on the current
blended family.

25. Urge both the custodial and
noncustodial parents to establish their respective
house rules for behavior
when the student is in resi-
dence.

26. Explore the student's relationship with his/her step-
grandparents and assign
him/her to describe the relationship in a personal journal entry or picture.

27. Meet with student and
his/her parents to discuss
any behavioral concerns
and to indicate that negative and self-defeating actions can be a symptom of
feelings of insecurity, split
loyalty, displacement, or
misplaced anger.

28. Counsel the parents on
symptoms and behavior
that indicate that the student is experiencing serious
adjustment difficulty (e.g.,
depression, withdrawal, excessive acting out, feelings
of resentment), and refer
them to a private family
therapist if necessary.

29. Refer the student to a support group for children living in blended families and

15. Express the needs and feelings that parents and stepparents experience during this time of transition. (30, 31)

16. List the many and unique strengths that exist among blended family members. (32)

17. Verbalize ambivalent or negative feelings toward members of the blended family as a normal part of the adjustment process. (3, 19, 33, 34)

discuss information and reactions in a counseling session.

30. Help the student to understand the feelings of confusion and frustration being experienced by parents as a result of the divorce, remarriage, and formation of the blended family.

31. Brainstorm with the student methods of resisting the desire for constant attention (e.g., complete homework, read a book, call a friend, or read e-mail) when parents need to spend time alone.

32. Ask the student to draw or write the name of each blended family member on a large sheet of paper, list several strengths or positive characteristics for each, and discuss in a counseling session.

3. View the video, *Sarah Plain and Tall Trilogy* (Sargent), and discuss the feelings of the children and adults when Sarah came to live with the family after the death of the mother and the length of time it took to adjust to one another.

19. Assign parents and stepparents to read *Living in Step* (Roosevelt and Lofas) for an understanding of how various family members react to the formation of a blended family and discuss with a counselor.

33. Assign the student to complete the activity "I Statements" from the *School Counseling and School Social Work Homework Planner* (Knapp) or role-play using "I" statements and active listening when discussing normal feelings (e.g., rejection, being discounted, jealousy, anger, or frustration), which occur in all families. (See *Parent Effectiveness Training* by Gordon.)

34. Meet with the parents to prepare them for actively listening to the student's feelings and to reinforce the importance of providing time for emotional expression.

18. Family members negotiate the division of household responsibilities and resolve conflict issues in a family forum. (35, 36)

35. Family members agree to hold weekly meetings during which family chores are delegated, family problems are discussed and resolved, allowance is distributed, and recognition for the efforts of each family member is given.

36. Assist the student in preparing for family meetings by discussing concerns and ideas in the counseling session and then recording them in a personal journal.

19. Parents and stepparents establish a proactive system of positive discipline that is balanced with love and designed to promote healthy

24. Teach the parents the importance of reinforcing positive behavior from all children, administering discipline to all children in an

self-esteem and responsible
behavior. (24, 37, 38, 39)

even-handed and logical
manner, and supporting
each other in child management issues.

37. Refer the parents to a child
management parenting
class (e.g., *Becoming a Love
and Logic Parent* by Fay,
Cline, and Fay, or *The Parent Talk System* by Moor-
man and Knapp).

38. Assign the parents to read
*Parenting with Love and
Logic* (Cline and Fay) for information about developing
responsible behavior in
their children.

39. Ask the parents to read a
book on parent communica-
tion (e.g., *Parent Talk* by
Moorman) and discuss with
a counselor how the pro-
posed strategies can help in
managing parent-child is-
sues in the blended family.

20. List the experiences that
have strengthened the
bonds with all new blended
family members.
(40, 41, 42)

40. Ask the student to list the
benefits of developing a
close relationship with all of
the family members in a
personal journal and to
identify methods of improving his/her interactions
with them (e.g., help and
support, reduction of personal stress, and family
harmony).

41. Assign the student to com-
plete the "New People in
My Family" activity in the
*School Counseling and
School Social Work Home-*

work Planner (Knapp) or to make a list of the new blended family members and relatives that have entered his/her life.

42. Assign the student to write a story entitled "A Day with My Mom or Stepmom" or "A Day with My Dad or Stepdad," and encourage the use of as many feeling words as possible.

21. Participate in activities that involve both the total family and one-to-one interaction among the family members. (43, 44, 45)

43. Assign student to play The Ungame (Zakich, Western Psychological Services) with members of the blended family.

44. Ask the student to make a date with each parent, stepparent, and sibling for participating in an interactive activity (e.g., dinner, a walk, reading a book, or playing a game), and discuss the experience during a counseling session.

45. Help the student plan for doing a personal favor that expresses love and caring for his/her parent and stepparent (e.g., cooking a meal, sitting for a younger sibling, or sending a note of appreciation).

22. Identify efforts from blended family members to create a loving, harmonious family atmosphere. (46)

46. Ask the student to identify several supportive and caring gestures made on his/her behalf by parents and other blended family members in an attempt to build a positive relationship.

23. List ways to cope with negative feelings related to adjusting to a blended family. (29, 47)

29. Refer the student to a support group for children living in blended families, and discuss information and reactions in a counseling session.

47. Ask the student to identify five feelings related to adjustment in a blended family, and then brainstorm five appropriate methods of expressing each feeling (e.g., anger—talk it out with a caring adult; jealousy—invite a parent to play a game; sadness—draw a picture expressing personal feelings).

24. Express affection and appreciation to all members of both the original and blended family. (48)

48. Discuss with the student methods of showing affection to all members of his/her original and blended family (e.g., hugs, high fives, smiles, winks, pats on the back, verbal recognition, conversation), and chart in a personal journal the number of times per week he/she engages in similar affectionate exchanges. Process the student's fear that expression of affection toward stepfamily members implies rejection of or disloyalty toward his/her biological family.

25. Parents and stepparents establish and reinforce clear boundaries for privacy and sexual taboos among blended family members. (49)

49. Assist the parents in establishing boundaries for intersibling sexual and personal contact behavior; suggest a family meeting requesting input from all family members regarding meeting privacy needs.

26. Verbalize an acceptance of the parent's decision to re-marry and recognition that this is an adult's, not a child's, determination. (50)

50. Brainstorm with the student all possible reasons for parent's decision to remarry and create a blended family, emphasizing that remarriage is an adult decision.

__. _____
_____
__. _____
_____
__. _____
_____

__. _____
_____
__. _____
_____
__. _____
_____

DIAGNOSTIC SUGGESTIONS

Axis I:
309.0	Adjustment Disorder With Depressed Mood
309.3	Adjustment Disorder With Disturbance of Conduct
309.24	Adjustment Disorder With Anxiety
309.81	Posttraumatic Stress Disorder
300.4	Dysthymic Disorder
V62.81	Relational Problem NOS
_____	_____

Axis II:
799.9	No Diagnosis on Axis II
V71.09	Diagnosis Deferred
_____	_____
_____	_____
_____	_____

CAREER PLANNING

BEHAVIORAL DEFINITIONS

1. Lack of awareness of various career pathways and options for future employment.
2. Failure to associate school-based curriculum with future career goals.
3. Immature or underdeveloped interpersonal skills.
4. Lack of awareness of professional etiquette that is necessary for success in the workplace.
5. Failure to consider personal learning styles, interests, and aptitudes in preparing for a future career.
6. Learning is viewed as a short-term product rather than a lifelong process.
7. Lack of competencies in work-related technologies, tools, and equipment.
8. Deficient communication at a professional level using speaking, listening, reading, and writing skills.
9. Absence of a comprehensive school-to-work transition plan.

__. _____
   _____
   _____
__. _____
   _____
   _____
__. _____
   _____

LONG-TERM GOALS

1. Verbalize an awareness of various career pathways and their educational or training prerequisites.

2. Complete an assessment of personal traits, interests, abilities, and learning styles to assist in determining career goals and work values.
3. Participate in a K-12 career awareness curriculum.
4. Demonstrate grade-level or above competencies in communication and literacy, including speaking, listening, reading, and writing.
5. Create an educational development plan (EDP) to assist in a successful transition from school to work.
6. Acquire competencies in technology and other work-related tools and equipment.
7. Demonstrate work-related social skills and the ability to interact appropriately with colleagues, clients, and managers.

—. _____
   _____
   _____
—. _____
   _____
   _____
—. _____
   _____

SHORT-TERM OBJECTIVES

1. List and describe various jobs in the community. (1, 2)

THERAPEUTIC INTERVENTIONS

1. Engage the student in a group or classroom discussion of the various jobs held by familiar adults. Create a list that includes job title, type of work, and necessary equipment (e.g., a carpenter builds things using a saw, hammer, nails, etc.; an accountant analyzes numbers using a calculator, computer, spreadsheets, etc.; a doctor diagnoses illnesses using a stethoscope, microscope, thermometer, etc.) (or assign the "Occupations Tasks and Tools" activity from the *School Counseling and School Social Work*

Homework Planner by Knapp).

2. Introduce the concept of broad occupational categories by having the student view a career cluster chart [e.g., *Career Pathways by the Michigan Occupational Information System* (MOIS) or *The Occupational Cluster Packet from the Missouri Comprehensive Guidance Model* (Gysbers)].

2. Describe positive work habits required for success in school and future jobs. (3, 4)

3. Invite parents representing several different occupational clusters to describe their personal work experience and to identify the positive work habits necessary for successful employment. Create a list with the student identifying personal habits that are important for success both at work and school (or assign the "Attributes for a Successful Career" activity from the *School Counseling and School Social Work Homework Planner* by Knapp).

4. Assign the student and other group members to create two role plays; one that demonstrates poor work habits (e.g., late for work or school, bored, too tired, gossiping, disrespect, off task) and one that demonstrates positive work or school habits (e.g., promptness, politeness, actively engaged in task).

3. Verbalize an awareness of why people work. (5, 6)

5. Ask the student to brainstorm reasons why his/her parent(s) and other adults work (e.g., earn money, help others, feel challenged, contribute to society, interact with others). Assign him/her to discuss ideas with two employed family members or other adults and seek additional motivations for working to add to the list.

6. Assign the student to record personal reasons for seeking future employment in a career awareness journal. Share these ideas during a class discussion.

4. Enroll in a curriculum designed to teach school to work-related competencies. (7, 8)

7. Engage the elementary school student in a classroom discussion of the relevance of each academic subject to obtaining future employment and life goals (e.g., math facilitates money management, measurement, scheduling, etc.; reading facilitates following directions, awareness of current events, awareness of work-related directives, etc.; writing facilitates communication with others, giving directions, requesting assistance, etc.).

8. Schedule the secondary school student in curriculum clusters designed specifically to prepare him/her for future educational and career goals.

5. Complete core curriculum requirements in reading, writing, speaking, and listening. (9, 10)

6. Complete academic testing required for graduation and enrollment in postgraduate studies or training. (11, 12)

7. Explore career pathways, occupational descriptions, and requirements through career development classes, job resource guides, computer programs, or the Internet. (13, 14, 15)

9. Assist the student in choosing language arts and communication courses that meet graduation requirements, and prepare him/her for college, postgraduation training, and occupational requirements.

10. Encourage the student to elect additional classes in the language arts and communications areas to supplement the basic requirements (e.g., foreign languages, theater arts, speech, debate, technical writing).

11. Assign the student to complete the state assessment tests, the ACT Assessment, the SAT, or other tests necessary for graduation and enrollment in postgraduate academic or work training programs.

12. Help the student prepare for selected academic tests by explaining their purpose, administering sample tests, answering questions, and referring him/her to school-sponsored or independent preparation classes.

13. Assign the student to explore options in his/her chosen career cluster using an Internet tool (e.g., *My Dream Explorer,* created by MOIS, or *Discover Career Guidance and Information Software System* by ACT). Instruct the student to save

careers of interest in his/her electronic careers folder or to record his/her choices in a career assessment journal.

14. Provide the student with a course and career guide that lists categories of careers and identifies required high school classes, electives, direct-experience opportunities (e.g., apprenticeships, job shadowing) and specific related careers; ask him/her to review the guide and to record several career categories of interest in his/her career assessment journal.

15. Meet with the student several times per year to review his/her future goals, course selections, academic credits, and grade point average to make sure he/she is on track for graduation and postgraduate transition to college or work.

8. Verbalize an awareness of personal interests and abilities that may influence a career choice. (16, 17)

16. Instruct the student to complete several interest, ability, and career-focus assessments [e.g., ACT, MBTI by Myers, O*NET Skills Assessment (available from MOIS), or the IDEAS Assessment by Johansson) to gain a better understanding of personality factors and aptitudes that should be considered when making career choices.

17. View the video *Self Image and Your Career* (Robbins and Ellis) with the student to help him/her consider personality types and values while planning for future careers and lifestyles.

9. Gather information regarding possible colleges to attend after graduation. (18, 19)

18. Instruct the student to complete a search of colleges using an Internet tool (e.g., My Dream Explorer, created by MOIS) to identify several colleges or training programs that meet specific career, financial, and geographical requirements, and list these colleges in a career assessment journal.

19. Ask the student to select several colleges that meet his/her personal goals and career criteria from a college resource guide (e.g., *The Fiske Guide to Colleges 2002* by Fiske) and to become more informed by writing, visiting, or interviewing representatives from the college.

10. Attend a career exploration workshop. (20)

20. Assign the student to attend a future careers workshop sponsored by the school to become better informed about available careers in the community and worldwide.

11. Develop a written or electronic EDP. (21, 22)

21. Assist the student in creating an Educational Development Plan (EDP), which includes future career and life goals, an interest and ability assessment, educational and achievement ex-

periences, work history, and college and training requirements.

22. Assign the student to complete a career self-assessment survey (e.g., Michigan Occupational Information System Self-Assessment Career Survey by MOIS) to determine categories of career interest and to include the results in an electronic or written EDP.

12. Develop technical competency and skills using office and industrial tools through school-sponsored technical instruction and after-school and summer employment. (23, 24)

23. Advise the student to enroll in core curriculum and recommended electives to acquire skills in technical areas of career preparation (e.g., computer, technical/industrial arts, computer-assisted design, multimedia productions).

24. Refer the student to after-school or summer programs offered by area schools, colleges, and businesses that teach technical skills, office machines, and use of other occupational tools.

13. Participate in extracurricular clubs or groups that teach individual and group problem-solving and project completion skills. (25, 26)

25. Encourage the student to participate in school- or community-sponsored extracurricular clubs or activities to develop essential work-related skills (e.g., 4-H, Junior Achievement, student government, school newspaper, foreign language club).

26. Encourage participation in activities that teach teamwork, problem solving, and

14. Complete an apprenticeship or additional study opportunities in an area of occupational interest and aptitude. (27, 28, 29)

15. Complete an ongoing self-assessment to evaluate adjustment to workplace requirements and culture. (30, 31)

social skills (e.g., sports, band, choir, honor society, yearbook, drama club).

27. Schedule the student in a career-based instruction (CBI) program that offers school credit for actual work experience with employers who provide on-the-job training and evaluation.

28. Enroll the student in a career/technical curriculum to acquire entry-level job skills in a trade, technical, medical, or business employment cluster (e.g., agriscience, business technology, construction, electromechanical technology, hospitality, manufacturing).

29. Invite the student who has completed core requirements to earn college credit by taking advanced placement classes from local colleges or by using on-line resources or distance learning facilities.

30. Assign the student to play the Career Interest Game (Holland) on the Internet (http://career.missouri .edu/holland/) to match interests and skills with similar careers.

31. Arrange for the student to meet regularly with a career development teacher, counselor, or workplace mentor to access emerging job skills and positive work attitudes and habits; ask

the student to summarize these meetings in his/her career assessment journal.

16. List the advantages of working together both at school and on the job. (32, 33, 34)

32. Ask the student to list the many work scenarios where people need to cooperate and work together (e.g., surgery, fire fighting, police investigation, office management, sales, social services).

33. Sponsor schoolwide diversity awareness activities (e.g., diversity theater, multicultural programs, videos, Internet exploration of diverse cultures) to promote tolerance for diversity both at school and in the workplace.

34. Assign the student to vary his/her lunch partners and sit with students belonging to different social, ethnic, and cultural groups. Instruct him/her to record the experiences in a career awareness journal and note how this activity can contribute to cohesion and cooperation both at school and in future work settings.

17. Enroll in a workplace- or school-based social skills class to develop interpersonal skills necessary for success in the workplace. (35, 36)

35. Brainstorm with the student the personal qualities that are required to work cooperatively with others (e.g., speaking and listening, problem solving, promptness, participation, acceptance, encouragement, following directions). Have the student list the

interpersonal qualities that are essential to the career cluster that he/she has selected.

36. Encourage the student to enroll in classes in psychology or sociology that offer insight into typical problems experienced as he/she attempts to adjust to the complexities of society and work experiences.

18. Predict several jobs or occupations of personal interest, which may be perused during the lifespan and list ongoing professional development requirements. (37, 38)

37. View the video *Dream Your Own Dream* (American Society of Civil Engineers) to evaluate the demand for specific careers in the future and the correlation between current academic courses of study and future employment.

38. Assign the student to list several careers that he/she may consider as he/she progresses through life. Ask him/her to consider careers for his/her 20s, 30s, 40s, 50s, 60s, and productive activities or employment that he/she may enjoy after retirement (or assign the "Careers for a Lifetime" activity from the *School Counseling and School Social Work Homework Planner* by Knapp).

19. List the personal benefits of lifelong learning and productive activities. (39, 40)

39. Conduct or enroll the student in a futuristic class designed to explore the future of careers and the world of work; teach him/her creative and critical thinking

skills as they relate to school, community, and worldwide problems.

40. Assign the student to review a catalogue of graduate classes, professional development, or community and adult education offerings and to select areas of continuing education to pursue at his/her leisure after completion of the initial career-related education or training; ask him/her to identify the positive aspects of learning as a lifelong pursuit.

—· _____   —· _____
    _____   _____
—· _____   —· _____
    _____   _____
—· _____   —· _____
    _____   _____

DIAGNOSTIC SUGGESTIONS

Axis I: 309.0   Adjustment Disorder With Depressed Mood
              309.24   Adjustment Disorder With Anxiety
              _____   _____

Axis II: V71.09   No Diagnosis on Axis II
              799.9   Diagnosis Deferred
              _____   _____
              _____   _____

CONFLICT MANAGEMENT

BEHAVIORAL DEFINITIONS

1. Engages in frequent confrontations with peers and adults.
2. Projects blame for misbehavior or mistakes onto others.
3. Refuses to listen to and understand different points of view.
4. Difficulty expressing personal thoughts and feelings.
5. Believes that to succeed (win) means the other person must fail (lose).
6. Gains satisfaction and gratification through power, control, and aggression.
7. Shows a lack of empathy for other people's situations and concerns.
8. Verbalizes a lack of confidence in personal problem-solving abilities.
9. Chronic conflicts interfere with family, social, and academic functioning.

___. _____
_____
_____

___. _____
_____
_____

___. _____
_____

LONG-TERM GOALS

1. Reduce the number of personal conflicts at home and school.
2. Learn conflict management skills to use at home, school, and in the community.
3. Acquire techniques for appropriate self-expression and active listening.

4. Assist others in resolving their interpersonal conflicts using the conflict management process.
5. Learn to differentiate between conflicts that can and cannot be resolved using the conflict management process.

—. _____
   _____
   _____
—. _____
   _____
   _____
—. _____
   _____

SHORT-TERM OBJECTIVES

1. Participate in a counseling group focused on developing personal conflict resolution skills. (1, 2)

2. Participate in a conflict management training designed to teach peer mediation skills. (3, 4, 5)

THERAPEUTIC INTERVENTIONS

1. Facilitate a conflict resolution group for students having difficulty with aggressive interactions either at home or at school.

2. Involve the student in a program designed to teach effective and peaceful means of solving disputes [e.g., *Peacemaking Skills for Little Kids* by Rizzo, Berkell, and Kotzen, *Solving Conflicts* (available from Sunburst Communications), *Mediation: Getting to Win-Win!* by Schmidt, or *Conflict Resolution Skills* (available from Sunburst Communications)].

3. Sponsor and coordinate a conflict managers' or peer mediation program that trains students to resolve disputes with their peers that occur in the educational setting.

4. Enlist the school administration and staff in supporting a conflict management program designed to promote social interaction skills, leadership qualities, critical thinking, and school harmony.

5. Arrange for an initial training of students selected to be peer mediators based on their personal qualities (e.g., verbal and listening skills, dependability, respect for others, and their right to confidentiality, leadership potential).

3. List the steps necessary to attain understanding of both sides of a conflict. (6, 7, 8)

6. Introduce the concept of *point of view* (individual perception) versus *factual information* (concrete data). Brainstorm with the student various situations where differing points of view can lead to conflict (e.g., who won the game, the grass needs cutting, it's my turn).

7. List for the student the steps necessary for understanding both points of view in a conflict (e.g., allow each person to state his/her point of view without interruption, repeat back each statement to check for understanding).

8. Ask the student to role-play several scenarios to portray one point of view, check for understanding, and then ask him/her to reverse roles

in order to advocate for and recognize both points of view.

4. Verbalize an understanding of empathy and how it can reduce conflict. (9, 10, 11)

9. Define empathy, understanding another's feelings and perceptions versus focusing only on our own thoughts and feelings; discuss with the student the role of empathy in conflict prevention or resolution.

10. Teach the student the importance of trying to predict the thoughts, feelings, and actions of others prior to the outbreak of a conflict.

11. Read a story involving conflict (e.g., *Nothing's Fair in Fifth Grade* by DeClement), and discuss with the student how empathy, communication, and awareness of another's point of view can prevent or reduce conflicts.

5. Define potential antecedents or triggers that create or intensify conflicts. (12, 13, 14)

12. Brainstorm with the student a list of conflicts that typically occur in life at home, school, or in the community. Identify possible conditions or triggers that preceded the actual conflict (e.g., shoving in the hallway, competition for grades or friends, vying for a parking spot).

13. Ask the student to identify actions and reactions of disputants that cause a conflict to intensify (e.g., physical contact, verbal

aggression, threats, facial expressions, body language); have the student describe a scenario from a TV program, movie, or book illustrating how a small negative reaction can escalate into a larger conflict.

14. Teach the student the "Rules for Fighting Fair" (see *Mediation: Getting to Win-Win!* by Schmidt): (1) Identify the problem; (2) focus on the problem; (3) attack the problem, not the person; (4) listen with an open mind; (5) treat the person's feelings with respect; (6) take responsibility for your actions.

6. Identify emotions that are commonly experienced during a conflict. (15, 16, 17)

15. Introduce a list of words that express feelings, and have the student select feelings commonly associated with conflict (or assign the "Feelings Vocabulary" activity from the *School Counseling and School Social Work Homework Planner* by Knapp).

16. Ask the student to list methods of supporting someone who is experiencing negative feelings (e.g., empathic listening, staying with them, asking how to help, seeking assistance from an adult).

17. Assign the student to identify personal feelings experienced in situations of conflict (e.g., teacher

confronts you about late homework, friend uses a put-down, peers exclude you from a game, sibling takes a personal possession of yours).

7. List social factors that contribute to conflict and methods of overcoming these factors. (18, 19, 20)

18. List some preexisting conditions that contribute to conflict (e.g., friendship cliques; feelings of exclusion; excessive competition; lack of cooperation; blaming problems on others; failure to emphasize a harmonious classroom, school, or family atmosphere).

19. Identify with the student some methods of promoting a harmonious school and family atmosphere [e.g., peer mediation, the TRIBES technique (see *TRIBES: A New Way of Learning and Being Together* by Gibbs), and using conflict resolution skills in personal disputes].

20. Read *The Cybil War* (Byars) and discuss the underlying causes of the conflict between friends and what could have prevented it.

8. List methods of resolving a conflict fairly and positively. (21, 22, 23)

21. Teach a simple process for younger students to use in resolving conflicts in their lives: (1) State the problem; (2) listen to the other's point of view; (3) share feelings about the problem; (4) brainstorm ideas for solving the problem; (5) agree to a solution and implement it.

22. Teach a conflict resolution process for older elementary school students to use in resolving personal disputes and in mediating the disputes of their peers: (1) Find a private place to talk; (2) discuss the problem without judging; (3) brainstorm possible solutions; (4) agree on a solution that works for both; (5) try the solution and agree to renegotiate if it is not effective.

23. Introduce a peer mediation process for secondary school students to use to resolve conflict: (1) Introduce yourself as a peer mediator; (2) ask the disputants if they are willing to mediate and agree to the mediation rules; (3) each disputant states the problem from his/her point of view without interruption; (4) brainstorm for solutions; (5) choose a mutually agreeable solution; (6) identify how this conflict could be avoided in the future; (7) congratulate the disputants for solving the problem.

9. Designate a time and place for working out conflicts. (24, 25)

24. Establish with the student and staff a designated place in the classroom or school where negotiation or mediation of conflicts can occur; this should be a private area where students can concentrate on conflict resolution and confidentiality can be maintained.

25. Brainstorm with the student appropriate places to resolve conflict in his/her home (e.g., kitchen table, bedroom, office or den, outside, or another area that is conducive to focusing on the problem away from the interference of activities or unnecessary input from uninvolved family members).

10. Implement techniques of active listening and effective questioning. (26, 27, 28, 29)

26. Define active listening (see *Teacher Effectiveness Training* by Gordon) for the student: listening without interruption, decoding the other person's message, and reflecting back both the perceived message and the underlying feelings to check for understanding. Demonstrate the process in role playing with the student, and then have him/her practice this technique by describing events of his/her day to an active listener and then reversing roles.

27. Introduce *effective questioning* (see *Mediation: Getting to Win-Win!* by Schmidt) to the student: using open-ended, nonjudgmental statements or questions to help the disputant explain his/her point of view (e.g., "I need information," "Help me understand," or "Tell me how it happened").

28. Assign the student to role-play several scenarios involving conflict, and exchange roles as the

speaker and the listener, using effective listening.

29. Ask the student to complete the "Listening Skills" activity in the *School Counseling and School Social Work Homework Planner* (Knapp) to practice the skill of active listening and reflecting the feeling.

11. Verbalize strategies for self-expression. (30, 31, 32)

30. Define "I" messages for the student: (1) State your concern in a nonblaming, nonjudgmental description; (2) state the concrete effect; and (3) state your feeling. Ask him/her to practice giving and receiving "I" messages in a group using the format: "I feel . . . when . . . and why. . . ." (See *Teacher Effectiveness Training* by Gordon.)

31. Have the student complete the "Speaking Skills" activity from the *School Counseling and School Social Work Homework Planner* (Knapp) to develop the skill of using "I" messages to state feelings, concerns, or frustrations.

32. Assign the student to complete the "Communication with Others" activity from the *School Counseling and School Social Work Homework Planner* (Knapp) to increase his/her awareness of appropriate times for talking and appropriate times for listening.

12. List examples of encouraging and discouraging nonverbal communication cues. (33, 34, 35)

33. Define nonverbal communication for the student, and indicate that facial expressions and body language can either encourage or discourage a peaceful solution to a conflict.

34. Brainstorm with the student the identification of nonverbal communication cues that encourage communication (e.g., smile, eye contact, leaning toward speaker, nodding the head) versus discouraging cues (e.g., rolling eyes, finger-pointing, eyebrows raised, arms folded); have him/her demonstrate and react to both types of nonverbal cues.

35. Ask the student to role-play conflict scenarios using encouraging nonverbal communication then discouraging nonverbal cues. Have him/her react and record his/her impressions in a conflict resolution journal (or assign the "Cases of Conflict" activity from the *School Counseling and School Social Work Homework Planner* by Knapp).

13. Implement the brainstorming process for seeking potential solutions. (36, 37, 38)

36. Introduce the concept of brainstorming to the student: (1) State any idea or possible solution and write it down; (2) no idea is laughed at or discarded; (3) consider the ideas on their merits; (4) choose a solution that everyone agrees upon.

37. Ask the student to use the brainstorming process to resolve several imagined conflicts. Act as an observer and guide the process to develop authenticity and teach the value of this technique (or assign the "Cases of Conflict" activity from the *School Counseling and School Social Work Homework Planner* by Knapp).

38. Assign the student to use brainstorming during the following week to resolve personal conflicts encountered at home or school. Report the results at the next group or individual session.

14. Identify potential roadblocks to the conflict mediation process and describe possible solutions. (39, 40, 41)

39. Discuss potential problems that could occur during mediation, and answer questions about how to handle difficult situations [e.g., What if the disputants won't agree to the mediation rules? (Find a teacher to intervene.) What if the disputants are too angry to talk? (Give them some time to cool off and set another time for mediation.) What if the disputants become physically aggressive? (Stop mediation and get an adult to intervene.)].

40. Meet with the educational staff to gain support and answer questions and concerns about the conflict management or peer mediation program. Indicate that having peers assist peers in

resolving conflict increases school harmony, builds a feeling of community, and reduces overall conflict in the educational environment.

41. Meet with the parents of group members and peer mediators to explain the benefits of using the conflict resolution process to solve disputes. Ask for their support in encouraging the student to resolve conflict in a peaceful, responsible, win/win manner.

15. Demonstrate the ability to work toward a mutually acceptable solution (win/win). (42, 43, 44)

42. Teach the difference between win/win (both parties are satisfied with the outcome) and win/lose (one person agrees with the outcome and the other person disagrees), and have the student identify situations reflecting each outcome. Create a list of each (e.g., Jimmy gets to go first and Janice doesn't versus Jimmy and Janice taking turns; Cynthia invites Shirley to play and ignores Latricia versus choosing an activity in which all three can participate), and ask the student to identify the resulting feelings of both the winner and the loser.

43. Read *Mop, Moondance, and the Nagasaki Knights* (Meyers) to illustrate how consensus problem-solving helps to unite people (win/win), whereas making

decisions without communication and consensus creates conflict (win/lose).

44. Assist the student in creating a conflict resolution chart that lists various ways to solve a dispute (e.g., share, take turns, listen, talk it over, apologize, get help, use humor, start over, flip a coin) on different segments of the chart. Instruct him/her to use this chart when having difficulty thinking of potential solutions to a conflict.

16. Practice the conflict resolution process with the program trainer and other peer mediators. (45, 46, 47, 48)

45. Introduce the prerequisites to which each disputant must agree before beginning mediation (e.g., agree to solve the conflict, tell the truth, listen without interrupting, no put-downs, and follow through with the solution); inform the conflict managers that if these ground rules are not agreed to, then mediation cannot proceed.

46. Divide the students into groups of four (two conflict managers and two disputants), and instruct them to role-play several conflicts using the conflict resolution process (or assign the "Cases of Conflict" activity from the *School Counseling and School Social Work Homework Planner* by Knapp).

47. Assign the student to practice the conflict resolution

process at home with family members, emphasizing win/win solutions, and to record the results of each mediation in their conflict management journal to share at future group or individual sessions.

48. Designate assigned times and places for the trained conflict managers to mediate disputes, working as a team in the school setting. This should be done as part of the peer mediation program with the full support of teachers and administrators.

17. List the benefits of using conflict resolution versus power struggles, anger, aggression, and arguments to solve disputes. (49, 50)

49. Brainstorm with the student the benefits of peaceful negotiations and problem solving (e.g., respect and dignity is maintained; problems are resolved rather than intensified; friendships continue or develop; social skills are learned) versus the results of conflict and power struggles (e.g., broken friendships, hostile school environment, suspicion, and aggression).

50. Request that the parents and teachers affirm the peer mediators verbally and in writing for their efforts in resolving conflicts and state specific positive results observed in the school or home environment. Read the positive comments at a monthly training session.

—. _____   —. _____
   _____   _____
—. _____   —. _____
   _____   _____
—. _____   —. _____
   _____   _____

DIAGNOSTIC SUGGESTIONS

Axis I: 313.81   Oppositional Defiant Disorder
                  312.8   Conduct Disorder
                  312.9   Disruptive Behavior Disorder NOS
                  314.01   Attention-Deficit/Hyperactivity Disorder
                                      Predominantly Hyperactive-Impulsive Type
                  314.9   Attention-Deficit/Hyperactivity Disorder NOS
                  303.02   Generalized Anxiety Disorder
                  V62.81   Relational Problem NOS
                  301.6   Dependent Personality Disorder

                  _____   _____
                  _____   _____

Axis II: 799.9   Diagnosis Deferred
                  V71.09   No Diagnosis on Axis II

                  _____   _____
                  _____   _____

DEPRESSION

BEHAVIORAL DEFINITIONS

1. Chronic feelings of sadness and/or crying.
2. Verbalizations of low self-esteem along with little or no eye contact.
3. Overwhelming pessimism and feelings of helplessness and hopelessness.
4. Lack of interest and participation in age-appropriate activities.
5. Forgetfulness, indecisiveness, and an inability to concentrate.
6. Irritability, frequent loss of temper, and overreactions to minor frustrations.
7. Problems sleeping at night and/or excessive daytime sleeping.
8. Changes in appetite, eating patterns, and fluctuation of weight.
9. Chronic fatigue, somatic complaints, and restlessness.
10. Preoccupation with morbid thoughts, death, and/or suicide.
11. Isolation from family and/or peers.
12. Deterioration of academic performance.
13. Unresolved guilt or grief issues.
14. Use of street drugs and/or alcohol to elevate mood.

—. _____

_____

—. _____

_____

—. _____

LONG-TERM GOALS

1. Identify and resolve the underlying causes of the depression.
2. Enhance level of self-esteem and reduce feelings of excessive fear, anxiety, and sadness.

3. Reduce level of irritability and antisocial behavior, and establish or reestablish positive relationships with significant others.
4. Resume participation in daily activities, school, and social events.
5. Stabilize mood swings and reduce regressive behavior and somatic complaints.
6. Establish normalized eating and sleeping patterns.
7. Develop feelings of optimism toward present circumstances and the future.

—. _____
   _____
   _____
—. _____
   _____
   _____
—. _____
   _____

SHORT-TERM OBJECTIVES

1. Cooperate with a comprehensive assessment of symptoms of depression and level of social/emotional functioning. (1, 2, 3)

THERAPEUTIC INTERVENTIONS

1. Have the student complete a personal information sheet that details pertinent personal data (or assign the "Personal Profile" activity from the *School Counseling and School Social Work Homework Planner* by Knapp).

2. Administer a depression inventory to the student [e.g., the Children's Depression Inventory (CDI), the Beck Depression Inventory (BDI), or the Center for Epidemiological Studies Depression Scale (CES-D)] to screen for symptoms and level of depression; give feedback to him/her regarding the results.

3. Complete a cumulative record perusal, and note any information that is relevant to the student's symptoms of depression and how these symptoms have affected his/her school adjustment and academic performance.

2. Parents and teacher(s) meet with the counselor to discuss their concerns about the student's symptoms of depression. (4, 5, 6)

4. Meet with the parents to gather a developmental history and to review the results of the depression inventories, which have been completed by the student and scored.

5. Assess concerns about the student's symptoms of depression, social/emotional, behavioral, or academic difficulties as described by the parents, referring teacher, and/or other educators.

6. Collaborate with the parents and teacher to complete the "Record of Behavioral Progress" from the *School Counseling and School Social Work Homework Planner* (Knapp) to analyze the student's behavior and to plan for specific intervention strategies that help him/her develop positive alternative behaviors.

3. Verbalize feelings of sadness, and identify the cause(s) for the depression. (7, 8)

7. Discuss questions and answers from the depression scales or the personal profile with the student, and begin the process of reframing to build a positive

self-image and a greater sense of empowerment. Have the student explain responses in more detail to establish and clarify possible causes of depression or melancholy.

8. Encourage the student to draw pictures, write songs or poems, play music, or use sculpting or sand play to describe his/her personal feelings of sadness and the source of the sadness. Assign the student to share these artistic expressions of personal feelings in a therapy group or during an individual counseling session.

4. Identify significant people and the degree of closeness or alienation felt. (9)

9. Ask the student to make a list of significant others in his/her life, including family members, friends, teachers, mentors, and role models, and to rate the degree of support given, closeness felt, or influence that person has (or assign the "Important People in My Life" activity from the *School Counseling and School Social Work Homework Planner* by Knapp).

5. Parents and other family members verbalize a deeper understanding of the student's depression, its causes, and treatment strategies after attending counseling sessions, joining a support group, or reading recommended literature

10. Refer the student and his/her parents to a mental health professional, clinic, or agency for individual and family counseling to assist in coping with the depression.

11. Direct the student and his/her family to informational

and viewing tapes about depression. (10, 11, 12)

resources offering state-of-the-art interventions and treatments for childhood and adolescent depression [e.g., American Academy of Child and Adolescent Psychiatry (www.aacap.org), Child and Adolescent Bipolar Foundation (www.bpkids.org), or the American Psychological Association (www.psych.org)].

12. Assign the student and his/her family to read literature that describes depression, its causes, and coping strategies (e.g., *Survival Guide to Childhood Depression* by Dubuque or *"Help Me I'm Sad": Recognizing, Treating and Preventing Childhood and Adolescent Depression* by Fassler and Dumas).

6. Teachers, parents, and other family members reassure the student about personal security, express an awareness and empathy for his/her fears, and affirm that they will maintain a supportive and loving relationship with him/her. (13, 14, 15)

13. Meet with the parents, family members, and teachers to prepare them for actively listening to the student's feelings and to reinforce the importance of providing time for emotional expression.

14. Assign the parents to read *How to Talk So Kids Will Listen and Listen So Kids Will Talk* (Faber and Mazlish) to develop additional positive communication skills with the student.

15. Help the parents or other family members plan for a time and method of

reassuring the student about personal security and expressing awareness and empathy for his/her fears and feelings of help-lessness and hopelessness. Role-play giving reassur-ance and expressing empa-thy.

7. Attend group sessions that are focused on increasing self-esteem, expressing feel-ings, and developing social skills. (16, 17)

16. Refer the student to group sessions that focus on build-ing social skills, healthy self-esteem, and expressing feelings.

17. Assign the student to par-ticipate in a conflict man-agement training program to develop interpersonal skills, appropriate as-sertiveness, and conflict resolution abilities.

8. Increase social interaction with classmates and friends. (18, 19, 20)

18. Using puppets or role play-ing, have the student prac-tice eye contact and smiles first with the puppets and then transfer this skill to the counselor and/or group members.

19. Assist the student in plan-ning for an after-school or weekend activity with a friend. Record the event in a personal journal with a photo, paragraph, or draw-ing describing the event.

20. Assign the student to join a group of friends for lunch daily, and discuss the expe-rience during the next coun-seling session.

9. Participate in several organized or informal extracurricular events or activities per month. (21, 22)

10. Increase daily participation in class, and assume responsibility for daily academic assignments. (23, 24, 25, 26)

21. Support the student in joining an extracurricular group sponsored by school, church, or community.

22. Assign the student to attend at least two school-sponsored functions per month with a friend or group of friends. Use the personal journal to plan for the event (or assign the "Planning for Fun" activity in the *School Counseling and School Social Work Homework Planner* by Knapp).

23. Assist the student in identifying methods of increasing classroom participation (e.g., listen actively, ask questions, prepare for input during study time), and have him/her create a graph in a personal journal to chart daily progress.

24. Encourage the student's teacher(s) to involve him/her in cooperative learning groups.

25. Help the student to create a plan for completing all classroom assignments and homework. Have him/her record the plan and progress in a journal.

26. Reinforce academic, family, and social successes by asking the student to draw or photograph a completed project that triggers personal pride (or assign the "Accomplishments I Am

Proud Of" activity from the *School Counseling and School Social Work Homework Planner* by Knapp).

11. Acquire a new skill, hobby, or interest that leads to increased social involvement. (27, 28)

27. Explore with the student his/her acquisition of a new hobby or outside activity that requires the development of a skill. Record progress and feelings in a journal with a descriptive paragraph, drawing, or photo.

28. Brainstorm with the student the interests that he/she now has, had in the past, and will have in the future. Compare the number of interests and activities listed in each developmental stage, and determine whether depression is correlated to a reduced interest level. Discuss how increasing one's personal level of activity can help to reduce depression.

12. Identify situations that have triggered feelings of fear, anxiety, or sadness concerning self, parents, family, school, or friends and verbalize more positive, realistic self-talk regarding these issues. (29, 30)

29. Council the parents to help the student reframe situations that trigger feelings of fear or sadness by discussing events rationally and logically with their child.

30. Use rational emotive techniques (or assign the "Reframing Your Worries" activity from the *School Counseling and School Social Work Homework Planner* by Knapp) to help the student identify situations

that have contributed to fearful feelings, and reevaluate these events in a more realistic and positive manner. (See *A New Guide to Rational Living* by Ellis.)

13. Participate in aerobic exercise on a regular basis to reduce tension and enhance energy level. (31, 32)

31. Encourage the student to participate in an aerobic exercise for one-half hour, three to four times per week.

32. Assign the student to enroll in a physical education class or sports activity to increase energy level and reduce tension.

14. Seek medical intervention to determine the need for antidepressant medication, and cooperate with recommendations. (33, 34)

33. Advise the student and/or his/her parents to consult with a physician to determine the need for antidepressant medication or other medical intervention to treat the depression.

34. Cooperate with the physician to monitor the effects of the antidepressant medication on the student's attitude and social/emotional adjustment.

15. Reduce excessive daytime sleep, and develop a regular nighttime sleep routine. (35, 36)

35. Help the student to develop a bedtime routine that reduces anxiety and encourages sleep (e.g., taking a bath or shower, playing soft music, reading a story, repeating a positive self-talk phrase, or counting backward until sleep occurs).

36. Plan with the student and/or his/her parents to increase the level of daytime

activities in order to reduce daytime sleep and promote normal nighttime sleep.

16. Verbalize the advantages of establishing balanced nutrition and implement healthy eating patterns. (37, 38)

37. Enroll the student in a class exploring nutrition and healthy eating and living habits.

38. Assign the student to monitor his/her eating habits by recording all food consumption in a personal journal, differentiating the healthy from the nonhealthy food.

17. Identify experiences of emotional pain that contribute to depression. (39, 40)

39. Explore the student's relationships with peers and family for sources of conflict, hurt, rejection, abuse, abandonment, or disappointment that may contribute to depression.

40. Report any suspicions of neglect or abuse of the student to the proper child protective services.

18. Openly acknowledge wishes for death or plans for suicide. (41, 42)

41. Explore the student's thoughts regarding death; ask specifically about his/her thoughts or plans to commit suicide.

42. Assess the degree of risk that the student will engage in self-harm; arrange for supervision of him/her 24 hours a day in a protective setting (e.g., psychiatric hospital, group home, residential treatment facility) if necessary.

19. Parents and teachers increase recognition and encouragement of the student

43. Teach the parents and the teacher(s) to recognize and affirm the student daily by

and reinforce his/her active attempts to effectively cope with depression. (43)

20. Implement problem-solving skills to reduce conflict. (44)

21. List strategies that peers have used to overcome depression. (45)

22. Identify people who can be sources of support for building confidence, giving empathy, and/or providing coping suggestions. (9, 46)

noticing small personal attributes and verbalizing an awareness of daily efforts and activities.

44. Assist the student in developing personal problem-solving skills by recording problems in a personal journal and completing the steps necessary for resolution (e.g., identify the problem, brainstorm solutions, list the pros and cons of each solution, select a solution, assess the outcome) (or assign the "Personal Problem-Solving Worksheet" from the *School Counseling and School Social Work Homework Planner* by Knapp).

45. Assign the student to interview three classmates or schoolmates who have overcome feelings of depression, and list the strategies that contributed to their successfully coping with this condition.

9. Ask the student to make a list of significant others in his/her life, including family members, friends, teachers, mentors, and role models, and to rate the degree of support given, closeness felt, or influence that person has (or assign the "Important People in My Life" activity from the *School Counseling and School Social Work Homework Planner* by Knapp).

23. Set personal goals, describe personal hopes and dreams, and express optimism for the future. (47, 48)

46. Have the student define a vision of his/her life five years in the future, focusing on possible relationships, family, career goals, and personal aspirations, and record this in a personal journal.

47. Assign the student to complete the "My Predictions for the Future" activity from the *School Counseling and School Social Work Homework Planner* (Knapp) to establish positive goals for the future.

48. Read *Lessons from Geese* (Clayton) to the student, and follow with a discussion of how people, like geese, can help one another cope in times of sadness, grief, or loss.

__. _____

__. _____

__. _____

__. _____

__. _____

__. _____

DIAGNOSTIC SUGGESTIONS

Axis I:	300.4	Dysthymic Disorder
	296.2x	Major Depressive Disorder, Single Episode
	296.3x	Major Depressive Disorder, Recurrent
	296.89	Bipolar II Disorder
	296.xx	Bipolar I Disorder
	301.13	Cyclothymic Disorder
	309.0	Adjustment Disorder With Depressed Mood

	309.28	Adjustment Disorder With Mixed Anxiety and Depressed Mood
	310.1	Personality Change Due to (Axis III Disorder)
	V62.82	Bereavement
	_____	_____
	_____	_____
Axis II:	799	Diagnosis Deferred
	V71.09	No Diagnosis on Axis II
	_____	_____
	_____	_____

DIVERSITY/TOLERANCE TRAINING

BEHAVIORAL DEFINITIONS

1. Lack of knowledge of various cultures, traditions, religions, rituals, and histories of people throughout the community and the world.
2. Tendency to negatively stereotype individuals who are perceived as being different.
3. Considers unfamiliar customs and behaviors as negatives to be avoided or eliminated.
4. Unwilling to associate with individuals from other ethnic, cultural, or social groups.
5. Views own social group as preferable and superior to other groups.
6. Discriminates against individuals and groups from different cultures, experiences, or backgrounds.
7. Overtly prejudiced toward people who are different from oneself, resulting in verbally degrading comments.
8. Hidden, often unconscious, biases that affect attitude and behavior toward others who are different.

—. _____

_____

—. _____

_____

—. _____

_____

LONG-TERM GOALS

1. Value diversity and place a high priority on becoming familiar with and experiencing various racial, ethnic, religious, and cultural groups.

2. Recognize the similarities and differences within many diverse social, religious, ethnic, and cultural groups, and eliminate stereotypical generalizations.
3. Develop self-awareness, a secure self-image, and the ability to accept and embrace differences in others.
4. Become aware of and eliminate conscious and unconscious biases and prejudices that affect behavior toward other groups and individuals.
5. Recognize own social identity group and how this affects behavior toward and reactions from other individuals and groups.
6. Build and nurture positive relationships with individuals and groups from different social and cultural backgrounds.
7. Work actively to build a sense of community within the school environment and eliminate discrimination, prejudice, and hidden biases toward any group or individual.

—. _____
   _____
   _____
—. _____
   _____
   _____
—. _____
   _____

SHORT-TERM OBJECTIVES

1. Identify personal biases learned in early childhood. (1, 2)

THERAPEUTIC INTERVENTIONS

1. Ask the student to list multicultural impressions developed at an early age in a diversity journal. Have him/her identify the source of these perceptions (e.g., comments from family members or friends, childhood books, toys, or games).

2. Direct the student to interview immediate and extended family members to assess their approach to multicultural and diversity issues.

2. List the similarities and differences of individuals in the classroom and/or school community. (3, 4, 5, 6, 7)

3. Assign the student to choose another student who is quite different from himself/herself, and list the characteristics they have in common. Then ask him/her to choose a classmate who seems quite similar to himself/herself and list their many differences.

4. Assign the student to complete the "Similar Yet Different" activity from the *School Counseling and School Social Work Homework Planner* (Knapp) to learn now people are the same and different.

5. View the video *Different and the Same: That's Us!* (by Alfred Higgins Productions) with the student, and ask him/her to describe a world in which all people are exactly the same.

6. Grant extra credit to the student if he/she varies his/her lunch partners and sits with students belonging to different social, ethnic, and cultural groups. Request that he/she record his/her experiences in a personal diversity journal and share during class discussion.

7. Play an imagination game with the student during which he/she imagines himself/herself as a person from another culture or group, and ask him/her describe

the events, concerns, joys, feelings, and frustrations experienced in a typical day.

3. Verbalize how stereotypes and biases interfere with just treatment and positive social interaction. (8, 9)

8. Brainstorm with the student many stereotypes that are commonly attributed to different cultural groups (e.g., African Americans are aggressive, Asians are industrious, Jews are conniving, Hispanics are hysterical); discuss how these stereotypes influence interpersonal thoughts and actions.

9. Assist the student in identifying instances from his/her own experience in which stereotyping and prejudice influenced his/her behavior.

4. Identify common positive and negative stereotypes currently prevalent in the school, community, and national culture. (8, 10, 11)

8. Brainstorm with the student many stereotypes that are commonly attributed to different cultural groups (e.g., African Americans are aggressive, Asians are industrious, Jews are conniving, Hispanics are hysterical); discuss how these stereotypes influence interpersonal thoughts and actions.

10. Show the video *Valuing Diversity: Multi-Cultural Communication* (by Film Ideas) as an introduction to a discussion about typical stereotypes and intolerance.

11. Assign the student to interview student, faculty, and community members from diverse backgrounds to

understand their perceptions about prejudice and intolerance in the community and the world.

5. List positive social aspects of the school community that promote feelings of respect, tolerance, and positive social interaction among students of divergent backgrounds. (12, 13, 14)

12. Brainstorm with the student roadblocks to unity in the school and community, and list methods of building bridges between diverse groups (e.g., share an ethnic meal, learn ethnic words and phrases, attend a multicultural festival, explore a different cultural custom, wear ethnic clothing).

13. Support an asset evaluation (*40 Developmental Assets* by the Search Institute) to determine the student body's perceptions of available support, encouragement, and unity in the school community.

14. Assign the student to solicit suggestions from diverse groups of classmates for creating cohesion and tolerance in the school or community. List the ideas on a school bulletin board.

6. List personal strengths and weaknesses that influence tolerance of diversity. (15, 16)

15. Instruct the student to list personal strengths and weaknesses that influence his/her ability to accept differences in others; ask him/her to select one intolerant behavior or perception to eliminate each week.

16. Assign the student to seek ideas and suggestions for more tolerant personal behavior from family

members, friends, and members of diverse cultural groups. Create a list of tolerance modifications, and include the ideas in a class newsletter.

7. Participate in activities or events featuring individuals or groups from various age groups, religious, social, ethnic, or racial backgrounds. (17, 18)

17. Assign the student to participate in an interfaith dialogue council or attend various churches, synagogues, and temples to learn about different religions and faiths.

18. Sponsor a trip to a senior citizens' center, and ask the student to interview the residents to gather information about aging and collect oral histories.

8. Learn a second language. (19, 20, 21)

19. Direct the student to enroll in a foreign language class and to share his/her knowledge during a multicultural group session.

20. Assign the student to learn sign language and to use this skill in communicating with hearing-impaired students and community members.

21. Teach the personal and interpersonal value of being multilingual, and have the student list the benefits in his/her "celebrating diversity" journal.

9. Participate in a diversity program or group at school, church/synagogue, or in the community. (22, 23)

22. Assign the student to a group to explore multicultural issues in the school, community, nation, and the world.

23. Invite presenters from various cultural heritages to discuss divergent histories, demonstrate ethnic rituals, and share traditional food with the student during a multicultural group session or class.

10. Teachers encourage sharing of various diverse cultural experiences as part of the regular class curriculum. (24, 25, 26)

24. Urge the teachers to schedule a regular multicultural show and tell featuring stories and artifacts that depict the various ethnic backgrounds of the students in the class or group and to develop with the class a bulletin board or mural identifying the many cultural groups that are represented.

25. Suggest that teachers create a class or group project to explore the multicultural background of the school and community, and assign the student to report on the history of local diversity.

26. Encourage the teachers to ask the student to bookmark websites that focus on multicultural issues and to share his/her finds in the class or group.

11. Recognize subtle biases or stereotypes used by the local and national media. (27)

27. Instruct the student to view popular forms of entertainment (e.g., TV programs, theater, videos, computer games, magazines), and rate them on a tolerance scale developed by the class (or assign the "Media Assessment" activity from the

School Counseling and School Social Work Homework Planner by Knapp).

12. Analyze the school community for prejudices and unconscious biases interfering with a positive school atmosphere. (28, 29)

28. Encourage the teachers to invite student, faculty, or community members from various ethnic or social backgrounds to join a class discussion of tolerance and diversity. Invite suggestions for valuing diversity in the classroom and school community and to answer questions from the student.

29. Assist the student in conducting an informal assessment of the school's support and acceptance of divergent groups (e.g., ethnic, cultural, physically disabled, sexual preference, family constellation, gender, religious preferences) (or assign the "Diversity Support Scale" activity from the *School Counseling and School Social Work Homework Planner* by Knapp).

13. Research own ethnicity and share with others in the school community. (30, 31, 32)

30. Assign the student to research his/her family's nation of origin, immigration to this country, and process of settling in the community; ask him/her to record results in a personal diversity journal and to share this history during group sessions.

31. Assist the student in creating a family tree that focuses on diversity and multicultural issues.

32. Encourage the student to collect stories about his/her ancestors' experiences and lifestyles, and share these with the class or group to illustrate the diverse nature of each student's family history.

14. Take a test of personal tolerance, bias, and prejudice. (33)

33. Direct the student to take a test for hidden bias (e.g., Black and White Race Bias, Age Bias, Gender Bias, Skin-Color Bias, Asian-American Race Bias, or Body Image Bias, all of which are available on the web at www.Tolerance.org) to identify subtle or unconscious bias or prejudice.

15. Identify the tolerance level of family, friends, acquaintances, and the school community. (34, 35)

34. Encourage the student to seek information about personal biases from his/her teachers, family, and friends, and to record the findings in his/her personal diversity journal.

35. Ask the student to rate his/her family, peer group, and the school as tolerant, progressing in tolerance, or intolerant, using a series of questions developed by the class (or assign the "Respect and Tolerance Rating Index" from the *School Counseling and School Social Work Homework Planner* by Knapp).

16. Plan activities with students of different cultural backgrounds. (6, 36, 37)

6. Grant extra credit to the student if he/she varies his/her lunch partners and sits with students belonging to different social, ethnic,

and cultural groups. Request that he/she record his/her experiences in a personal diversity journal and share during class discussion.

36. Organize a brown-bag lunch activity to involve the student in multicultural activities and discussions during his/her lunch break.

37. Encourage the student to communicate with students living in another part of the nation or world by organizing a pen pal program. (See http://Tolerance.org:Forums.)

17. Participate in multicultural cooperative learning groups and activities. (38)

38. Organize a TRIBES (see *TRIBES: A New Way of Learning and Being Together* by Gibbs) program in the classroom, which engages the student in cooperative groups for the purpose of problem solving, socialization, and learning to work together.

18. Engage in interethnic peer tutoring. (39, 40, 41)

39. Sponsor a peer tutoring or mentoring program, which pairs older and younger students and creates a supportive and positive relationship between interethnic and culturally diverse students.

40. Encourage the group members to volunteer their services at an elementary school or in a special-needs or special education classroom.

19. Work to eliminate racial slurs, intolerant actions, and ethnic put-downs. (42, 43)

20. Administrators, board members, parents, students, and staff support the confidential reporting of intolerant actions and subsequent interventions for both victims and perpetrators. (44, 45)

21. Promote and publicize the strengths and benefits of diversity in the school community. (46, 47)

41. Engage the student in a volunteer program at a local nursing or retirement home to assist the residents with their social or daily living needs.

42. Ask the student to record any prejudicial statements or cultural slurs that he/she hears in a multicultural journal. Role-play appropriate responses to use the next time he/she is confronted with bias speech.

43. Promote a conflict resolution or peer mediation program in the school to deal with student disagreements and conflict. Encourage the student to participate as a conflict manager and to use the process during times of personal conflict.

44. Actively support a comprehensive harassment policy in the school, and assist the student in using the process whenever he/she feels bullied or victimized by ethnic, racial, cultural, social, or sexual harassment.

45. Work with both victims and perpetrators of harassment to improve their social interaction skills, develop appropriate assertiveness, and alleviate the need or tendency to bully and intimidate or refer to a social skills group.

46. Assign the student to create a diversity all-star bulletin

board that features students who have promoted multicultural activities and unity within the school community. Honor a different all-star student each month, and describe his/her efforts to celebrate diversity.

47. Help the student organize a multicultural festival that features food, art, activities, and performances from different cultures in the community and the world.

—. _____

_____

—. _____

_____

—. _____

_____

—. _____

_____

—. _____

_____

—. _____

_____

DIAGNOSTIC SUGGESTIONS

Axis I: V71.02   Child/Adolescent Antisocial Behavior
             V62.81   Relational Problem, NOS
             V71.09   No Diagnosis

             _____   _____

Axis II: 799.9   Diagnosis Deferred
             V71.09   No Diagnosis on Axis II

             _____   _____

             _____   _____

DIVORCE

BEHAVIORAL DEFINITIONS

1. Parents' marital separation has led to fear of abandonment, feelings of insecurity, shock, deep loss, and vulnerability.
2. Parents' divorce has precipitated strong feelings of anger toward one or both parents.
3. Guilt, a sense of responsibility for the divorce, and an unrealistic desire to reunite the parents.
4. Internal conflict over issues of loyalty to one parent over another.
5. Absentmindedness, forgetfulness, and a temporary loss of organizational skills.
6. Mood swings, weariness, depression, and a tendency to withdraw since parental divorce.
7. Disillusionment with current and future family and personal relationships.
8. Aggressive, acting-out behavior, impulsivity, and oppositional reactions.
9. Excessive physical complaints.
10. Declining grades and a lack of interest in school and social activities.
11. Attempts to regain control through repetitive, compulsive behavior.
12. A tendency to regress to a safer, more infantile stage of development.
13. Self-defeating and self-destructive behavior (e.g., truancy, running away, substance abuse, mutilation, inappropriate sexualized actions).

—. _____

_____

—· _____
  _____
  _____
—· _____
  _____

LONG-TERM GOALS

1. Accept parents' decision to separate or divorce without feelings of rage, guilt, or depression.
2. Develop a sense of personal security and an assurance of love and involvement from parents.
3. Stabilize mood swings and reduce regressive, oppositional, or aggressive behavior.
4. Reduce physical complaints and self-defeating behaviors.
5. Reestablish interest and involvement in school and social activities.
6. Express feelings about divorce to parents and counselor.
7. Parents agree to discuss divorce with student in a truthful manner and not involve the student in the conflict.

—· _____
  _____
  _____
—· _____
  _____
  _____
—· _____
  _____

SHORT-TERM OBJECTIVES

1. Discuss the parents' decision to separate, and verbalize areas of personal fear and feelings of loss. (1, 2, 3, 4, 5)

   Family Portrait drawing- share. Who is in your family?

THERAPEUTIC INTERVENTIONS

1. Ask the student to share the effect of his/her parents' divorce on his/her life by describing family life before, during, and after the divorce.

2. Brainstorm the effects of divorce on children in general

and specifically regarding the student.

3. Assist the student in listing all fears and personal feelings of loss related to his/her parents' divorce.

4. Show the student pictures of faces expressing feelings from a book about divorce (e.g., *Divorce Illustrated* by Minnick), and ask him/her to draw a face reflecting strong feelings related to the divorce.

5. Assist the student in entering personal thoughts, feelings, and fears in a personal journal, which will reflect through activities, writing, and drawing the divorce adjustment process.

2. Parents discuss their current separation or divorce with a counselor and indicate its effect on the student and the family. (6, 7, 8)

6. Meet with both parents jointly, or separately (if necessary), to discuss the current family situation and the effects of the separation or divorce on the student (e.g., daily routines, emotional stability, school adjustment, relationship with parents).

7. Ask the parents to detail immediate plans for the student including custody, visitation, possible moves, and so forth.

8. Assign the parents to read a book that describes the effects of divorce on children (e.g., *Helping Children Cope with Divorce* by Teyber).

3. Parents reassure the student about personal security,

8. Assign the parents to read a book that describes the

express an awareness and empathy for the student's fears, and affirm that they will maintain a close, loving relationship with him/her. (8, 9, 10)

effects of divorce on children (e.g., *Helping Children Cope with Divorce* by Teyber).

9. Help the parents to plan for a time and method of reassuring the student about personal security and expressing awareness and empathy for the student's fears and feelings.

10. Discuss and role-play with the parents the techniques of "I" statements and active listening to use with the student when discussing the divorce and family plans. (See *Parent Effectiveness Training* by Gordon and *How to Talk So Kids Will Listen and Listen So Kids Will Talk* by Faber and Mazlish.)

4. Verbalize and acknowledge the many people in life who care and are supportive. (11, 12)

11. Assign the student to complete the "Important People in My Life" activity in the *School Counseling and School Social Work Homework Planner* (Knapp), or have the student list a number of supportive people that remain in his/her life.

12. Ask the student to identify several supportive and caring gestures made on his/her behalf by his/her parents, family members, and other concerned people to assist him/her in coping with the divorce.

5. Explore divorce-related feelings, and identify

13. Ask the student to identify five divorce-related feelings,

appropriate methods for expressing these feelings. (13, 14, 15)

and then brainstorm an appropriate method of expressing each of these feelings (e.g., anger: talk it out with a caring adult; jealousy: invite a parent to play a game; sadness: draw a picture expressing personal feelings).

14. Help the student to devise a plan for managing a strong negative feeling during the following week, and discuss his/her progress during the next counseling session.

15. Play the Talking, Feeling, and Doing Game (Gardner, Western Psychological Services) during a counseling session to help the student to identify and express feelings related to the divorce.

6. Verbalize a plan for an appropriate time to share divorce-related feelings with the parents. (16, 17)

16. Help the student to plan for an appropriate time to invite each parent to discuss family-related issues of concern, and role-play this parent-child interaction to rehearse methods of expressing feelings.

17. Assign the student to play The UnGame (Zakich, Western Psychological Services) with each parent and the siblings to facilitate the expression of feelings within the family.

7. Parents express acceptance of the student's feelings and encourage him/her to continue appropriate expression of feelings. (18)

18. Meet with the parents to prepare them for actively listening to the student's feelings and to reinforce the importance of providing

8. Identify divorce as a parental decision, not as the result of any child-based activity. (19, 20)

9. Acknowledge the permanence of the parents' decision to divorce and the futility of attempts to create a reunion. (20, 21)

10. Develop and describe methods of improving the relationship with both parents. (22, 23)

time for emotional expression.

19. Brainstorm with the student all possible reasons for his/her parents' divorce, emphasizing that divorce is an adult decision and that kids do not cause divorce.

20. Read an excerpt from *The Boys and Girls Book about Divorce* (Gardner) to reduce the student's guilt about causing the divorce and to reinforce the futility of his/her attempts to reunite his/her parents.

20. Read an excerpt from *The Boys and Girls Book about Divorce* (Gardner) to reduce the student's guilt about causing the divorce and to reinforce the futility of his/her attempts to reunite his/her parents.

21. Engage the student in mutual storytelling to describe his family's life after the divorce and to accept the permanence of his/her parents' decision.

22. Ask the student to make a date with each parent for participating in an interactive activity (e.g., dinner, a walk, reading a book together, or playing a game).

23. Help the student to plan for doing a personal favor that expresses love and caring for each parent (e.g., cooking a meal, sitting for a

11. Describe interactions with the siblings, and list methods of strengthening these relationships. (24, 25)

12. Outline methods of seeking support from extended family members. (26, 27)

13. Verbalize feelings related to the custody and visitation arrangements. (28, 29, 30)

younger sibling, or sending a note of appreciation).

24. Help the student to predict or describe divorce-related feelings and reactions experienced in his/her relationship with his/her siblings and to write them in a personal journal.

25. Assist the student in listing activities that could strengthen his/her relationship with his/her siblings (e.g., take a walk together, play a game together, create a collage of feelings pictures together, make cookies or dessert together).

26. Ask the student to phone a grandparent, aunt, or uncle and to request a social outing.

27. Assist the student in writing a letter or sending a card to an extended family member that shares feelings and expresses a need to spend time together.

28. Explore the student's feelings about the custody and visitation arrangements; encourage the student to share these feelings with both parents.

29. Assign the student to write a story entitled, "A Day with My Mom" or "A Day with My Dad," and encourage the use of as many feeling words as possible.

14. Parents identify for the student the reasons for the divorce, and calmly discuss family issues as they relate to the student. (31)

15. Parents express awareness that divorce can create severe emotional disruption for children of all ages and that their working together and limiting volatility and change can help to reduce distress. (8, 32, 33)

16. Identify constructive ways to express underlying feelings and fears that trigger self-defeating behaviors. (34, 35)

30. Ask the student to list the benefits of maintaining a close relationship with both parents and to identify methods of improving his/her interactions with them.

31. Facilitate the parents meeting with the student to outline the reasons for their divorce in terms that the student can understand and that absolve him/her of any responsibility for the decision to divorce.

8. Assign the parents to read a book that describes the effects of divorce on children (e.g., *Helping Children Cope with Divorce* by Teyber).

32. Meet with the parents, and encourage them to keep emotional volatility to a minimum and to plan for discussing necessary changes with the student.

33. Help the parents to develop a postseparation plan for cooperatively managing school-related issues (e.g., attendance of school functions, review of progress reports, school conferences, and receiving school information.

34. Explore the student's emotional reactions (e.g., screaming, hitting, withdrawing, or destroying property), and suggest a more rational method of expressing his/her feelings (e.g., using an "I" statement,

writing in a personal journal, drawing a feelings picture, or taking a walk).

35. Brainstorm with the student methods of reducing underlying fears and frustrations (e.g., sharing feelings with his/her parents, counselor, empathetic friend, or supportive adult).

17. Express awareness that negative emotions and fears can trigger physical distress. (36, 37)

36. Explore the student's somatic complaints (e.g., headache, stomach ache, or neck pain), and identify possible emotional triggers (e.g., parents' argument, fear of abandonment, anger toward parent).

37. Encourage the student to participate in physical stress-reducing activity (e.g., walking, running, playing basketball, jumping rope, lifting weights, aerobics).

18. Increase the frequency of age-appropriate reactions, and reduce the frequency of inappropriate or regressive behaviors. (38)

38. Encourage the student to substitute age-appropriate behavior for regressive actions (e.g., sleeping in his/her own bed instead of sleeping in his/her parents' bed, taking the bus to school instead of his/her parent driving him/her to school, using bathroom facilities independently instead of with parent supervision, or getting himself/herself dressed in the morning instead of demanding parental assistance), and to graph his/her

19. Participate in several organized and informal extracurricular events or activities per month. (39, 40)

20. Participate in a support group for children of divorce. (41)

21. Complete class assignments and homework on time. (42, 43)

22. Discuss divorce and its impact on school performance with the teacher(s) and develop strategies for improvement. (44, 45)

progress toward independence in a personal journal.

39. Encourage the student to join an athletic team, school club, church, or interest group; monitor his/her subsequent participation.

40. Devise a plan with the student for inviting a friend to participate in a social activity.

41. Refer the student to a children-of-divorce support group, and discuss this information with him/her and his/her reactions in a counseling session.

42. Assist the student in developing a chart that prioritizes homework and assigns a work schedule and completion time; review this chart periodically and give him/her recognition for positive efforts and guidance in areas of deficits.

43. Request progress notes from the teacher(s) to monitor the student's efforts, and review these notes with him/her during the counseling session.

44. Encourage the student to report the effects of divorce on school and organizational skills to classroom teachers and to request helpful input and support from them.

45. Brainstorm with the student useful strategies for focusing

on schoolwork (e.g., complete work at school, challenge himself/herself to improve his/her grades, reward himself/herself for work completion, request tutoring from the teacher).

23. Verbalize an awareness of the consequences for positive and negative actions and an understanding of cause-and-effect thinking. (46, 47)

46. Discuss incidents of both positive and negative behavior, and ask the student to indicate the resulting consequence; assign the student to record the scenarios in a personal journal.

47. Ask the student to complete the "Positive and Negative Consequences" activity in the *School Counseling and School Social Work Homework Planner* (Knapp) to help establish the relationship between his/her personal actions and their consequences.

24. Express empathy for parents' decision to divorce. (48, 49)

48. Use role reversal techniques to help the student to predict feelings being experienced by his/her parents as a result of divorce and to empathize with their pain and fears.

49. Ask the student to describe the divorce from each parent's perspective to develop an awareness of the underlying reasons for the decision.

25. Ask three schoolmates how they have successfully coped with a divorce in their family. (50)

50. Assign the student to interview three classmates or schoolmates who have experienced a divorce at least one year prior and to

determine how they have
successfully coped with the
changes in their families.

—. _____   —. _____
   _____   _____
—. _____   —. _____
   _____   _____
—. _____   —. _____
   _____   _____

DIAGNOSTIC SUGGESTIONS

Axis I: 309.0   Adjustment Disorder With Depressed Mood
            309.24   Adjustment Disorder With Anxiety
            308.38   Adjustment Disorder With Mixed Anxiety and
                       Depressed Mood
            308.21   Adjustment Disorder With Disturbance of
                       Conduct
            308.22   Adjustment Disorder With Mixed Disturbance
                       of Emotions and Conduct
            299.31   Dysthymic Disorder
            299.02   Generalized Anxiety Disorder
            308.21   Separation Anxiety Disorder
            312.81   Oppositional Defiant Disorder
            300.82   Undifferentiated Somatoform Disorder

            _____   _____

            _____   _____

Axis II: V71.09   No Diagnosis on Axis II
            799.9   Diagnosis Deferred

            _____   _____

            _____   _____

GRIEF/LOSS

BEHAVIORAL DEFINITIONS

1. Loss of a significant relationship due to death, physical separation, divorce, or emotional abandonment.
2. Declining grades and a lack of interest in school and social activities.
3. Profound grief over the loss of a loved one prevents the resumption of normal daily routines.
4. Feelings of shock, deep loss, and vulnerability.
5. Mood swings, weariness, depression, and a tendency to withdraw.
6. Feelings of isolation, confusion, and fear.
7. Moving through the stages of grief—from intense pain to deep sorrow, to sadness mixed with acceptance, and peace.
8. Overwhelming emotional reactions triggered by internal memories or reactions to external reminders of the lost relationship.
9. Impulsivity, acting out, and/or self-defeating or compulsive behavior.
10. Difficulty expressing deep feelings of grief related to the loss of the prominent relationship.

—. _____
   _____
—. _____
   _____
—. _____
   _____

LONG-TERM GOALS

1. Identify feelings of profound grief and loss, and express them to the counselor and/or parents.

2. Resume interest in daily activities, school, and social events.
3. Gradually accept the loss of the significant relationship.
4. Establish or reestablish positive relationships with significant others.
5. Stabilize mood swings and reduce regressive behavior and somatic complaints.
6. Gain a sense of self-control over inappropriate or self-defeating behavior, and find positive outlets for anger, confusion, and uncertainty.
7. Develop feelings of optimism toward the future.

—. _____
_____
—. _____
_____
—. _____
_____

SHORT-TERM OBJECTIVES

THERAPEUTIC INTERVENTIONS

1. Describe the loss to caring, empathetic, and supportive listeners. (1, 2)

1. Ask the student to share the story of the death or loss in a counseling session, and encourage him/her to repeat the story to other empathetic listeners; encourage him/her to write about the loss and/or to bring in photographs of the loved one.

2. Encourage the student to describe personal and family life before, during, and after the loss to define how these patterns have been altered.

2. Explore feelings related to the loss and identify appro-

3. Ask the student to write a letter to the lost loved one

priate methods for expressing these feelings. (3, 4, 5)

expressing personal feelings, questions, fears, and perceptions about the loss; process the content of the letter during the next counseling session.

4. Encourage the student to draw pictures, write songs or poems, play music, or use sculpting or sand play to describe his/her personal reactions to the loss; ask him/her to share these artistic expressions of loss with the counselor or members of a grief-and-loss support group.

5. Help the student to devise a plan for managing strong emotional reactions during the week (e.g., talk with a friend or family member, draw a picture, write in a journal, take 10 deep breaths), and discuss his/her progress during the next counseling session.

3. Define grief and the grief process. (6, 7)

6. Offer a simple definition of grief to the student (e.g., a personal reaction to change or a loss), and assist him/her in developing a more personalized working definition.

7. Brainstorm the effects of death or loss on children in general and specifically regarding the student (or assign the "My Evolving Feelings about Change, Loss, and Grief" activity from the *School Counseling*

4. Parents or other family members express acceptance of the student's feelings and encourage ongoing expression of feelings. (8, 9)

5. Verbalize an understanding that grieving and adjusting to a loss take time and effort. (10, 11)

and School Social Work Homework Planner by Knapp).

8. Meet with the parents, family members, and teachers to prepare them for actively listening to the student's feelings and to reinforce the importance of providing time for emotional expression.

9. Assign the parents to read *How to Talk So Kids Will Listen and Listen So Kids Will Talk* (Faber and Mazlish) to develop additional positive communication skills with the student.

10. Teach the student the process of working through grief (e.g., accepting the loss, experiencing the pain, adjusting to the change, and investing in an altered life pattern). Have him/her determine which stage is currently being experienced, and plan for stages yet to come (or assign the "Climb the Mountain" activity from the *School Counseling and School Social Work Homework Planner* by Knapp).

11. Watch *The Secret Garden* (Playhouse Video) with the student individually or in a group, and discuss the stages of grief experienced in the video by the children and their guardian or father after the death of loved

ones. Ask the student to identify the stages of grief and coping mechanisms used by the adults and children.

6. Join a grief support group. (12)

12. Refer the student to or conduct a grief support group that includes the student and several other students experiencing significant losses.

7. Plan coping strategies for difficult days or periods of heightened grief. (13, 14)

13. Brainstorm with the student ideas for facing holidays, birthdays, and the anniversary of the loss (e.g., plan an activity with a friend, share fond memories with a family member, visit the cemetery and talk to the lost loved one, say a prayer, write a poem of thanks for the memories, do something kind for another person).

14. Help the student to plan a memorial or designated period of grief on the anniversary of the loss, birthday, or holiday during which special memories, stories, and experiences involving the lost loved one are shared; suggest that he/she invite family members or special friends to share in the ritual.

8. List common reactions to grief and loss. (15, 16)

15. Identify for the student the common reactions to grief and loss (e.g., shock, anger, guilt, shame, lack of focus, behavioral changes, mood swings, regression, and preoccupation); ask him/her to

add any symptoms personally experienced or observed in family members or friends.

16. Play the Talking, Feeling, and Doing Game (Gardner) during a counseling or group session to help the student to identify and express feelings related to the death or loss.

9. Identify sources of comfort within the family, school, and community. (17, 18, 19)

17. Assign the student to complete the "Important People in My Life" activity from the *School Counseling and School Social Work Homework Planner* (Knapp) to identify a personal support system.

18. Ask the student to identify several supportive and caring gestures from family and friends designed to help him/her cope with the death or loss.

19. Ask the student to phone a grandparent, aunt, uncle, or other close family member and request a conversation or a social outing.

10. Meet with clergy to discuss the spiritual perspective of death and/or loss. (20, 21)

20. Arrange a meeting with the family's rabbi, priest, minister, or church youth leader to discuss the loss from a spiritual perspective and to give guidance and support.

21. Encourage the student to join a support group sponsored by the family's church, mosque, temple, or synagogue.

11. Parents or family members express an awareness and empathy for the student's fears and affirm that they will maintain a close, loving relationship with him/her. (22, 23)

22. Assign the parents to read a book that describes the effects of grief and loss on children (e.g., *Explaining Death to Children* by Grollman or *The Way Children Grieve* by Bissler).

23. Help the parents or other family members plan for a time and method of reassuring the student about personal security and expressing awareness and empathy for his/her fears and feelings of grief.

12. Parents and teachers respond to the student's grieving from an informed developmental perspective. (24, 25)

24. Assign the student's parents and teachers to read the *Developmental Considerations Concerning Children's Grief* (Metzgar) or *The Way Children Grieve* (Bissler).

25. Assist the parents and teachers in providing age-appropriate, positive interventions to help the student deal with grief (e.g., active listening, frequent affirmations, answer questions, read books about grief and loss together, continually express support and encouragement).

13. Parents and teachers adopt strategies to help the student deal with grief. (26, 27, 28)

26. Ask the teacher to discuss the death or loss with the class during the student's absence and to request compassion and support from his/her classmates.

27. Meet with the parents and teachers to suggest helpful strategies to assist the stu-

dent in dealing with grief (e.g., be open and tell the truth, don't hesitate to express personal feelings of grief, reassure the student that death or loss was not his/her fault, recognize that the grief process can involve an extended period of time).

28. Encourage the parents and teachers to read books or watch videos with the student about grief and loss (e.g., *The Fall of Freddie the Leaf* by Buscaglia, *The Lion King* from Walt Disney Productions, or *Don't Despair on Thursdays* by Moser), and discuss thoughts and emotions that are triggered by the stories.

14. Discuss the negative effects of grief on concentration and organization with the teachers and request their assistance. (29)

29. Encourage the student to discuss the negative effects of the loss upon his/her school and organizational skills with the classroom teacher(s) and to request helpful input and support.

15. Participate in several organized and informal extracurricular events or activities per month. (30, 31)

30. Encourage the student to avoid social withdrawal by joining an athletic team, school club, church, or interest group; monitor his/her subsequent participation and discuss personal reactions during a counseling session.

31. Devise a plan with the student for inviting a friend to participate in a social activity.

16. Parents and teachers list danger signals that the grief process is not progressing normally. (32, 33)

32. Help the student's parents and teachers to watch for prolonged or abnormal grief reactions (e.g., sustained disinterest in daily activities, loss of appetite, difficulty sleeping, extended regression, withdrawal from relationships, refusal to attend school or to participate successfully in academics), and encourage them to discuss concerns with a mental health professional.

33. Ask the parents to keep a daily journal of the student's grief reactions, and discuss them during a counseling session or refer them to a private family therapist.

17. Share and reframe magical thinking. (34, 35, 36)

34. Ask the student to record all thoughts, theories, and feelings about the loss in a personal grief journal; discuss the entries during the next counseling session using interpretation to reframe any magical thinking.

35. Help the student to reframe any erroneous ideas or perceptions about the death or loss by seeking accurate information from an authoritative figure in the family or community.

36. Use a mutual storytelling technique with the student to dispel harmful magical thinking (e.g., I caused the loss because I once wished

he would die), and encourage a healthier interpretation of the death or loss of a loved one.

18. Increase the frequency of age-appropriate reactions, and reduce the number of inappropriate or regressive behaviors. (37)

37. Encourage the student to substitute age-appropriate behavior for regressive actions (e.g., sleeping in his/her own bed instead of sleeping in his/her parents' bed, taking the bus to school instead of his/her parent driving him/her to school, using bathroom facilities independently instead of with parent supervision, or dressing himself/herself independently in the morning instead of demanding parental assistance). Ask him/her to graph his/her progress toward independence in a personal journal.

19. Identify constructive ways to express underlying feelings and fears that trigger self-defeating behaviors. (38, 39)

38. Explore the student's emotional overreactions (e.g., screaming, hitting, withdrawal, or destruction of property); ask him/her to substitute a more rational method of expressing grief (e.g., using "I" statements, writing in a personal journal, drawing a feelings picture, or taking a walk).

39. Brainstorm with the student methods of reducing underlying fears and frustrations (e.g., sharing feelings with his/her parents, counselor, empathetic friend, or supportive adult).

20. Express awareness that negative emotions and fears can trigger physical distress. (40, 41)

21. Recognize that losses are an essential part of life. (42, 43)

22. Plan ways to turn despair into positive, productive effort. (44, 45, 46)

40. Explore the student's somatic complaints (e.g., headache, stomachache, or neck pain), and identify possible emotional triggers (e.g., argument with a parent, fear of abandonment, feelings of guilt, upcoming holiday, or special event).

41. Assign the student to participate in physical activity (e.g., walking, running, playing basketball, jumping rope, lifting weights, performing aerobics) to reduce stress levels.

42. Assign the student to create a family time line of significant events (e.g., births, deaths, marriages, graduations) to gain a visual perspective of the give-and-take of life, or assign the "Ebb and Flow" activity from the *School Counseling and School Social Work Homework Planner* by Knapp).

43. Assist the student in constructing a family loss history (see *Do a Loss History* by Overbeck) by gathering and recording information to become familiar with previous family losses and how these losses have been experienced and dealt with by family members.

44. Assign the student to bookmark helpful grief-and-loss websites and to compile a

list for others who experience a death or other significant loss in their lives.

45. Encourage the student to write an article about a personal grief experience and to share it with members of a grief support group or submit it to a grief newsletter or website.

46. Brainstorm with the student methods of turning a traumatic event into a positive effort (e.g., volunteer to help others who are grieving; work for a significant charity; start a project for change, such as Mothers Against Drunk Drivers, banning cell phones while driving, wearing helmets while biking, or enforcing the seatbelt law).

23. Set personal goals. Describe hopes and dreams, and express optimism for family and personal relationships in the future.
(47, 48, 49, 50)

47. Have the student describe himself/herself and his/her family five years in the future, focusing on the personal relationships within and outside of the family, and record this in a personal journal.

48. Assign the student to interview three classmates or schoolmates who have experienced a death or loss at least one year prior and to determine how they have successfully coped with the changes in their lives.

49. Assign the student to complete the "My Predictions for the Future" activity

from the *School Counseling and School Social Work Homework Planner* (Knapp) to establish positive goals for the future.

50. Read the book *Lessons from Geese* (Clayton) to the student, and follow with a discussion of how people, like geese, can help one another cope in times of grief and loss.

__. _____   __. _____

__. _____   __. _____

__. _____   __. _____

DIAGNOSTIC SUGGESTIONS:

Axis I:	296.2x	Major Depressive Disorder, Single Episode
	296.3x	Major Depressive Disorder, Recurrent
	V62.82	Bereavement
	309.0	Adjustment Disorder With Depressed Mood
	309.4	Adjustment Disorder With Mixed Disturbance of Emotions and Conduct
	300.4	Dysthymic Disorder
	____	_____
	____	_____
Axis II:	799.9	Diagnosis Deferred
	V71.09	No Diagnosis on Axis II
	____	_____
	____	_____

LEARNING DIFFICULTIES

BEHAVIORAL DEFINITIONS

1. Learning difficulties in reading, math, or written language, and inadequate (below age and grade level) or inconsistent progress in school.
2. Below-average intellectual functioning in one or several areas as measured by an individually administered, standardized IQ test.
3. Academic performance significantly below overall ability level as measured by an individually administered, standardized IQ test.
4. Difficulty with personal organization, time management, and study skills.
5. Auditory processing deficits and/or developmental speech and language delays.
6. Requires accommodations to progress satisfactorily in school or work environment.
7. Inadequate cause-and-effect thinking or inability to learn from consequences.
8. Becomes confused with directions and spatial orientation.
9. Short- and long-term memory deficits.
10. Short attention span, easily distracted, and impulsive.
11. Immature behavior, lack of social skills, and difficulty picking up social cues from others.
12. Low self-esteem and feelings of inadequacy in academic, social, and independent functioning.

—. _____

—. _____

—. _____

LONG-TERM GOALS

1. Participate in a complete social, psychological, and medical assessment of symptoms.
2. Acquire an understanding of the learning disabilities (LD) or mentally impaired (MI) syndromes along with parents and teachers.
3. Participate in special education programs designated by the individualized education planning and placement committee (IEPC) to enhance academic progress and independent functioning.
4. Work with the teachers and special educators to develop accommodations to promote academic, social, and behavioral success.
5. View self as a unique individual with many strengths and abilities.
6. Acquire appropriate social skills, including self-advocacy and empathy for others.
7. Learn time management and organizational skills.
8. Demonstrate independent and responsible behavior.

—. _____

_____

—. _____

_____

—. _____

_____

SHORT-TERM OBJECTIVES

1. Complete psychological, social/emotional, and medical testing to determine causes for learning difficulties. (1, 2)

THERAPEUTIC INTERVENTIONS

1. Gather information about the student's academic performance and social or behavioral difficulties from discussions with the student and his/her parents, referring teacher, or special educator.

2. Collaborate with the school or a private psychologist to complete a social/emotional and psychological evaluation of the student if deemed appropriate by the

2. Participate in individual or group counseling to acquire a general and personal awareness of learning differences, their management strategies, and social/emotional effects. (3, 4, 5)

3. Parents and teachers verbalize an understanding of the effects of learning differences upon the student and possible management strategies from the special educators, counselor, or other resources. (6, 7, 8)

parents and the school child study team.

3. Include the student in a learning differences counseling group at school, which discusses the nature of LD or MI, associated problems, and strategies for coping successfully.

4. Have the student begin a personal journal entitled *Coping with Learning Differences,* which contains thoughts, feelings, successes, and challenges of living with learning problems.

5. Read children's literature with the student that explains learning differences, explores feelings, and suggests management strategies (e.g. *What Do You Mean, I Have a Learning Disability?* by Dwyer or *The Don't-Give-Up Kid and Learning Differences* by Gehret).

6. Assign the parents to read *Helping Your Dyslexic Child: A Step-by-Step Program for Helping Your Child Improve Reading, Writing, Spelling, Comprehension, and Self-Esteem* (Cronin), *The Misunderstood Child: A Guide for Parents of Children with Learning Disabilities* (Silver), or other literature to prepare for subsequent discussions with the student concerning the nature of learning differences.

7. Refer the student's parents to an LD or MI parent support group [e.g., *Council for Exceptional Children, Division of Learning Disabilities* (703-620-3660 or www.cec.sped.org) or Learning Disabilities Association of America (LDA) (412-341-1515 or www.ldanatl.org)].

8. Meet with the teacher regularly to review strategies from *Teaching Kids with Learning Difficulties in the Regular Classroom* (Winebrenner) or other best-practice literature offering classroom techniques for teaching and encouraging students with learning differences.

4. Accept recommendations for individualized or small-group instruction in areas of academic deficits. (9, 10, 11)

9. Attend the IEPC meeting, and participate in the determination of the student's eligibility for special education services.

10. Assist in establishing performance goals and objectives for the student at the IEPC in areas of learning and social/behavioral deficits.

11. Work with other IEPC members to identify special programs that may be helpful to the student (e.g., total pullout program, resource room, individual or small-group instruction, mainstream classroom support).

5. Participate in speech, occupational, physical, or social work therapy. (12, 13)

12. Refer the student for assessments by the speech, occupational, or physical

therapist and the school social worker to determine eligibility for services in these areas.

13. Advocate for the student to receive school-based services from the speech, physical, or occupational therapist, as well as the school social worker at the IEPC, if deemed appropriate, or refer him/her for private therapy.

6. Participate in programs designated to enhance self-care, independent functioning, and future employment. (14, 15, 16)

14. Encourage the student to select classes that prepare him/her for future independence (e.g., child development, independent living, home economics, personal finance).

15. Enroll the student in community-based instruction or school career programs that are designed to provide employment skills and work experience.

16. Refer the student to skill-based technical programs (e.g., auto mechanics, construction, fashion and design, hospitality and guest services, or cosmetology training).

7. Use accommodations and adapted technology to enhance ability to receive instruction, complete assignments, and take tests. (17, 18)

17. Work with special educators to provide adapted technology (e.g., tape recorder, computer, calculator, teacher voice enhancer) to assist the student in daily academic performance and assessment.

18. Consult with the student, teacher(s), and parents regarding necessary accommodations to encourage academic success (e.g., give one task at a time, monitor frequently, use an affirming attitude, modify assignments as needed, allow extra time if necessary).

8. Participate in a functional analysis to determine specific academic and behavior goals and to design strategies to support goal achievement. (19, 20)

19. Complete a functional analysis of the student to define learning and behavior concerns, analyze the probable causes, and develop reinforcement interventions to correct the problems.

20. Collaborate with the multidisciplinary evaluation team (MET) members to complete the "Record of Behavioral Progress" from the *School Counseling and School Social Work Homework Planner* (Knapp) to analyze the student's behavior and plan for specific intervention strategies that help him/her to develop positive alternative behaviors.

9. Verbalize the awareness that all people are unique, learn differently, and have various strengths and weaknesses. (21, 22, 23, 24)

21. Explain the theory of multiple intelligences (Gardner), which stipulates that people are smart in different ways, and ask the student to identify his/her personal areas of greater and lesser intelligences; have him/her add to his/her personal ability list by accepting affirmations from other students in the group or from the counselor.

22. Ask the student to complete the "Skill Assessment" activity from the *School Counseling and School Social Work Homework Planner* (Knapp) to evaluate existing abilities in terms of multiple intelligences (Gardner).

23. Assign the student to determine personal learning styles [e.g., visual (or seeing what is being learned), auditory (or hearing or saying what is being learned), or kinesthetic (or needing motion to learn, through self-observation and observations from parents and teachers)]. Instruct the student to use his/her primary learning style while preparing for the next quiz or test and to report the results during a subsequent counseling session.

24. Ask the student to complete the "Building on Strengths" activity from The *School Counseling and School Social Work Homework Planner* (Knapp) to identify personal strengths and to discover how these strengths can be used to reach goals.

10. Participate in a social skills group. (25)

11. Implement communication techniques to build social relationships. (26, 27)

25. Refer the student to a social skills counseling group.

26. Teach the student to use "I" messages and reflective listening. [See *Teaching Children Self-Discipline* by

Gordon, or the Bug-Wish Technique ("It bugs me when you . . . I wish you would. . . .").]

27. Use the *Peacemaking Skills for Little Kids Student Activity Book* (Schmidt, Friedmann, Brunt, and Solotoff) to develop social assertiveness and conflict management skills.

12. Actively seek friendships among peer group. (28, 29)

28. Encourage the student's teacher(s) to involve the student in cooperative learning groups.

29. Support the student in joining an extracurricular social group sponsored by the school, church, or community.

13. Develop positive relationships with the parents, teachers, and other significant adults. (30, 31)

30. Use puppets or role playing to help the student prepare for appropriate sharing of his/her feelings with significant adults.

31. Assign the student to discuss a personal concern with a parent, teacher, or friend, and process the results during the next counseling session.

14. Increase completion of in-class assignments and homework. (32, 33, 34)

32. Assign the student to use a study planner to list all assignments, record working time, and check off when completed.

33. Play Study Smart (ADHD Warehouse) with the student to assist him/her in the development of study skills,

comprehension, test taking, and memory.

15. Establish a routine or schedule to prioritize and organize key daily activities. (35, 36)

16. Implement problem-solving strategies to improve social interaction, school performance, and personal satisfaction. (37, 38)

17. Parents and teachers empower the student by emphasizing personal responsibility and the benefits of

34. Ask the parents and teachers to monitor the student's assignment planner daily and to give encouragement and direction as needed.

35. Assist the student in listing and prioritizing key daily activities at home, school, and in the community; assign times for completion and record in a Learning Differences journal or an assignment planner.

36. Instruct the student to place a star, sticker, or smiley face on a chart next to each chore, task, or assignment that is completed and share accomplishments with parents, teacher(s), or counselor.

37. Assist the student in completing the "Personal Problem-Solving Worksheet" from the *School Counseling and School Social Work Homework Planner* (Knapp) to outline a strategy for solving personal problems.

38. Introduce activities from the program *I Can Problem-Solve* (Shure, ADHD Warehouse) to teach problem solving and predicting the result of specific actions.

39. Encourage the teacher(s) and parents to use positive discipline strategies for helping the student to develop responsibility (e.g.,

considering the consequences before acting. (39)

18. Verbalize an increased awareness of how personal choices and behavior create specific results. (38, 40)

19. Parents, teachers, and counselor affirm the student for progress in assuming responsibility and acquiring independence. (41, 42)

20. Mentor other students who are coping with learning differences and academic problems. (43, 44)

chores, assignments and tasks, learning from mistakes, consequences, choices, and a chance to try again next time).

38. Introduce activities from the program *I Can Problem-Solve* (Shure) to teach problem solving and predicting the result of specific actions.

40. Have the student complete the "Decision Making" activity from the *School Counseling and School Social Work Homework Planner* (Knapp) either individually or in a small-group session to increase awareness of the connection between personal choices and specific results.

41. Encourage the teachers and parents to give frequent affirmations to the student for progress noted in a private, low-key manner.

42. Allow time during the counseling sessions for the student to develop personal affirmations for progress in school, home, and social adjustment, and to share successes with his/her parents, teacher(s), counselor, and group members.

43. Arrange with the teacher to have the student assist classmates or younger students who are coping with various learning differences.

44. Invite the student to share personal strategies and successes with students of a newly formed learning differences group.

___. _____   ___. _____
   _____   _____
___. _____   ___. _____
   _____   _____
___. _____   ___. _____
   _____   _____

DIAGNOSTIC SUGGESTIONS

Axis I:	315.00	Reading Disorder
	315.1	Mathematics Disorder
	315.2	Disorder of Written Expression
	315.9	Learning Disorder NOS
	317	Mild Mental Retardation
	318.0	Moderate Mental Retardation
	299.00	Autistic Disorder
	299.80	Rett's Disorder
	299.80	Asperger's Disorder
	299.10	Childhood Disintegrative Disorder
	_____	_____
	_____	_____
Axis II:	799.9	Diagnosis Deferred
	V71.09	No Diagnosis on Axis II
	_____	_____
	_____	_____

OPPOSITIONAL DEFIANT DISORDER (ODD)

BEHAVIORAL DEFINITIONS

1. Difficulty with anger management, quick to anger, easily frustrated.
2. Engages in frequent confrontation and arguments with adults.
3. Refusal to comply with adult directions or requests.
4. Deliberately tries to upset or annoy people and is easily angered or annoyed by others.
5. Projects blame for misbehavior or mistakes upon others.
6. Pervasive angry or resentful attitude.
7. Seeks revenge, is spiteful or vindictive.
8. Lack of self-calming strategies.
9. Extreme need for being in control.
10. Significant difficulty in family, social, or academic functioning.

—. _____

_____

—. _____

_____

_____

—. _____

_____

LONG-TERM GOALS

1. Increase cooperative behavior with adults and peers.
2. Reduce temper outbursts.
3. Develop a positive and trusting attitude toward authority figures.
4. Assume responsibility for own behavior.

5. Use conflict management and appropriate interpersonal skills in social interaction.
6. Gain a sense of self-control and a willingness to share control with others.

—. _____
   _____
   _____

—. _____
   _____
   _____

—. _____
   _____
   _____

SHORT-TERM OBJECTIVES

1. Cooperate with a complete psychosocial evaluation. (1, 2, 3, 4, 5)

THERAPEUTIC INTERVENTIONS

1. Explore the student's oppositional and defiant behavior with parents, referring teacher, and other involved educators.

2. Complete a cumulative record perusal, and note any information relevant to the student's oppositional defiant disorder (ODD) symptomatology and how this affects his/her school adjustment.

3. Meet with the student's parents to gather a developmental history and review the school's concerns or the results of the child study committee's recommendations.

4. Request the parents' permission to obtain any relevant assessment information regarding a current diagnosis of the student, or

discuss the possibility of an independent psychological assessment to determine or rule out the existence of ODD.

2. Participate in individual or group counseling to acquire an awareness of ODD, its management strategies, and social/emotional effects. (6, 7, 8)

5. Arrange for a complete social/emotional and psychological evaluation of the student within the school or by a private psychotherapist.

6. Discuss treatment options with the parents, teachers, and student (e.g., medical intervention as prescribed by a physician, individual or group counseling for the student, behavioral interventions, structuring the environment, or a combination of the preceding strategies).

7. Meet with the student to explore feelings, answer questions, and seek his/her cooperation and involvement in the successful management of ODD symptoms.

8. Include the student in an ODD counseling group at school, which discusses the nature of ODD, associated problems, and strategies for coping successfully.

3. Record in a journal situations that trigger ODD and the feelings associated with those situations. (9, 10, 11)

9. Have the student begin a personal journal entitled *Peaceful Coexistence* to record thoughts, feelings, successes, and the challenges of living with ODD symptoms.

10. Ask the student to list in a personal journal daily situations that cause irritation.

11. Assign the student to select feelings from a feelings chart that describes emotions he/she commonly experiences. Record the feelings in the personal journal and process these during individual or group counseling sessions.

4. Identify underlying feelings of anger and anxiety, and plan for appropriate resolution of these feelings. (12, 13)

12. Assess the student's current level and areas of anxiety and frustration by administering an objective inventory (e.g., the Revised Children's Manifest Anxiety Scale by Reynolds and Richmond, available from Western Psychological Services). Process specific responses during subsequent counseling sessions.

13. Read with the student children's literature that explains ODD, explores feelings, and suggests management strategies (e.g., *Hands Are Not for Hitting* by Agassi or *The Teenagers Guide to School Outside the Box* by Greene).

5. Participate in family counseling sessions that focus on rebuilding relationships and establishing family harmony. (14, 15, 16)

14. Assign the parents to read literature explaining ODD (e.g., *It's Nobody's Fault: New Hope and Help for Difficult Children* by Koplewicz) to acquire insight and strategies for coping with ODD.

15. Meet with the parents on a monthly basis to discuss the challenges of ODD for the student and family, develop strategies to help the student and family to adjust, or refer them to a private therapist or agency for family counseling.

16. Suggest that the parents and the student meet weekly at a designated time to review progress, give encouragement, note continuing concerns, and keep a written progress report to share with counselor or private therapist.

6. Verbalize a plan for improved compliance with rules at home and school. (17, 18, 19)

17. Review family rules with the student, and identify areas of compliance and noncompliance. Help the student to formulate a plan for improved compliance in challenging areas, and chart his/her progress.

18. Meet with the parents and the student to review family rules. Help the student and the parents to formulate a plan for compliance, using structured positive and negative reinforcement principals, and instruct the student to chart his/her progress.

*19. Discuss the school rules with the student in either individual or group counseling sessions, and identify those that are difficult to comply with and those that create few problems.

7. List authority conflict problems and steps necessary for resolution. (20)

20. Ask the student to draw or write about an authority conflict or problem that needs to be resolved and to identify any support persons or groups who can assist with resolution (or assign the "Problem Ownership" activity from the *School Counseling and School Social Work Homework Planner* by Knapp).

8. Learn and implement relaxation or stress reduction techniques to reverse the escalation of emotional distress. (21, 22, 23, 24)

21. Ask the student to identify areas on an image of the human body where excessive anger or frustration is most commonly reflected (or assign the "Physical Receptors of Stress" activity from the *School Counseling and School Social Work Homework Planner* by Knapp).

22. Teach the student how to relax different areas of the body by first tightening and then relaxing muscles, paying particular attention to areas where anger or irritation is typically manifested (e.g., jaw, neck, shoulders, stomach).

23. Ask the student to hold a soft rubber ball and practice squeezing and relaxing his/her arm and fist while breathing in and out at an even pace and to use this technique during times of frustration.

9. Increase the frequency of aerobic exercise to four times per week to reduce anxiety and tension. (25)

10. Identify triggers and targets for angry outbursts and positive resolution techniques for these situations. (26, 27)

11. Self-monitor personal behavior and interactions with adults and peers using a chart to record improvement in the ability to remain appropriate. (28)

12. Participate in an extracurricular club, team, or church/synagogue group for a

24. Assign the student to practice deep, even breathing and muscle relaxation daily during times of emotional distress.

25. Encourage the student to participate in an aerobic exercise for one-half hour, three to four times per week.

26. Ask the student to identify triggers and targets for emotional outbursts and to record these in a personal journal.

27. Brainstorm with the student appropriate, socially acceptable methods of dealing with the triggers and targets for angry outbursts (e.g., use an "I" statement, walk away, use humor, take a personal time-out).

28. Ask the student to create self-monitoring charts that are kept on his/her classroom desk or in a personal planner to track emotional reactions, behaviors, and social interactions (or assign the "Student Self-Report" activity from the *School Counseling and School Social Work Homework Planner* by Knapp). Review his/her self-monitoring charts, giving affirmations for progress made and guidance in areas of no or little progress.

29. Explore with the student various interest groups (e.g., sports, hobby, church/

designated period of time and chart progress. (29, 30)

synagogue, exercise), select one to join, determine a reasonable time duration, and chart participation.

(30.) Assist the student in identifying the positive aspects and challenges of sustained involvement in a friendship or activity group, and record ideas in a personal journal in either written or picture form.

13. Parents attend parenting classes and read parenting literature to enhance positive family discipline. (31, 32)

31. Refer the parents to a parenting class (e.g., *Systematic Training for Effective Parenting* by Dinkmeyer and McKay, *Discipline with Love and Logic* by Cline and Fay, or *The Parent Talk System* by Moorman and Knapp) to acquire techniques of positive discipline to use with the student.

32. Meet with the parents to help them initiate parenting strategies of positive discipline learned in parenting classes or from recommended parenting books or tapes (e.g., *Your Defiant Child: Eight Steps to Better Behavior* by Barkley or *Parent Talk* by Moorman).

14. Parents convene weekly family meetings to discuss issues of conflict and progress. (33)

33. Encourage the parents to initiate weekly family meetings to discuss concerns, reflect upon positive events, coordinate activities, review values, answer questions, and plan for positive interaction.

15. Coauthor behavior plans for school and home that focus on cooperative, successful participation in each environment. (34, 35, 36)

34. Assist the student in formulating ideas for a behavior management plan at school or home using a plan sheet that outlines the problem and a proposed solution (or assign the "Problem Solving Worksheet" from the *School Counseling and School Social Work Homework Planner* by Knapp).

35. Caution the student and his/her parents and teachers to be realistic in expectations expressed in behavior plans to increase the success level and avoid defeat (e.g., target specific behaviors, recognize incremental progress, revise the plan frequently to reflect progress and address remaining problems).

36. Advise the student and his/her parents and teachers that a behavior plan addressing an existing problem must be completed by the student and accepted by the parents or teacher before the student is able to enjoy or participate in any family or school activities (e.g., recess, TV, computer, meals with the family or classmates, playing games, using supplies). If the plan is ineffective, privileges are again suspended until a workable plan is in place.

16. List and implement strategies for breaking the cycle

37. Ask the student to draw the cycle of negative behavior and the resulting

of oppositional behavior. (37, 38)

consequences (e.g., event, student reacts negatively, adult criticizes the student, student escalates the negative reaction), and then list strategies for breaking the cycle (e.g., count to 10, engage in positive self-talk, write instead of verbalize reaction, take a short mental time-out).

38. Assign the student to establish a verbal or nonverbal cue with his/her parents and teachers to signal the need to break the cycle of negative behavior by implementing a prearranged strategy (e.g., time-out, change seats, take a walk, or switch activities).

17. Increase the frequency of positive interactions with the parents and educators. (39, 40, 41)

39. In an individual or group session, have the student complete the "Criticism, Praise, and Encouragement" activity from the *School Counseling and School Social Work Homework Planner* (Knapp) to gain insight regarding the effects of positive and negative attention-seeking behavior.

40. Make a list with the student entitled "Things I Do for Good Attention" and "Things I Do for Bad Attention." Compare the length of the lists and brainstorm how to add substantially to the "good attention" list. Assign the student to implement "good attention" behaviors.

41. Read *Everything I Do You Blame on Me* (Aborn) during an individual or group session to help the student to understand the importance of taking responsibility for personal actions.

18. Complete household chores. (42, 43, 44)

42. Ask the student to complete the "Responses to Praise, Criticism, and Encouragement" activity from the *School Counseling and School Social Work Homework Planner* (Knapp) to assist him/her in learning appropriate responses to adults' evaluations of their actions.

43. Assign the parents and the student to create a list of household chores and to designate an appropriate number to each family member, taking into consideration age, maturity, and ability level.

44. Create and assign the use of a chore chart, which monitors the student's weekly chores, time spent on task, and a grade given by both the parents and the student (or assign the "Chore Report Card" from the *School Counseling and School Social Work Homework Planner* by Knapp).

19. Verbalize how personal decisions affect consequences. (45)

45. Ask the student to complete the "Decision Making" activity from the *School Counseling and School Social Work Homework Planner*

(Knapp) to recognize the effects of positive and negative decisions upon his/her quality of life.

20. Maintain an acceptable level of competence in academic performance. (46, 47, 48)

46. Brainstorm with the student, in either an individual or group session, strategies that encourage sustained academic effort and task completion (e.g., self-monitoring, taking a short break, scheduling a specific time, prioritizing jobs, stretching muscles, standing while working), and share personal successes or challenges with this goal.

47. Discuss with the student and his/her parents and teachers his/her academic potential, and determine a mutually agreed-upon level of academic performance that must be maintained to earn privileges at home or school.

48. Arrange a meeting with the teacher(s), parents, and the student to determine accommodations that encourage successful academic performance (e.g., supervise the student closely during times of transition; seat the student near the teacher's desk, in an area of low distractions, or near a good role model; involve the student in lesson discussions, giving simple and clear instructions).

21. Establish friendships and positive relationships with peers. (49, 50)

49. Use children's literature to explore the causes for and effects of behavior upon

interpersonal relationships (e.g., *Don't Pop Your Cork on Mondays!* by Moser and Pilkey or *Don't Feed the Monster on Tuesday!* by Moser and Thatch).

50. In an individual or group session, have the student review an experience in which an impulsive choice created a negative interpersonal problem, and then select a more appropriate action and predict the probable result (or assign the "Rewind Game" activity in the *School Counseling and School Social Work Homework Planner* by Knapp).

__. _____   __. _____
   _____   _____
__. _____   __. _____
   _____   _____
__. _____   __. _____
   _____   _____

DIAGNOSTIC SUGGESTIONS

Axis I:	313.81	Oppositional Defiant Disorder
	312.8	Conduct Disorder
	312.9	Disruptive Behavior Disorder NOS
	314.01	Attention-Deficit/Hyperactivity Disorder, Predominantly Hyperactive-Impulsive Type
	314.9	Attention-Deficit/Hyperactivity Disorder NOS
	V62.81	Relational Problem NOS
	_____	_____
Axis II:	799.9	Diagnosis Deferred
	V71.09	No Diagnosis on Axis II
	_____	_____
	_____	_____

PARENTING SKILLS/DISCIPLINE

BEHAVIORAL DEFINITIONS

1. Irresponsible behavior at home and school.
2. Lack of respect for self, parents, and others as shown by oppositional behavior patterns.
3. Inability to function independently at home, school, and in the community.
4. Prevalent symptoms of anger, unhappiness, and depression.
5. High levels of stress and anxiety.
6. Low self-esteem and feelings of inadequacy.
7. Fails to follow home and classroom rules for conduct (e.g., take turns, listen, complete tasks, line up, stay in seat).
8. Parents put stress on the marriage and foster dependency by creating a child-centered rather than a couple-centered family.
9. Parents lack the skills that are necessary to set reasonable limits.
10. Parents waver between overprotective or harsh and aggressive interactions with the student.

—. _____
   _____

—. _____
   _____

—. _____
   _____

LONG-TERM GOALS

1. Follow rules and procedures at home, school, and community.
2. Develop self-reliance and responsibility.
3. Demonstrate respect and regard for self and others.

4. Acquire positive and moral character traits.
5. Parents acquire positive discipline strategies that set limits and encourage independence.
6. Family atmosphere is peaceful, loving, and harmonious.

—. _____

_____

—. _____

_____

—. _____

_____

SHORT-TERM OBJECTIVES

1. Parents meet with the counselor to seek assistance with discipline and family harmony concerns. (1, 2)

2. Parents attend classes and read parenting literature that teach the techniques of positive discipline. (3, 4)

THERAPEUTIC INTERVENTIONS

1. Meet with the parents to obtain information about discipline, family harmony, and the student's developmental history.

2. Complete a cumulative record review, and note any information relevant to the family's current discipline problems.

3. Refer the parents to a parenting class (e.g., *Systematic Training for Effective Parenting* by Dinkmeyer and McKay, *Discipline with Love and Logic* by Cline and Fay, or *The Parent Talk System* by Moorman and Knapp) to acquire techniques of positive discipline to use with the student.

4. Assign the parents to read literature about implementing strategies of positive discipline in the family

(e.g., *Kids Are Worth It!* by Coloroso or *Children: The Challenge* by Dreikurs and Stoltz).

3. Parents and student participate in family counseling sessions that focus on rebuilding relationships and establishing family harmony. (5, 6, 7)

5. Meet with the parents to help them initiate parenting strategies of positive discipline learned in parenting classes or from recommended parenting books or tapes (e.g., *Discipline for Home and School* by Ford, *Your Defiant Child: Eight Steps to Better Behavior* by Barkley, or *Parent Talk* by Moorman).

6. Meet with the parents on an ongoing basis to discuss disciplinary challenges for the student and the family; develop strategies to help the student and the family adjust, or refer them to a private therapist or agency for family counseling.

7. Suggest that the parents and the student meet weekly at a designated time to review progress, give encouragement, note continuing concerns, and keep a written progress report to share with a counselor or private therapist.

4. Student participate in a social/emotional assessment, focusing on issues of self-esteem, self-control, responsibility, and respect. (8, 9)

8. Have the student complete the "Personal Profile" informational sheet from the *School Counseling and School Social Homework Planner* (Knapp), which details pertinent personal data, or gather personal

information in an informal interview with the student.

9. Give the student the Goals of Misbehavior Inventory (Manly) or another index to identify his/her current wrong assumptions that motivate inappropriate behavior according to Dreikur's theory of misbehavior (see *Children: The Challenge* by Dreikurs and Stoltz).

5. Parents initiate strategies that help the student to develop responsibility. (10, 11, 12)

10. Assist the parents in implementing the "Four Steps to Responsibility" (see *Parenting with Love and Logic* by Cline, Fay, and Fay): (1) Give the student a task he/she can handle; (2) if he/she fails, view his/her mistakes as learning opportunities; (3) let consequences and empathy do the teaching; (4) give the same task again. Ask the student to repeat this process continually as he/she begins to develop responsibility and independence.

11. Ask the parents to use the Red Light, Green Light technique (see *Parent Talk* by Moorman) to turn an irresponsible behavior into a responsible behavior: (1) Describe the inappropriate behavior to the child (red light)—screaming, kicking, clinging, whining, and so on; (2) describe the expected behavior (green light)—smiling, waving good-bye,

opening door, going into school.

12. Ask the parents to assign the student one new responsibility or challenge each month, asking him/her to record his/her progress in a personal discipline journal and to share the content with the counselor during the next session.

6. Parents set limits using positive discipline strategies. (13, 14, 15)

13. Discuss and role-play with the parents the use of "I" statements (e.g., "I feel . . . when . . . because. . . .") with the student as a first step in addressing behavior that disturbs them. (See *Parent Effectiveness Training* by Gordon.)

14. Instruct the parents to use controlled choice (see *Parent Talk* by Moorman) to limit the options the student has according to his/her maturity and level of responsibility (e.g., "Would you like hot dogs or grilled cheese?" versus "What would you like to eat?").

15. Teach the parents to use enforceable statements (see *Parenting with Love and Logic* by Cline, Fay, and Fay) to direct behavior in a positive manner (e.g., "Feel free to go outside when your homework is finished" versus "You're not going outside until your homework is finished").

7. Parents teach the student appropriate behavior through modeling and defining what is expected. (16, 17, 18)

16. Assign the parents to use the Parent Talk statement (see *Parent Talk* by Moorman), "Next time . . . ," to help the student picture himself/herself engaged in appropriate rather than inappropriate behavior (e.g., "Next time you need my help, please ask in a polite tone of voice").

17. Teach the parents to use the Describe, Describe, Describe technique (see *Parent Talk* by Moorman) to help the student replace negative behaviors with positive actions. Instruct the parents to (1) describe the problematic situation to the student (your bike is outside in the driveway); (2) describe the parent's feeling ("I feel annoyed"); (3) describe what needs to be done to correct the problem (put the bike in the garage).

18. Ask the student to review an experience in which impulsive words or actions created a negative interpersonal problem, and then select a more appropriate statement or action and role-play the probable result (or assign the "Rewind Game" activity from the *School Counseling and School Social Work Homework Planner* by Knapp). Have the student teach this technique to his/her parents for use during family conflicts.

8. Parents allow the student to learn from his/her mistakes. (18, 19)

18. Ask the student to review an experience in which impulsive words or actions created a negative interpersonal problem, and then select a more appropriate statement or action and role-play the probable result (or assign the "Rewind Game" activity from the *School Counseling and School Social Work Homework Planner* by Knapp). Have the student teach this technique to his/her parents for use during family conflicts.

19. Assign the parents to allow the child to live with the consequences of personal choices in at least three instances during the week and to report the outcome in the next counseling session. If the student is unhappy with the choice he/she has made, council the parents to say, "Don't worry, next time you'll have a chance to make a different choice."

9. Parents use natural and logical consequences to redirect the student's behavior. (20, 21)

20. Define natural (naturally occurring in the environment) and logical (created by parents or teacher) consequences for the parents, and outline their effectiveness as part of a positive discipline strategy (e.g., teach the student appropriate behavior, allow him/her to learn from mistakes, encourage the parent to model effective problem-solving

behavior, urge the parent to be both kind and firm).

21. Help the parents to design several logical consequences to deal with chronic behavior that is disrupting family harmony (e.g., the student forgets to make his/her bed: no TV until the bed is made; the student is late for curfew: curfew hour is reduced the following weekend; the student forgets his/her lunch: the parent instructs him/her to borrow from friends or wait until dinner to eat; the student wastes time at bedtime: bedtime hour is reduced the following evening).

10. Parents report a reduction in power struggles resulting from strategies designed to enlist the student's cooperation. (22, 23)

22. Ask the parents to practice methods of sidestepping power struggles (e.g., use broken record, "I" statements, choices, enforceable statements, refusing to argue, time-outs, and natural and logical consequences), and ask them to record progress in a discipline journal and report progress during a subsequent counseling session.

23. Ask the student to draw the cycle of negative behavior and resulting consequences (e.g., event, student reacts negatively, adult criticizes the student, student escalates the negative reaction), and then list strategies for breaking the cycle (e.g., count to 10, engage in

positive self-talk, write instead of verbalize reaction, take a short mental time-out).

11. Parents express awareness that all behaviors have a social purpose and all misbehavior is goal-oriented. (24, 25, 26)

24. Discuss the four goals of misbehavior (see *Children: The Challenge* by Dreikurs and Stoltz) (e.g., attention, power, revenge, and displaying feelings of inadequacy) with the parents, and identify the goals of the student's current misbehavior. Ask the parents to reflect upon how they are reinforcing this misbehavior by their reactions, and determine more appropriate responses that encourage appropriate behavior.

25. Collaborate with the parents and teachers to complete the "Record of Behavioral Progress" activity from the *School Counseling and School Social Work Homework Planner* (Knapp) to analyze the student's behavior and plan for specific intervention strategies that help the child develop positive alternative behaviors.

26. Encourage the parents and teachers to involve the student in activities that enhance his/her feelings of belonging and self-worth (e.g., one-to-one chats, high fives, daily greetings, reciprocal smiles, interactive tasks or activities, "caught being good," or low-key personal affirmations).

12. Parents differentiate between their own problems and those belonging to the student. (27, 28)

27. Work with the student and the parents to differentiate problems that belong to the student (e.g., grades, friends, homework) from problems that belong to the parents (e.g., messy kitchen, disrespectful behavior at home, misplaced belongings of parents).

28. Guide the parents in using proactive discipline strategies (e.g., "I" statements, consequences, enforceable statements, or choices) to modify behavior that is creating a problem for them and supportive interventions (e.g., active listening, encouragement, brainstorming, or problem-solving strategies) to assist when the problem belongs to the student.

13. Parents allow the student to solve his/her own problems with guidance. (29, 30)

29. Advise the parents and teachers to use the empowering statement, "I think you can handle it," when the student is becoming overly dependent and asking for too much assistance in solving problems that he/she is capable of managing.

30. Introduce the parents to the five-step process for "Guiding the Child to Solve the Problem" (see *Parenting with Love and Logic* by Cline, Fay, and Fay): (1) empathy (active listening); (2) send the power message, "What do you think you're

going to do?"; (3) offer choices (options for solving the problem); (4) have the student state the consequences (of the possible solutions); (5) give permission for the student to either solve the problem or not solve the problem. Assign the parents to use this process when the student has a problem and seeks assistance from them.

14. Parents promote independent behavior using encouragement and support. (29, 31, 32)

29. Advise the parents and teachers to use the empowering statement, "I think you can handle it," when the student is becoming overly dependent and asking for too much assistance in solving problems that he/she is capable of managing.

31. Request that the parents and teachers use the Act As If technique (see *Teacher Talk* by Moorman and Moorman) to encourage the student to make an effort, despite his/her fear of failure (e.g., act as if you felt great about going to school; pretend you really like your teacher and classmates; play like you've done this before; or fake it till you make it).

32. Ask the parents to use the Check Yourself statement (see *Parent Talk* by Moorman) (e.g., "This is sharing day at school, check yourself to make sure you have what you need when it's

your turn to share") to help the student develop the ability to prepare successfully for upcoming events and personal experiences.

15. Parents involve the student in designing his/her own plan for correcting inappropriate behaviors. (33, 34, 35, 36)

33. Assign the student to complete the "Problem Ownership" activity from the *School Counseling and School Social Work Homework Planner* (Knapp) to gain a sense of problems that can be solved independently and those that require assistance; ask him/her to share the results with his/her parents.

34. Assist the student in completing the "Personal Problem-Solving Worksheet" activity from the *School Counseling and School Social Work Homework Planner* (Knapp) to outline a strategy for solving personal problems; encourage him/her to communicate this process with his/her parents.

35. Instruct the student to complete the "Problem-Solving Worksheet" activity from the *School Counseling and School Social Work Homework Planner* (Knapp) to analyze a rule violation at home or at school and to plan for a more appropriate response. Advise the parents and teachers to use this worksheet with the student whenever a rule is violated.

36. Advise the parents and teachers to use a behavior modification plan to address a target behavior that must be modified by the student before he/she is able to enjoy or participate in family or school activities (e.g., recess, TV, computer, meals with his/her family or classmates, play games, use supplies); if the plan is ineffective, privileges are again suspended until a workable plan is in place.

16. Parents help the student recognize personal attributes and talents. (31, 37)

31. Request that the parents and teachers use the Act As If technique (see *Teacher Talk* by Moorman) to encourage the student to make an effort, despite his/her fear of failure (e.g., act as if you felt great about going to school; pretend you really like your teacher and classmates; play like you've done this before; or fake it till you make it).

37. Empower the student to take ownership for both positive and negative events in his/her life by encouraging both the parents and teachers to use attribute awareness (see *Parent Talk* by Moorman) to point out how behaviors produce results (e.g., "You earned an A on this paper, what do you attribute that to?" "You can't find your rollerblades. What caused

that?" "Your teacher says your handwriting is improving. How come?").

17. Parents verbalize an awareness of the problems created by overfunctioning as a parent. (38, 39)

38. Encourage the parents and teachers to allow the student to seek his/her own solutions with guidance even if it requires some struggle and learning from mistakes. Recommend that the parents and teachers listen to the student's problems with empathy and give guidance or assistance only when requested; discuss the results of this approach in a subsequent counseling session.

39. Discuss with the parents how overprotection and overparenting can contribute to feelings of inadequacy and dependency; encourage them to strengthen the student's independent functioning by allowing him/her to practice problem solving, experience consequences, and learn from his/her mistakes.

18. Parents promote positive character development through family discussions, analyzing literature and media examples, loving interactions, spiritual training, and community involvement. (40, 41)

40. Encourage the family to view TV or video programs that are consistent with their personal family values and to discuss the outcome, meaning, and moral value of the program, allowing each family member to express his/her viewpoint without criticism.

41. Discuss with the student and the parents the significance of regular family

attendance at church, synagogue, or other spiritual organization of their choice for character development, moral training, and family cohesion; encourage regular participation by the entire family.

19. Parents convene weekly family meetings to discuss family issues, make family plans, and create a feeling of connectedness. (42, 43)

42. Assign the parents to read about the family council (see *Children: The Challenge* by Dreikurs and Stoltz) or the family meeting (see *Systematic Training for Effective Parenting* by Dinkmeyer and McKay) to understand the process of family members discussing important family issues together at a weekly designated time and place.

43. Encourage the parents to initiate weekly family meetings to discuss concerns, reflect upon positive events, coordinate activities, review values, answer questions, discuss responsibilities, and plan for positive interaction.

20. Parents work to maintain a strong, couple-centered family environment. (44, 45, 46)

44. Assign the parents to read *The Seven Habits of Highly Effective Families* (Covey) to learn strategies for attaining a positive family atmosphere through maintaining a couple-centered approach.

45. Brainstorm with the parents ideas for strengthening their marriage and maintaining a couple-centered family (e.g., support each

other during child interactions, keep a weekly date night, engage in daily personal discussions using active listening, affirm one another frequently).

46. Refer the parents to a marriage counselor or a skills-based marital program [e.g., Prevention and Relationship Enhancement Program (PREP) by Markman, Stanley, and Blumberg (www.prepinc.com)] to strengthen the marital relationship through improved communication and conflict resolution.

21. Family members work together to establish a loving, respectful, cooperative family atmosphere. (47, 48)

47. Identify with the parents and student any triangulation or sabotaging that is occurring in the family, and make plans to end it through open discussions, mutual problem solving, and parents presenting a united front.

48. Discuss with the student cooperative efforts and group projects at home and in the community. Encourage positive efforts and offer guidance in areas of problematic or reluctant participation.

___. _____

___. _____

___. _____

___. _____

___. _____

___. _____

DIAGNOSTIC SUGGESTIONS

Axis I:

300.4	Dysthymic Disorder
314.01	Attention-Deficit/Hyperactivity Disorder, Predominantly Hyperactive-Impulsive Type
314.9	Attention-Deficit/Hyperactivity Disorder, NOS
313.81	Oppositional Defiant Disorder
312.30	Impulse Control Disorder, NOS
301.6	Dependent Personality Disorder
300.02	Generalized Anxiety Disorder
309.21	Separation Anxiety Disorder
V71.02	Child Antisocial Behavior
V61.20	Parent-Child Relational Problem
_____	_____

Axis II:

799.9	Diagnosis Deferred
V71.09	No Diagnosis on Axis II
_____	_____
_____	_____

PHYSICAL DISABILITIES/CHALLENGES

BEHAVIORAL DEFINITIONS

1. Existence of a physical impairment that substantially limits one or more major life activities and affects educational performance.
2. Diagnosed by a physician as having a physical disability.
3. Requires specific accommodations to progress successfully in the academic environment and qualifies for Section 504 services.
4. An ongoing history of a chronic physical condition.
5. Low self-esteem and feelings of inadequacy in academic or social functioning.
6. Qualifies for special education under Individuals with Disabilities Education Act (IDEA).
7. Problems with transitions from one life phase or environment to another.

—. _____

_____

_____

—. _____

_____

_____

—. _____

_____

LONG-TERM GOALS

1. Participate in a complete medical, social, and psychological assessment of symptoms.
2. Parents, teachers, and student acquire an understanding of the physical disability or condition.

3. Participate in and achieve academic success through special education programs or accommodations designated by the IEPC or the Section 504 plan.
4. View self as a unique individual with many strengths and capabilities.
5. Develop appropriate social skills including self-advocacy and empathy for others.
6. Develop organizational skills and demonstrate independent functioning.
7. Develop future career goals and plan for an independent lifestyle.

—. _____
   _____
   _____

—. _____
   _____
   _____

—. _____
   _____

SHORT-TERM OBJECTIVES

1. Complete medical, psychological, and social/emotional assessment to determine eligibility for special education, related services, and necessary accommodations. (1, 2)

THERAPEUTIC INTERVENTIONS

1. Meet with the student, parents, and school staff members to gather background information, discuss educational needs and resources, and determine if more information or assessment is necessary.

2. Collaborate with the student's physician and the school's special service providers (e.g., psychologist, social worker, physical and occupational therapists, speech and language pathologist) to complete a medical, social/emotional, and psychological evaluation of the student if deemed appropriate by the parents and school child study team.

2. Participate in individual or group counseling to acquire a general and personal awareness of the disability, social/emotional effects, and potential management strategies. (3, 4, 5)

3. Include the student in a "succeeding with disabilities" counseling group at school that discusses the nature of disabilities, associated problems, and strategies for coping in school and in life.

4. Have the student begin a personal journal, entitled *Coping with My Disability,* that contains thoughts, feelings, successes, and challenges of living with a chronic physical condition.

5. Read children's literature or view a video with the student that explains various or specific disabilities, explores feelings, and suggests management strategies (e.g., *Reach for the Moon* by Abeel or *Just Look At Us Now* from the South Carolina Educational TV Network).

3. Parents and teachers gain an awareness of the ramifications of the disability upon the student and helpful accommodations and management strategies from special educators, special therapists, or other resources. (6, 7)

6. Refer the parents to a support group, such as one sponsored by the Council for Exceptional Children (703-620-3660 or www.cec.sped.org) or the National Information Center for Children and Youth with Disabilities (NICHCY) (800-695-0285 or www.nichcy.org).

7. Meet with the teacher regularly to review strategies from best-practice literature offering classroom techniques for promoting

4. Verbalize acceptance of a program of individualized or small-group instruction from special educators in the areas of physical, academic, or social deficits. (8, 9, 10)

disability awareness and successfully promoting inclusion in the classroom (e.g., *Disability Awareness in the Classroom: A Resource Tool for Teachers and Students* by Charles C. Thomas Publishers).

8. Attend the Individualized Education Planning and Placement Committee (IEPC) meeting, and participate in the determination of the student's eligibility for special education and related services.

9. Assist in establishing performance goals and objectives for the student at the IEPC in areas of his/her disability and social/behavioral deficits.

10. Assist the IEPC members in identifying special programs that may be helpful to the student (e.g., inclusion with supportive services, total pullout program, resource room, individual or small-group instruction).

5. Participate in assessments for speech, occupational, physical, or social work therapy and/or other related services. (11, 12)

11. Refer the student for assessments by the speech, occupational, or physical therapist; school social worker; and other related service providers to determine his/her eligibility for services in these areas.

12. Advocate for school-based related services and accommodations at the IEPC if deemed appropriate or refer

the student for private therapy.

6. Use accommodations and adapted technology to enhance ability to receive instruction, complete assignments, and take tests. (13, 14)

13. Provide adapted technology (e.g., tape recorder, computer, calculator, phonic ear) to assist the student in daily academic performance and assessment.

14. Consult with the student and his/her teacher(s) and parents regarding necessary accommodations to encourage academic success (e.g., give one task at a time, head phones, hand fidgets, monitor frequently, use an affirming attitude, modify assignments as needed, allow extra time if necessary).

7. Cooperate with a functional analysis of behavior. (15, 16)

15. Complete a functional analysis of the student to define physical, social, learning, and behavioral deficits, analyze the probable causes, and develop reinforcement interventions to correct the problems.

16. Collaborate with the multidisciplinary evaluation team (MET) members to complete the "Record of Behavioral Progress" activity from the *School Counseling and School Social Work Homework Planner* (Knapp) to analyze the student's behavior and to plan for specific intervention strategies that help him/her develop positive alternative behaviors.

8. List own unique learning style and various strengths and abilities. (17, 18, 19)

17. Explain the theory of multiple intelligences (see *Intelligence Reframed* by Gardner), pointing out that people are smart in different ways and asking the student to identify his/her personal areas of greater and lesser intelligences and talents. Have the student add to his/her personal ability list by accepting affirmations from other students or from the counselor.

18. Assign the student to determine his/her personal learning style [e.g., visual (or seeing what is being learned), auditory (or hearing or saying what is being learned), kinesthetic (or needing motion to learn, through self-observation and observations from parents and teachers)]. Instruct the student to use his/her primary learning style while preparing for the next quiz, test, or assignment and to report the results during a subsequent counseling session.

19. Ask the student to complete the "Building on Strengths" activity from The *School Counseling and School Social Work Homework Planner* (Knapp) to identify personal strengths and discover how these strengths can be used to reach his/her goals.

9. Verbalize an increased awareness of how personal choices and behavior create specific results. (20, 21)

20. Have the student complete the "Decision Making" activity from the *School Counseling and School Social Work Homework Planner* (Knapp) to increase his/her awareness of the connection between personal choices and specific results.

21. Introduce activities from the program *I Can Problem-Solve* (Shure) to teach the student problem solving and predicting the result of specific actions.

10. Reframe negative self-talk into positive, realistic messages. (22, 23)

22. Teach the student to use a journal to reframe negative thinking or predicting by having him/her describe an event or problem involving his/her disability and then rewrite the scenario to reflect a more positive outcome.

23. Assist the student in identifying his/her propensity for negative self-talk by reviewing situations in which he/she felt anxious, inferior, or rejected; reframe his/her thinking into more positive, realistic self-talk.

11. Participate in a social skills group. (24, 25, 26)

24. Refer the student to a social skills therapeutic group.

25. Teach the student to use "I" messages and reflective listening. [See *Teaching Children Self-Discipline* (Gordon) or the Bug-Wish Technique (whereby the student says, *"It bugs me*

when you . . . I wish you would stop").]

26. Use *Peacemaking Skills for Little Kids Student Activity Book* (Schmidt, Friedman, Brunt, and Solotoff) to teach the student to develop social assertiveness and conflict management skills.

12. Actively seek friendships among peer group. (27, 28)

27. Encourage the teacher(s) to involve the student in cooperative learning groups that will enhance socialization.

28. Involve the student in a circle-of-friends group, involving classmates or peers who provide support, interaction, free-time activity engagement, and friendship to him/her during the school day.

13. Develop positive relationships with the parents, teachers, and other significant adults. (29, 30)

29. Use puppets or role playing to teach the student how to appropriately share his/her feelings with significant adults.

30. Assign the student to discuss a personal concern with a parent, teacher, or friend; process the results during the next counseling session.

14. Mentor other students who are coping with disabilities and related issues. (31, 32)

31. Arrange with the teacher to have the student assist classmates or younger students who are coping with physical conditions or disabilities.

32. Invite the student to share personal strategies and successes with students of a

15. Successfully complete school assignments and homework. (33, 34, 35)

16. Establish a routine or schedule to prioritize and organize key daily activities. (36, 37)

17. Parents and teachers empower the student by emphasizing personal responsibility and the benefits of considering the consequences before acting. (38, 39)

newly formed succeeding-with-disabilities group.

33. Assign the student to use a study planner to list all assignments, record working time, and check off when completed.

34. Play Study Smart (ADHD Warehouse) with the student to assist him/her in developing study skills, comprehension, test taking, and memory.

35. Ask the parents and teachers to monitor the student's assignment planner daily and to give encouragement and direction as needed.

36. Assist the student in listing and prioritizing key daily activities at home, school, and in the community; assign times for completion, and record the results in a personal journal or an assignment planner.

37. Instruct the student to place a star, sticker, or smiley face on a chart next to each chore, task, or assignment that is completed and to share these accomplishments with his/her parents, teacher(s), or counselor.

38. Assist the student in completing the "Personal Problem-Solving Worksheet" activity from the *School Counseling and School Social Work Homework Planner* (Knapp) to

outline a strategy for solving personal problems.

39. Encourage the teacher(s) and parents to use positive discipline strategies for helping the student to develop responsibility (e.g., assign chores and tasks that he/she is capable of handling; allow him/her to learn from mistakes and to experience relevant and logical consequences and allow a chance to try again).

18. Parents, teachers, and counselor affirm the student for progress in assuming responsibility and acquiring independence. (40, 41)

40. Discuss with the teachers and the parents the importance of giving frequent affirmations to the student for progress noted in a private, low-key manner.

41. Allow time during the counseling sessions for the student to develop personal affirmations for progress in school, home, and social adjustment and to share these successes with his/her parents, teacher(s), counselor, and group members.

19. Participate in programs designated to enhance self-care, independent functioning, and future employment. (42, 43)

42. Encourage the student to select classes that prepare him/her for future independence (e.g., child development, independent living, home economics, personal finance).

43. Enroll the student in community-based instruction or school-to-career programs that are designed to provide employment skills and work experience.

20. Establish career goals, mentors, and role models to assist in the transition from school to work. (44, 45, 46)

44. Teach the student to use goal setting by recording daily, weekly, and monthly goals in a personal journal and listing the steps that are necessary to achieve each goal; meet with him/her to evaluate his/her progress and to revise either the goal or the process when indicated.

45. Work with the student to assess career goals and to plan a curriculum that is consistent with these goals.

46. Brainstorm with the student role models, mentors, and family or community members who are available to support the achievement of personal and career goals; list them in a personal journal (or assign the "Inspirations" activity from the *School Counseling and School Social Work Homework Planner* by Knapp).

—. _____
    _____

—. _____
    _____

—. _____
    _____

—. _____
    _____

—. _____
    _____

—. _____
    _____

DIAGNOSTIC SUGGESTIONS

Axis I: 299.00   Autistic Disorder
299.80   Rett's Disorder
299.80   Asperger's Disorder
299.10   Childhood Disintegrative Disorder
299.80   Pervasive Developmental Disorder NOS
315.4   Developmental Coordination Disorder
315.31   Expressive Language Disorder
315.32   Mixed Receptive-Expressive Language
Disorder
315.39   Phonological Disorder

_____   _____

_____   _____

Axis II: V71.09   No Diagnosis on Axis II
799.9   Diagnosis Deferred

_____   _____

_____   _____

PHYSICAL/SEXUAL ABUSE

BEHAVIORAL DEFINITIONS

1. Self-report of physical, sexual, or emotional aggression resulting in injury or emotional trauma from a parent or caregiver.
2. Bruises or wounds as evidence of victimization.
3. Frequent and prolonged periods of depression, irritability, anxiety, and/or apathetic withdrawal.
4. Marked distrust in others as manifested by social withdrawal and problems with establishing and maintaining close relationships.
5. Feelings of guilt, shame, and low self-esteem.
6. Significant increase in the frequency and severity of aggressive behaviors toward peers or adults.
7. Absence of minimum care, supervision, emotional support, and nurturing required for normal childhood development.
8. Parents lack emotional, affective, or mental ability and/or the knowledge base to perform appropriate parenting behaviors.
9. Parents or caregivers were abused or neglected in their own childhood and are repeating a generational cycle of abuse and neglect.
10. Parent condones or ignores abuse, neglect, or maltreatment from his/her spouse or another caregiver.
11. Parental expectations exceed the student's maturity and ability level.
12. Family secrecy and isolation are valued, promoted, and demanded.

—. _____

_____

—. _____

_____

—. _____

_____

LONG-TERM GOALS

1. Disclose incidents of abuse or neglect to a supportive educator and/or child protection investigator, and work to terminate the abuse.
2. Obtain protection from any further victimization.
3. Access social and mental health services for self, parents, and other family members.
4. Enhance self-worth and build a sense of self-reliance and empowerment.
5. Parents develop empathy for the student's needs and enhance bonding, communication, and proper boundaries.
6. Parents acquire parenting skills and knowledge about home management and child development.
7. Parents adopt reasonable expectations of their parenting skills and the student's behavior, abilities, and level of maturity.

—. _____
   _____

—. _____
   _____

—. _____
   _____

SHORT-TERM OBJECTIVES

1. Discuss family issues and disclose experiences of mistreatment, neglect, or abuse. (1, 2, 3)

THERAPEUTIC INTERVENTIONS

1. Meet with the student to discuss concerns about improper treatment from family members or other caregivers; use a supportive, low-key approach to assure the student that disclosure is the first step in getting help to terminate the abuse.

2. Gather enough information to determine if there is reason to suspect abuse; document the actual words used

by the student to include in the abuse referral report.

2. Share feelings about the abuse and dysfunctional family relationships. (4, 5, 6)

3. Peruse the student's cumulative records to determine if any previous abuse or maltreatment has been reported or suspected.

4. Reassure the student that disclosure takes courage, and encourage him/her to express and process the associated feelings (e.g., fear, guilt, confusion, anger, resentment, love, and hate).

5. Assign the student to complete the "My Secret Story" activity from the *School Counseling and School Social Work Homework Planner* (Knapp) to disclose the story of the abuse and associated feelings.

6. Affirm continuing positive regard for the student, and set up regular counseling appointments to ensure counseling support throughout the abuse reporting, investigation, and intervention process.

3. Verbalize an acceptance of the fact that contact must be made with the child protection agency to report all known facts and suspicions of the abuse. (7, 8, 9, 10)

7. Support the teacher or other educator suspecting abuse, review the circumstances, and assist him/her in completing the necessary report forms and contacting the proper child protection authorities.

8. Report any suspected abuse to the state-authorized child protection services (CPS)

agency or local police department. Keep notes on the student's behaviors, physical marks, or other suspicious evidence, and complete an oral and/or written report according to the state's child protection laws and guidelines.

9. Review the school or school board policy regarding abuse reporting, and notify the student's parents and the school administration if indicated in the policy.

10. Indicate to the CPS caseworkers the school's desire to be informed during the investigation and willingness to provide support and assistance to the student and his/her family (e.g., diagnosis and assessment of specific problems, development of individualized educational plans, and related services).

4. Move to a safe living environment while the abusive situation is being investigated. (11)

11. Provide background information to the CPS caseworkers to facilitate the student's placement with relatives, friends, or in foster care if deemed necessary.

5. Parents/caregivers and the student cooperate with family therapy designed to eliminate the abusive behaviors and work together after the disclosure of the abusive situation. (12, 13, 14)

12. Meet with the parents on an ongoing basis to discuss disciplinary challenges for the student and to discuss techniques learned in parenting classes or from recommended books or tapes (e.g., *Discipline for Home*

and School by Ford, *Parenting with Love and Logic* by Cline and Fay, or *Parent Talk* by Moorman).

13. Suggest that the parents and the student meet weekly at a designated time to review progress, give encouragement, note continuing concerns, and keep a written progress report to share with a school counselor or private therapist.

14. Refer the student and his/her family to a private therapist or agency to help heal the family disruption and dysfunctional relationships created by the abuse and to begin to reconstruct positive family functioning and feelings of love and trust.

6. Openly share and record emotional reactions to the abuse on a daily basis. (15, 16)

15. Initiate a feelings checkup with the student each morning, and record the results on a graph; ask him/her if immediate supportive counseling is necessary, and set up an appointment for that day if necessary.

16. Ask the student to complete the "Measuring My Feelings" activity in the *School Counseling and School Social Work Homework Planner* (Knapp) to use as a daily barometer of how he/she is coping with the ramifications of the abuse.

7. Parents attend parent education classes and read parenting literature that teaches techniques of positive discipline. (17, 18)

17. Refer the parents to a parenting class (e.g., *Systematic Training for Effective Parenting* by Dinkmeyer and McKay, *Becoming a Love and Logic Parent* by Fay, Cline, and Fay, or *The Parent Talk System* by Moorman and Knapp) to help them replace abusive parent-child interactions with techniques of positive discipline.

18. Assign the parents to read literature about implementing strategies of positive discipline in their family (e.g., *Baby Wise* by Ezzo and Bucknam, *Kids Are Worth It!* by Coloroso, or *Children: The Challenge* by Dreikurs and Stoltz).

8. Parents verbalize an awareness of the problems created by overly punitive, abusive, and inconsistent parenting. (19, 20, 21)

19. Assign the parents to listen to the audiotape *Helicopters, Drill Sergeants, and Consultants* (Fay) to identify their own style of parenting and recognize the advantages of allowing children to problem-solve; meet with the parents to discuss the information and apply it to their specific discipline issues.

20. Encourage the parents to allow the student to seek his/her own solutions with guidance even if it requires some struggling and learning from mistakes. Recommend that the parents listen to his/her problems with empathy and give guidance or assistance only when requested. Assign the

parents to use this approach and discuss the results in a subsequent counseling session.

21. Assist the parents in identifying common reactions of children to overly punitive parenting (e.g., feelings of inadequacy, dependency, resentment, and rebellion).

9. Single parents seek support, encouragement, and respite from coparent, family, and friends. (22, 23, 24)

22. Brainstorm with the single parent a list of support people whom he/she can call on to baby-sit, console, listen, and help out in case of emergency or burnout.

23. Identify with the single parent community agencies available to offer assistance and support (e.g., community mental health, respite care, social services for financial assistance, school and church organizations, single-parent support groups).

24. Discuss with the single parent or parents the importance of cooperation in the coparenting process, and offer to mediate any current roadblocks or refer to a private counselor for coparenting skills training.

10. Parents and student connect with social service agencies able to provide support, guidance, and respite. (25, 26)

25. Refer the student and his/her family to community agencies and services designed to support families struggling with parent-child or abuse issues (e.g., Visiting Nurses Association,

Head Start, mental health clinics, and family abuse counseling services), or refer them to a national support resource [e.g., Childhelp, U.S.A. (800-4CHILD) or Parents Anonymous (800-421-0353)].

26. Refer the parents to a marriage counselor or a skills-based marital program [e.g., Prevention and Relationship Enhancement Program (PREP), described in *Fighting for Your Marriage* by Markman, Stanley, and Blumberg, or see www .prepinc.com] to strengthen the marital relationship through improved communication and conflict resolution.

11. Increase social interaction with classmates and friends. (27, 28)

27. Plan with the student for various social interactions with his/her classmates and friends; record the plan and outcome in a journal.

28. Encourage the student to join a social group or club; brainstorm options and help the student to make a selection.

12. Family members reduce their social isolation by becoming involved in school activities. (29)

29. Encourage the family to become involved with social activities at the student's school (e.g., PTA, open house, holiday bizarre, festivals, fairs, sports events, concerts) to reduce their isolation.

13. Parents promote positive character development

30. Assign the parents to read stories from *Where the*

through family discussions, analyzing literature and media examples, loving interactions, spiritual training, and community involvement. (30, 31, 32)

Heart Is (Moorman) or *Chicken Soup for the Soul* (Canfield, Hansen, and Kirberger) to stress family togetherness and the important roles or each family member.

31. Encourage the family to view TV or video programs that are consistent with their personal family values and to discuss the outcome, meaning, and moral value of the program, allowing each family member to express his/her viewpoint without criticism.

32. Discuss with the student and his/her parents the significance of regular family attendance at the church, synagogue, or other spiritual organization of their choice for character development, moral training, and family cohesion.

14. Extended family members support the parents' attempts to use positive parenting strategies to create family harmony. (33, 34)

33. Suggest that the parents invite the grandparents and other involved family members to parenting classes or a counseling session to help them understand the discipline strategies being used to establish emotional health and family harmony.

34. Recommend that the parents give *Grandparenting with Love and Logic* (Fay and Cline) to their parents as a holiday or special event gift; advise the parents to discuss particular aspects of

15. Parents grant specific freedoms consistent with the student's maturity and level of self-control. (35, 36)

this book with their own parents on a regular basis.

35. Define *parenting inside the funnel* (see *Baby Wise* by Ezzo and Bucknam), which extends freedoms to a child only after developmental maturity has been attained to illustrate the importance of waiting until the necessary self-control in acquired before granting specific privileges.

36. Teach the parents the phrase "Soon you'll be on your own" (see *Parent Talk* by Moorman) to encourage the student to earn freedom from parental monitoring by demonstrating the ability to complete a task or chore independently. When the student complains about too much supervision, instruct the parents to reply, "When you show me you can handle it, you'll be on your own."

16. Parents report a reduction in power struggles resulting from strategies designed to enlist the student's cooperation. (37, 38)

37. Ask the parents to practice methods of sidestepping power struggles (e.g., using techniques such as the broken record, "I" statements, choices, enforceable statements, refusing to argue, taking a time-out, and natural and logical consequences); recommend that they record the progress in a discipline journal and report the progress during subsequent counseling sessions.

38. Assist the student and his/her parents in establishing a verbal or nonverbal cue to signal the need to break the cycle of negative behavior followed by an abusive reaction by implementing a prearranged strategy (e.g., taking a time-out, changing location, taking a walk, or switching activities).

17. Participate in a social/emotional assessment, focusing on issues of self-esteem, self-control, responsibility, respect, and empowerment. (39, 40)

39. Have the student complete the "Personal Profile" activity information sheet from the *School Counseling and School Social Work Homework Planner* (Knapp), which details pertinent personal data, or gather personal information in an informal interview with the student.

40. Administer a self-concept inventory to the student (e.g., the Piers-Harris Self-Concept Scale or the Coopersmith Self-Esteem Inventory) to determine specific areas of low self-esteem, lack of internal control, and feelings of hopelessness.

18. Cooperate with community agencies to acquire long-term living arrangements that are safe, nurturing, and promote the growth and development of love, trust, and healthy self-esteem. (41, 42, 43)

41. Help the student to deal with court involvement with the family by providing information about the process, taking a field trip to the courtroom, or interviewing a supportive judge or lawyer.

42. Initiate immediate contact with the student's foster

parents to plan for a smooth transition, offer support, and cooperate on school issues.

43. Assist the student in acclimating to new short- or long-term living arrangements by encouraging the expression of grief and loss, dealing with adjustment issues, and identifying the positive aspects of living in a healthy, abuse-free environment.

—. _____   —. _____
   _____   _____

—. _____   —. _____
   _____   _____

—. _____   —. _____
   _____   _____

DIAGNOSTIC SUGGESTIONS

Axis I:	309.81	Posttraumatic Stress Disorder
	308.3	Acute Stress Disorder
	300.4	Dysthymic Disorder
	296.xx	Major Depressive Disorder
	309.21	Separation Anxiety Disorder
	995.53	Sexual Abuse of Child (Victim)
	311	Depressive Disorder NOS
	300.02	Generalized Anxiety Disorder
	307.47	Nightmare Disorder
	313.81	Oppositional Defiant Disorder
	312.8	Conduct Disorder/Childhood-Onset Type
	300.6	Depersonalization Disorder
	300.15	Dissociative Disorder
	_____	_____
	_____	_____
Axis II:	799.9	Diagnosis Deferred
	V71.09	No Diagnosis on Axis II
	_____	_____
	_____	_____

POVERTY/ECONOMIC CONCERNS

BEHAVIORAL DEFINITIONS

1. Family receives welfare payments, food stamps, Medicaid, and/or qualifies for free or reduced-fee school meal programs.
2. Family resides in transient or subpar housing.
3. Parents are unemployed or earn income below the poverty level.
4. Lack of transportation, phone, medical assistance, school supplies, and other essential resources.
5. Family has recently become impoverished.
6. Family has been in poverty for more than one generation.
7. Parents place a low value on education and are minimally involved in the education process.
8. Predominance of single-parent families with a matriarchal structure and inconsistent involvement from the father.
9. People are seen as personal resources, and extra money is shared with family and friends rather than saved to meet emergencies or plan for future goals.
10. Child discipline is designed to generate penance and forgiveness, not a change in behavior.
11. Strong belief in fate or destiny.
12. High incidence of teen pregnancies in the extended family.

—. _____

_____

—. _____

_____

—. _____

_____

LONG-TERM GOALS

1. Family and student access community and social services that provide social, economic, and medical resources.
2. Family implements employment and financial counseling and other resources that will lead to increased self-reliance.
3. Participate in school and attain academic success.
4. Prepare for transition from school to work.
5. Abstain from substance abuse and other self-defeating behaviors.
6. Consistently use birth control or abstinence, and adopt long-term family planning goals.
7. Reduce stress and emotional negativity caused by poverty conditions.

__. _____
   _____
__. _____
   _____
   _____
__. _____
   _____

SHORT-TERM OBJECTIVES

1. Family members attend school- or community-based support groups. (1, 2)

THERAPEUTIC INTERVENTIONS

1. Involve the student and his/her family in a support group [e.g., Families and Schools Together (FAST), developed by the Alliance for Children and Families] to strengthen the parent-child relationship, to build a partnership between the parents and the school, and to provide ongoing encouragement for him/her and his/her family.

2. Develop coping strategies or an advisory group that will meet weekly with family members to discuss issues

and problem-solve to assist the student in dealing with concerns involving his/her school, family, peer group, and community.

2. Family members participate in literacy education programs. (3)

3. Organize a schoolwide reading program that links volunteer tutors with students and parents needing assistance and encouragement with literacy.

3. Parents identify and access available public assistance resources and services. (4, 5)

4. Assist the student and his/her family in developing a plan for obtaining needed economic assistance and services. Note roadblocks (e.g., transportation, day care, appropriate clothing), and assist them in planning to overcome these hurdles.

5. Refer the family to agencies that provide social, financial, and economic services (e.g., public assistance, food stamps, Medicaid, Head Start), and help the family to apply for these resources.

4. Identify negative self-talk regarding school-related issues, and develop more positive, realistic messages. (6, 7, 8)

6. Use a journal to reframe a negative thinking process by having the student describe an event in his/her life, and then assist him/her in rewriting the scenario to reflect a healthier interpretation.

7. Brainstorm positive statements of encouragement that could be applied by the student to himself/herself, the school setting, academic abilities, or acceptance from others. Ask the student to

record them in a journal, and have him/her record actual encouraging statements received from others during the course of the week.

8. Assist the student in identifying his/her propensity for negative self-talk regarding school, his/her abilities, social acceptance, or teachers by reviewing situations in which he/she felt anxious, inferior, or rejected; reframe his/her thinking into more positive, realistic self-talk.

5. Take classes that teach skills necessary for attaining economic independence and self-sufficiency in the future. (9)

9. Encourage the student to select classes that will prepare him/her for future independence (e.g., child development, career development, independent living, home economics, personal finance, etc.).

6. Identify the negative consequences of poverty on daily functioning in the school setting. (4, 5, 10, 11)

4. Assist the student and his/her family in developing a plan for obtaining needed economic assistance and services. Note roadblocks (e.g., transportation, day care, appropriate clothing), and assist them in planning to overcome these hurdles.

5. Refer the family to agencies that provide social, financial, and economic services (e.g., public assistance, food stamps, Medicaid, Head Start), and help the family to apply for these resources.

10. Explore how family poverty has affected the student in the school setting (e.g., lack of proper clothing or nutritional meals, rejection by peers, frequent geographic moves).

11. Explore and process the student's emotional reaction to living in poverty (e.g., anger, shame, fear).

7. List the positive value of education on overcoming poverty and enriching satisfaction with mastery over life. (12, 13)

12. Teach the student the multifaceted value of education (e.g., appreciating the many nuances of different people and cultures, gaining mastery over his/her own destiny, exploring and expanding his/her personal interests).

13. Explore and reframe negative attitudes regarding education that the student has learned from his/her extended family and the neighborhood.

8. Participate in family planning and child development classes provided by the school or community clinics. (14)

14. Refer the student to community clinics, church programs, or medical workshops that focus on family planning, prenatal self-care, birthing classes, and infant child care to acquire the skills necessary for planning and assuming his/her future role as a parent.

9. Identify future family goals, and create a plan for their attainment. (15, 16, 17)

15. Assist the student in determining future parental and family goals and to develop a plan for preventing teen pregnancy.

16. Arrange for the student to meet with role models and mentors who have postponed marriage and child bearing until after graduation and employment goals have been attained.

17. Brainstorm the positive effects of postponing reproduction until becoming self-supporting and the negative aspects of teen parenthood.

10. Family members and the student establish long- and short-term personal and family goals. (18, 19)

18. Meet with the student and his/her family to take a family history, clarify family issues and concerns, and identify long- and short-term goals.

19. Assist the student and his/her family members in planning for goal attainment through the following steps: (1) listing goals, (2) identifying resources and roadblocks, and (3) creating a strategy for success (or assign the "Goal Achievement" activity from The *School Counseling and School Social Work Homework Planner* by Knapp).

11. Student and his/her family members report that a trusting relationship has developed with school staff members. (20, 21, 22)

20. In-service the school staff on issues of poverty by introducing ideas from *A Framework for Understanding Poverty* (Payne).

21. Promote *looping,* or allowing a group of students to remain with the same teacher for two or more years, to enhance a feeling of belonging and community.

22. Monitor relationships among the staff and the student and his/her family to encourage connectedness and trust. Discuss areas of conflict with both the staff and the student, and offer encouragement and mediation of problems.

12. Parents attend classes focused on teaching them effective parenting techniques. (23)

23. Refer the parents to a parenting class (e.g., *Systematic Training for Effective Parenting* by Dinkmeyer and McKay, *Becoming a Love and Logic Parent* by Fay and Cline, or *The Parent Talk System* by Moorman and Knapp) to acquire techniques of positive discipline to use with the student.

13. Parents participate in group discussions of their concerns regarding school programs. (24, 25)

24. Sponsor a forum for parent discussions of their concerns regarding school issues. Provide a meeting place, child care, and refreshments. Use conflict management and mediation techniques to allow the discussion to be free-flowing, but respectful.

25. Provide school information and parent education through videos that explain school policy and procedures and that are lent to families for viewing; follow up with question-and-answer sessions facilitated by school staff members.

14. Parents attend school conferences focused on the student's behavior and

26. Organize student-led conferences that involve an exchange of information about

academic performance.
(26, 27, 28)

school issues and progress between the student and his/her parents, with the teacher assuming the role of observer and facilitator.

27. Arrange for transportation (e.g., bus, taxi vouchers, or car rides) for parents who need assistance in getting to school events.

28. Initiate team planning sessions involving the parents and school staff members to identify methods of helping the student become more successful in school. Encourage the parents to take an active role in the strategy sessions.

15. Attend a social skills training group. (29)

29. Refer the student to or conduct a social skills therapeutic group that focuses on developing feelings of belonging and participating appropriately in the school milieu.

16. Attend school on a consistent basis. (30, 31)

30. Encourage the teachers to involve the student in cooperative learning groups and to promote participation in classroom social activities.

31. Assist the student in identifying concerns or roadblocks to regular school attendance (e.g., lack of food, clothing, or sleep; family disruption; requested to baby-sit; view school as irrelevant); brainstorm solutions and offer assistance (e.g., referral to community agencies, home-

work support, child care, transportation).

17. Establish career goals and use mentors and role models to assist in the transition from school to work. (32, 33, 34)

32. Teach the student to use goal setting by recording daily, weekly, and monthly goals in a personal journal and listing the steps necessary to achieve each goal. Meet with the student to evaluate his/her progress, and revise either the goal or the process when indicated.

33. Assist the student in assessing his/her career goals and planning a curriculum consistent with these goals.

34. Brainstorm with the student what role models, mentors, and family or community members are available to support his/her achievement of academic and career goals.

18. Participate in classes that teach school-to-work skills. (35, 36)

35. Assist the student in choosing between a college prep curriculum and a skill-based technical program, depending on career goals, aptitude, and interest.

36. Enroll the student in community-based instruction or school-to-career programs designed to provide employment skills and work experience.

19. Cooperate with the school classroom rules and discipline structure. (37, 38, 39)

37. Include the student in a group that teaches appropriate classroom and school behavior (e.g., listening to instruction without interrupting, raising hands to

comment, staying seated, taking notes, completing assignments); practice and role-play these behaviors weekly in group sessions.

38. Brainstorm with the student how school rules differ from family or street rules, and discuss the necessity of adhering to different rules in different situations (or assign the "Home/School Rules Comparison" activity from The *School Counseling and School Social Work Homework Planner* by Knapp).

39. Assist the school staff in developing a positive system of discipline that incorporates a set of clearly defined principals and structure enforced by logical consequences that are designed to teach appropriate and responsible behavior.

20. Achieve grade-level or individualized academic expectations in the school curriculum. (40, 41)

40. Support a schoolwide schedule that groups students by skill level in reading and math to encourage teaching to the ability level and optimal academic progress for each group.

41. Support teachers in addressing the student's learning styles, constantly checking for learning, using multisensory techniques, concrete experiences, and relevant curriculum.

21. Participate in substance abuse prevention and

1. Involve the student and his/her family in a support

wellness programs at school or in the community. (1, 42)

group [e.g., Families and Schools Together (FAST), developed by the Alliance for Children and Families] to strengthen the parent-child relationship, to build a partnership between the parents and the school, and to provide ongoing encouragement for him/her and his/her family.

42. Teach substance abuse prevention programs in the classroom as part of the K-12 curriculum.

22. Family members and/or the student attend substance abuse assessment and/or treatment services. (43, 44)

43. Refer the student and/or his/her parents to community programs or services for assessment and treatment of substance abuse (e.g., Alcoholics Anonymous, Al-Anon, psychiatric hospitals, detox programs, or private therapy).

44. Discuss lifestyle choices with the student, and support and encourage healthy choices that avoid substance abuse.

23. Use problem-solving skills to address economic, family, and social issues. (45)

45. Teach the student to use a simple problem-solving process by (1) stating the problem, (2) listing potential solutions, (3) predicting the possible result, and (4) choosing an intervention to deal with the situation. Assign him/her to use this process to solve daily dilemmas and to report the results during the next counseling or group session.

—. _____   —. _____
   _____   _____
—. _____   —. _____
   _____   _____
—. _____   —. _____
   _____   _____

DIAGNOSTIC SUGGESTIONS

Axis I: 309.24   Adjustment Disorder With Anxiety
309.0   Adjustment Disorder With Depressed Mood
309.28   Adjustment Disorder With Mixed Anxiety and
         Depressed Mood
300.00   Anxiety Disorder NOS
300.02   Generalized Anxiety Disorder

_____   _____

_____   _____

Axis II: V71.09   No Diagnosis on Axis II
799.9   Diagnosis Deferred

_____   _____

_____   _____

RESPONSIBLE BEHAVIOR TRAINING

BEHAVIORAL DEFINITIONS

1. Does not complete age-appropriate tasks, chores, or schoolwork.
2. Demonstrates poor organizational skills.
3. Undependable and relies excessively on others for support, direction, and guidance.
4. Reports strong feelings of inadequacy and lack of self-confidence.
5. Fearful of new situations or of taking risks.
6. Careless with personal property and others' belongings.
7. Uncooperative or unproductive during group projects.
8. Lack of persistence in challenging situations.
9. Refuses to follow rules at home or at school.
10. Demonstrates reluctance in taking the initiative or assuming a leadership role.

—. _____
   _____

—. _____
   _____
   _____

—. _____
   _____

LONG-TERM GOALS

1. Complete chores at home and assignments at school.
2. Learn to organize assignments, activities, and self-care.
3. Demonstrate self-reliance and the ability to problem-solve.
4. Develop feelings of capability, adequacy, and healthy self-esteem.
5. Take care of the belongings of self and others.

6. Participate in cooperative group activities, and assume appropriate workload.
7. Continue to work or participate in challenging situations until they are resolved or completed.

—. _____
    _____

—. _____
    _____

—. _____
    _____

SHORT-TERM OBJECTIVES

THERAPEUTIC INTERVENTIONS

1. Parents and teacher(s) meet with the counselor to discuss their concerns about the student's lack of demonstrating responsibility. (1, 2, 3)

1. Meet with the parents and teachers to discuss their concerns about the student's lack of responsibility at school and at home.

2. Gather developmental history information, and create a list of behaviorally specific goals which define an age-appropriate level of responsibility.

3. Collaborate with the parents and teacher to complete the "Record of Behavioral Progress" activity from the *School Counseling and School Social Work Homework Planner* (Knapp) to analyze the student's behavior and plan for specific intervention strategies that will help the student to develop positive alternative behaviors.

2. Verbalize an honest evaluation of strengths, weaknesses, and goals for

4. Meet with the student individually or in group sessions which focus on

demonstrating responsibility. (4, 5)

helping him/her to develop goals in areas of family and school involvement, personal care, recognize capabilities, and acquire a pattern of taking responsibility for his/her behavior.

5. Ask the student to complete the "Skill Assessment" activity from the *School Counseling and School Social Work Homework Planner* (Knapp) to evaluate existing abilities in terms of multiple intelligences. (See *Intelligence Reframed: Multiple Intelligences for the 21st Century* by Gardner.)

3. Parents and teacher(s) attend workshops and read literature focusing on teaching children to become responsible. (6, 7, 8)

6. Refer the parents to a class that focuses on helping children to develop responsible behavior (e.g., *Systematic Training for Effective Parenting* by Dinkmeyer and McKay, *Becoming a Love and Logic Parent* by Fay, Cline, and Fay, *The Parent Talk System* by Moorman and Knapp).

7. Refer the teachers to workshops designed to promote independence and responsible behavior in children (e.g., *Discipline with Love and Logic* by Cline and Fay, *Teacher Talk* by Moorman and Moorman, or *Positive Discipline, What Does and Does Not Work* by Knapp).

8. Assign the teachers and the parents to read child development literature that addresses promoting

responsibility in children (*Children: The Challenge* by Dreikurs and Stoltz, *The Underachievement Syndrome* by Rimm, *Parent Talk* by Moorman, or *Teaching with Love and Logic* by Fay and Funk).

4. Parents initiate strategies at home designed to foster responsible behavior. (9, 10)

9. Assist the parents in implementing "the Four Steps to Responsibility:" (1) give the child a task he/she can handle; (2) if he/she fails, view mistakes as learning opportunities; (3) let consequences and empathy do the teaching; (4) give the same task again. Ask the student to repeat this process continually as he/she begins to develop responsibility in chore completion. (See *Parenting with Love and Logic* by Cline and Fay.)

10. Ask the parents to use the Red Light, Green Light technique (see *Parent Talk* by Moorman) to turn an irresponsible behavior into a responsible behavior: (1) describe the inappropriate behavior to the child (red light), such as an unmade bed, wet towels on the floor, or dirty dishes in the family room; (2) describe the expected behavior (green light), such as bed made before school, towels on the rack, dishes in dishwasher.

5. Teacher(s) implement classroom interventions that encourage the student to be self-reliant, organized,

11. Ask the teachers to substitute the phrase "Next time" for "Don't" in order to shape positive future efforts from

and self-confident. (11, 12)

the student (e.g., "Next time you turn in a paper, make sure your name is at the top" versus "Don't turn in a paper without your name at the top"). (See *Teacher Talk* by Moorman and Moorman.)

12. Request that the teachers use "Act as if" to encourage the student to make an effort, despite the fear of failure (e.g., "Act as if you know how to draw that tree"; "Pretend you can jump rope"; "Play like you've done this before"; or "Fake it till you make it"). (See *Teacher Talk* by Moorman and Moorman.)

6. Complete assigned chores at home. (13, 14)

13. Create a chore chart that monitors the student's weekly chores, time spent on the task, and that includes a grade given by both the parents and the student (or assign the "Chore Report Card" activity in the *School Counseling and School Social Work Homework Planner* by Knapp).

14. Brainstorm with the student, in either an individual or a group session, strategies that encourage sustained effort and task completion (e.g., self-monitoring, taking a short break, scheduling a specific work time, prioritizing jobs, stretching his/her muscles, standing while he/she works), and ask him/her to

7. Increase completion of in-class assignments and homework. (15, 16, 17, 18)

8. Establish a routine or schedule to prioritize and organize key daily activities. (19, 20)

share personal successes or challenges with this goal.

15. Assign the student to use an in-class and homework planner to list all assignments, record working time, and check off each assignment when it is completed.

16. Play Study Smart (ADHD Warehouse) with the student to assist him/her in the development of study skills, comprehension, test taking, and memory.

17. Ask the parents and teachers to monitor the student's assignment planner daily and give encouragement and direction as needed.

18. Consult with the teacher(s) and parents regarding necessary accommodation to encourage the student's success, (e.g., give one task at a time; monitor progress frequently; use an affirming attitude; modify assignments as needed; allow extra time if necessary).

19. Assist the student in listing and prioritizing key daily activities at home, school, and in the community; ask him/her to assign times for completion and to record his/her experiences in a personal journal or an assignment planner.

20. Instruct the student to place a star, sticker, or smiley face on a chart next to

each chore, task, or assignment that is completed to share accomplishments with his/her parents, teachers, or counselor.

9. Assume responsibility for personal care in the morning and prior to bedtime. (19, 21)

19. Assist the student in listing and prioritizing key daily activities at home, school, and in the community; ask him/her to assign times for completion and to record his/her experiences in a personal journal or an assignment planner.

21. Develop a self-care chart listing personal responsibilities for getting ready in the morning and preparing for bed at night.

10. Parents and teachers establish regular communication between them to assist the student in organizing and monitoring assignments and school responsibilities. (22, 23)

22. Consult with the parents and teachers to devise a communication schedule that provides for weekly, monthly, or as-needed interchange between school and home.

23. Encourage the teachers and parents to exchange written notes on a daily, weekly, or monthly basis, using a behavior journal or checklist to monitor the student's progress both at school and home.

11. Solve personal problems at home or at school independently or with the help of the parents, teachers, or counselor. (24, 25)

24. Assign the student to complete the "Problem Ownership" activity in the *School Counseling and School Social Work Homework Planner* (Knapp) to gain a sense of problems that can be solved independently

and those that require assistance.

25. Assist the student in completing the "Personal Problem-Solving Worksheet" activity in the *School Counseling and School Social Work Homework Planner* (Knapp) to outline a strategy for solving personal problems.

12. Teacher(s), counselor, student, and the parents collaborate to devise a plan for helping the student become more successful in the classroom. (26, 27, 28)

26. Meet with the parents to discuss strategies that will encourage the student to gain independence, complete chores and homework, engage in cooperative behavior, and gain independence (e.g., maintain eye contact with the student when delivering instructions; encourage questions; offer guidance on an as-needed basis; simplify directions; and ask him/her to describe what type of assistance is needed).

27. Arrange a meeting with the teachers, the parents, and the student to determine accommodations that will encourage the student's successful participation in classroom activities (e.g., supervising him/her closely during times of transition; seating him/her near the teacher's desk in an area of low distractions or near a good role model; involving him/her in lesson discussions; giving him/her simple, clear instructions).

28. The teacher and/or counselor meet with the student weekly to affirm progress and determine necessary changes in classroom strategies.

13. Teachers and the parents help the student break tasks and assignments into manageable steps. (29)

29. Assign the student the "Task Buster" activity in the *School Counseling and School Social Work Homework Planner* (Knapp) to teach him/her the skill of subdividing assignments and chores into manageable steps.

14. Verbalize an increased awareness of how personal choices and behavior create specific results. (30, 31, 32)

30. Have the student, in either an individual or a small-group session, complete the "Decision Making" activity in the *School Counseling and School Social Work Homework Planner* (Knapp) to increase his/her awareness of the connection between personal choices and specific results.

31. Use cartooning [see "Cartooning as a Counseling Approach to a Socially Isolated Child" by Sonntag in the *School Counselor* (1985, vol. 32, pp. 307–312)] by having the student begin a cartoon story that is completed with the counselor in progressive cartoon frames, which can be interpreted and can eventually result in a solution to a personal dilemma.

32. Introduce activities from the program *I Can Problem-Solve* (Shure, available from

the ADHD Warehouse) to teach the student problem solving and predicting the result of specific actions.

15. Parents and teachers demonstrate confidence in the student's ability to function independently. (33, 34, 35)

33. Encourage the parents and teachers to allow the student to seek his/her own solutions with guidance even if it requires some struggling and learning from mistakes. Recommend that the parents and teachers listen to the student's problems with empathy and give guidance or assistance only when requested.

34. Advise the parents and teachers to use the empowering statement, "I think you can handle it," when the student is becoming overly dependent and asking for too much assistance.

35. Ask the parents to use the Check Yourself technique (e.g., "This is sharing day at school, check yourself to make sure you have what you need when it's your turn to share") to help the student to develop the ability to prepare successfully for upcoming events and personal experiences. (See *Parent Talk* by Moorman.)

16. Organize personal belongings at home and school and treat them with care. (36, 37)

36. Teach the student methods of organizing personal belongings and space in the home, and devise a plan for keeping possessions neat and well organized [e.g., list possessions in categories (toys, clothes, study

materials, sports equip-
ment, reading material);
designate a specific place
for each category (desk,
closet, bookshelf, labeled
boxes, drawers, hooks,
garage); throw away un-
wanted articles; put all remaining articles in the
designated place; clean and
reorganize all possessions
and personal areas on a designed schedule)].

37. Ask the student to complete
the "Personal Organization
Chart" activity in the
*School Counseling and
School Social Work Home-
work Planner* (Knapp) as a
guide to organizing per-
sonal materials at home
and school.

17. Follow rules and procedures
that pertain to home, classroom, and school.
(38, 39, 40, 41)

38. Discuss the school rules
with the student in either
individual or group counseling sessions, and identify
those that are difficult to
comply with and those that
create few problems.

39. Instruct the student to
complete the "Problem-
Solving Worksheet" activity
in the *School Counseling
and School Social Work
Homework Planner* (Knapp)
to analyze a rule violation
at home or at school and to
plan for a more appropriate
response; advise the par-
ents and teachers to use
this worksheet with the
student whenever a rule is
violated.

40. Encourage the parents and the teacher to use practice as a remedy for procedural violations (e.g., running in the hall, talking during quiet-study time, inappropriate table manners, pushing ahead in line); this process involves having the student practice appropriate behavior during his/her free time.

41. Review family rules with the student, and identify areas of compliance and noncompliance. Help the student formulate a plan for improved compliance in challenging areas and chart his/her progress.

18. Parents develop household rules that are responsible and positive in expectation. (42)

42. Advise the parents to establish household rules with the student by brainstorming necessary rules and framing them in positive, rather than negative language (e.g., hang coats in the closet; arrive on time for dinner; be in by 8:30; observe weekend curfew).

19. Mentor other students who are coping with responsibility deficits. (43, 44)

43. Arrange with the teacher to have the student assist classmates or younger students who are resisting the development of responsible behavior patterns.

44. Invite the student to share personal strategies and successes with students of a newly formed responsible behavior training group.

20. Identify the rewards and challenges of developing

45. Explore with the student, in either an individual or a

responsible behavior.
(45)

21. Parents, teachers, and counselor affirm the student for progress in assuming responsibility and acquiring independence. (46, 47)

group session, the personal joys and challenges of developing responsible behavior.

46. Assign the student to affirm himself/herself for progress made in developing personal responsibility at home, school, and in the community and to share successes with his/her parents, teachers, and counselor.

47. Discuss with the teachers and the parents the importance of giving frequent affirmations to the student for progress noted in a private, low-key manner.

__. _____
    _____

__. _____
    _____

__. _____
    _____

__. _____
    _____

__. _____
    _____

__. _____
    _____

DIAGNOSTIC SUGGESTIONS

Axis I:	300.4	Dysthymic Disorder
	314.01	Attention-Deficit/Hyperactivity Disorder
	313.81	Oppositional Defiant Disorder
	301.6	Dependent Personality Disorder
	300.02	Generalized Anxiety Disorder
	309.21	Separation Anxiety Disorder
	____	_____
	____	_____
Axis II:	799.9	Diagnosis Deferred
	V71.09	No Diagnosis on Axis II
	____	_____
	____	_____

SCHOOL REFUSAL/PHOBIA

BEHAVIORAL DEFINITIONS

1. Persistent and pervasive reluctance to attend school.
2. Numerous somatic complaints used to justify school nonattendance.
3. Emotional outbursts involving crying, whining, excessive clinging, and refusal to separate from parents.
4. Negative comments and stories involving the academic program, teachers, and classmates, designed to focus blame on the school.
5. Underlying fear that a potential disaster may occur upon leaving home and family.
6. High anxiety, low self-esteem, and absence of age-appropriate responsible behavior.
7. Fear of failure in school and related activities.
8. Intensified school refusal following illnesses, weekends, or vacations from school.
9. Immature social skills with peers and adults.
10. Verbalizes overly dependent thoughts, feelings, and actions related to a highly symbiotic relationship with one or both parents.
11. A tendency to generalize school refusal and fears to other areas of independent functioning.

—. _____
   _____

—. _____
   _____

—. _____
   _____

LONG-TERM GOALS

1. Attend school on a regular basis.
2. Significantly reduce level of anxiety and emotional reactions related to school attendance and other independent functioning.
3. Establish positive perceptions about school, classmates, and teachers.
4. Eliminate the underlying fear of leaving home and parents.
5. Recognize personal strengths and abilities related to school performance.
6. Acquire age-appropriate social skills and confidence.
7. Parents implement strategies to develop the student's responsible and independent behavior, including regular school attendance.

—. _____

_____

—. _____

_____

—. _____

_____

SHORT-TERM OBJECTIVES	THERAPEUTIC INTERVENTIONS
1. Parents, student, and teachers describe how the student's fears and/or resistance interfere with school attendance and other daily functioning. (1, 2)	1. Meet with the parents, teacher, and the student (if appropriate) to access the school refusal problem in terms of home and school behaviors.
	2. Gather background information about the student from his/her parents, including pertinent medical, vision, hearing, and developmental history.
2. Identify the intensity of and triggers for anxiety related to school attendance. (3, 4, 5)	3. Explore how the student's anxiety and avoidance reaction interferes with his/her daily functioning, particularly school attendance.

4. Assess the student's current level of triggers for anxiety by administering an objective inventory (e.g., The Revised Children's Manifest Anxiety Scale by Reynolds and Richmond, available from Western Psychological Services).

5. Use a therapeutic game (e.g., The Talking, Feeling, Doing Game, available from Creative Therapeutics, or The Ungame, available from the Ungame Company) to expand the student's awareness of his/her own feelings and the triggers for these feelings.

3. Parents agree to ensure that the student attends school on a daily basis. (6, 7, 8)

6. Advise the parents of the critical importance of the student's daily participation in school to eradicate the school refusal syndrome, and contract with them to ensure daily school attendance by the student.

7. Advise the parents to have the nonsymbiotic parent transport the student to school to reduce intensified anxiety and long emotional good-byes.

8. Support and prepare the parents to face resistance from the student when they insist on school attendance; suggest methods of coping with the resistance (e.g., speak calmly but firmly, keep repeating, "I'm sorry you feel that way, but you

4. Teachers, administrators, and/or counselor assist the student and his/her parents with the initial transition to the school day. (9, 10)

must go to school"; say, "I'll be so happy to see you after school"; don't argue with any of the complaints the student is making).

9. Work with the parents, the school staff, and the student (if appropriate) to devise a plan for greeting the student upon arrival at school, allowing the parent to depart, and then transitioning the student to the classroom.

10. Assist the student in developing a self-monitoring chart, which is kept on his/her classroom desk or in a personal planner, to track the length of time taken for the morning good-bye, time spent in the classroom during the day, and the number of days attended per week (or assign the use of the "Attending School Self-Report" activity from the *School Counseling and School Social Work Homework Planner* by Knapp).

5. Prioritize and reduce the number of generalized worries. (11)

11. Brainstorm with the student an extensive list of personal worries, and ask him/her to prioritize them from the most to the least troubling, eliminating duplications and consolidating overlapping items.

6. Establish a morning routine designed to help organize and prepare for the school day. (12)

12. Assign the student to complete the "Do I Have What I Need?" activity from the *School Counseling and*

School Social Work Homework Planner (Knapp) to aid in planning for the school day and to reduce anxiety caused by feelings of being unprepared.

7. Report a visualization of self as successfully participating in the school day. (13, 14)

13. Ask the student to visualize what a perfect day in school would look, feel, smell, and sound like, and to record his/her ideas in a personal journal. Compare the perfect day description with the student's actual experiences and brainstorm ways to improve each school day.

14. Assign the student to complete the "School Days in a Perfect World" activity from the *School Counseling and School Social Work Homework Planner* (Knapp) to encourage him/her to see himself/herself as successfully participating in the school curriculum.

8. Reframe feelings of guilt, anxiety, fear, or jealousy concerning self, parents, family, school, or friends, which may be contributing to the school refusal. (15, 16, 17)

15. Suggest alternative methods for the student to interpret and cope with each school situation that creates stress (e.g., listing several positive options for dealing with the situation, recording the situation in a personal journal, deciding to delay any corrective action until after a discussion with a trusted adult).

16. Use rational emotive techniques (or assign the "Reframing Your Worries" activity from the *School*

Counseling and School Social Work Homework Planner by Knapp) to help the student to identify thoughts and feelings that have contributed to school avoidance and to reevaluate these assumptions in a more realistic and positive manner. (See *A New Guide to Rational Living* by Ellis.)

17. Conduct a family session to identify anxieties or phobias that may be unintentionally reinforced by the parents' words or actions; counsel the parents to help the student to reframe perceptions that trigger feelings of fear and resistance by discussing events rationally and logically with him/her.

9. Focus on one anxiety- or fear-producing situation and develop problem-solving and decision-making skills for that situation. (18, 19, 20)

18. Engage the student in mutually telling a story, entitled "My Day at School"; focus on the transition from home to school, and guide the story toward a successful outcome.

19. Direct the student to identify one source of anxiety to work on during the week; then brainstorm possible remedies to the troubling situation, choose an option that is most likely to reduce his/her level of concern, and explore the outcome of implementation during the next counseling session.

20. Use children's literature (e.g., *Don't Pop Your Cork*

on Mondays! by Moser and Pilkey or *Don't Feed the Monster on Tuesdays!* by Moser and Thatch) to explore common feelings that children have about school and their methods of successfully dealing with everyday stress.

10. List the present and future benefits of school attendance and the negatives of nonattendance. (21)

21. Brainstorm with the student the current and future benefits of attending school and the negative results of limited attendance or nonattendance; have him/her list these ideas in a personal journal.

11. Verbalize feelings of attachment and belonging to the school entity and the classroom unit. (22, 23, 24)

22. Refer the student to or conduct a social skills therapeutic group that focuses on developing feelings of belonging and participating appropriately in the school milieu.

23. Encourage the student's teacher(s) to involve him/her in cooperative learning groups and to promote participation in classroom social activities.

24. Brainstorm options and then support the student in joining an extracurricular group sponsored by the school, church, or community.

12. Increase daily participation in class, and assume responsibility for daily academic assignments. (25, 26)

25. Help the student to create a schedule for completing all classroom assignments and homework; have him/her record the plan and progress in a journal.

26. Reinforce the student's academic, family, and social successes by drawing or photographing a completed project that triggers personal pride (or assign the *"Accomplishments I Am Proud Of"* activity from the *School Counseling and School Social Work Homework Planner* by Knapp).

13. Demonstrate success in test-taking performance. (27, 28, 29)

27. Engage the student in identifying and recording several self-talk statements, which can be used during test-taking to ward off worry (e.g., "I am prepared for this test"; "I can handle this subject"; "I practiced for this at home"; or "I've done well on tests like this before").

28. Teach the student studying methods used to prepare for a test (e.g., set a study schedule; outline the material; read, write, and verbalize; study smaller sections; create flash cards for key ideas; develop pneumonic devices); assess effectiveness and revise the preparation routine to prepare for the next test.

29. Teach the student how to relax different areas of the body by first tightening and then relaxing muscles, paying particular attention to areas where stress is typically manifested (e.g., jaw, neck, shoulders, stomach); encourage him/her to use this relaxation technique during tests.

14. Identify how stress is manifested in physical symptoms. (30, 31, 32)

30. Ask the student to note in a journal several incidents of elevated stress and related physical symptoms (e.g., rapid heartbeat, headache, stomach distress, sweaty palms).

31. Help the student to heighten his/her awareness of anxious moments by wearing a biodot (biofeedback stress patch available from the Biodot Company) and to record times of stress and accompanying physical reactions in a journal.

32. Assist the student in identifying areas on an image of the human body where his/her personal stress is most commonly reflected (or assign the "Physical Receptors of Stress" activity from the *School Counseling and School Social Work Homework Planner* by Knapp).

15. Implement relaxation techniques during periods of stress. (29, 33)

29. Teach the student how to relax different areas of the body by first tightening and then relaxing muscles, paying particular attention to areas where stress is typically manifested (e.g., jaw, neck, shoulders, stomach); encourage him/her to use this relaxation technique during tests.

33. Ask the student to hold a stress ball and practice squeezing and relaxing his/her arm and fist while

breathing in and out at an even pace; encourage deep breathing during tests to reduce anxiety.

16. Discuss somatic complaints with a physician to determine physical or emotional causes. (34)

34. Request that the parents and the student consult with the student's physician to review physical and behavioral symptoms related to school refusal and seek information and guidance regarding physical and emotional causes.

17. Increase social interaction with classmates and friends. (22, 24, 35, 36)

22. Refer the student to or conduct a social skills therapeutic group that focuses on developing feelings of belonging and participating appropriately in the school milieu.

24. Brainstorm options and then support the student in joining an extracurricular group sponsored by the school, church, or community.

35. Teach the student the importance of good eye contact, smiling, and appropriate physical touching in making friends, gaining acceptance, and building relationships; ask him/her to practice eye contact, smiles, and high-fives or handshakes throughout the week with his/her family and friends and during subsequent counseling sessions.

36. Plan with the student for an after-school or weekend activity with a friend; record the event in a

18. Recognize and acknowledge encouraging comments from others. (37, 38)

19. Parents verbalize and implement strategies designed to promote independence and responsible behavior. (39, 40, 41, 42)

journal with a photo, paragraph, or drawing.

37. Brainstorm positive statements of encouragement that could be applied by the student to himself/herself; ask him/her to record them in a journal, in addition to actual encouraging statements received from others at school during the course of the week.

38. Role-play social encounters in which the student receives compliments or encouragement from others; emphasize the need to not discount such affirmation but to accept it, thank the giver, and integrate the message into his/her self-concept.

39. Ask the parents to use the Red Light, Green Light technique (see *Parent Talk* by Moorman) to turn an irresponsible behavior into a responsible behavior: (1) describe the inappropriate behavior to the child (red light), such as screaming, kicking, clinging, and whining; (2) describe the expected behavior (green light), such as smiling, waving good-bye, opening the door, and going into school.

40. Ask the teachers to substitute the phrase "Next time" (see *Teacher Talk* by Moorman and Moorman) for

"don't" in order to shape positive future efforts from the student (e.g., "Next time you go to school, smile at your counselor and teacher and wave good-bye to Dad," versus, "Don't cry when you go to school, it only makes things worse").

41. Request that the parents and teachers use the Act As If technique (see *Teacher Talk* by Moorman and Moorman) to encourage the student to make an effort despite his/her fear of failure (e.g., "act as if you felt great about going to school"; "pretend you really like your teacher and classmates"; "play like you've done this before"; or "fake it till you make it").

42. Refer the parents to a parenting class that focuses on helping children to develop responsible behavior (e.g., *Systematic Training for Effective Parenting* by Dinkmeyer and McKay, *Becoming a Love and Logic Parent* by Fay, Cline, and Fay, or *The Parent Talk System* by Moorman and Knapp).

20. Parents attend a class or didactic series focusing on positive parenting. (42, 43, 44)

42. Refer the parents to a parenting class that focuses on helping children to develop responsible behavior (e.g., *Systematic Training for Effective Parenting* by Dinkmeyer and McKay, *Becoming a Love and Logic Parent* by Fay, Cline, and

Fay, or *The Parent Talk System* by Moorman and Knapp).

43. Assign the parents to listen to the audiotape *Helicopters, Drill Sergeants and Consultants* (Fay) to identify their own style of parenting and recognize the advantage of allowing their children to resolve their problems without overprotection; discuss this in a subsequent counseling session.

44. Discuss with the parents in a counseling session how overprotection and overparenting can contribute to feelings of inadequacy and dependency. Encourage them to strengthen the student's independent functioning through allowing him/her to practice problem solving, experience consequences, and learn from mistakes.

21. Parents and teachers establish regular communication to assist the student in organizing and monitoring assignments and school responsibilities and in maintaining regular school attendance. (45, 46)

45. Consult with the parents and teacher(s) to devise a communication schedule that provides for weekly, monthly, or as-needed interchange between school and home.

46. Encourage the teachers and parents to exchange written notes on a daily, weekly, or monthly basis using a behavior journal or checklist to monitor the student's progress both at school and at home.

22. Parents, teachers, and counselor increase recognition and encouragement of the student and reinforce his/her active attempts to attend school and build positive self-esteem. (47, 48)

47. Teach the parents and the teacher(s) to use the one sentence intervention (e.g., "I noticed that you get up on time each morning," "I noticed that you enjoy hot lunch") with the student daily along with can-do messages and replacing criticism with encouragement. (See *Parenting with Love and Logic* by Cline and Fay.)

48. Review with the student his/her strategies for maintaining regular school attendance and give recognition for progress made and guidance in remaining areas of concern. Ask the student to record both the successful and in-progress behavioral strategies in a personal journal.

23. Acknowledge personal progress toward the development of healthy self-esteem and independent, responsible behavior. (49, 50)

49. Assign the student, in either an individual or a group session, to complete the "Growing and Changing" activity from the *School Counseling and School Social Work Homework Planner* (Knapp), which is designed to acknowledge current progress and create an awareness that learning, changing, and self-improvement is a lifelong process.

50. Assign the student, in either an individual or a group session, to complete the "My Predictions for the Future" activity from the

School Counseling and School Social Work Homework Planner (Knapp) to help him/her to establish positive goals for the future.

—. _____   —. _____
    _____   _____
—. _____   —. _____
    _____   _____
—. _____   —. _____
    _____   _____

DIAGNOSTIC SUGGESTIONS

Axis I: 309.21   Separation Anxiety Disorder
               300.02   Generalized Anxiety Disorder
               296.xx   Major Depressive Disorder
               300.4   Somatization Disorder
               300.81   Undifferentiated Somatoform Disorder
               309.81   Posttraumatic Stress Disorder

               _____   _____

Axis II: 799.9   Diagnosis Deferred
               V71.09   No Diagnosis on Axis II

               _____   _____
               _____   _____

SELF-ESTEEM BUILDING

BEHAVIORAL DEFINITIONS

1. Verbalization of many personal weaknesses and few strengths.
2. An expressed desire to become someone else or change numerous personal qualities.
3. Feels disliked by peers.
4. Pervasive feelings of failure.
5. Feeling pressured or pushed by the expectations of the parents, peers and/or teachers and fearful of disappointing them.
6. Reluctant to try new things.
7. Lack of pride in schoolwork and reluctance to participate in class.
8. Feeling unhappy.
9. Dependent on others for making decisions.
10. Feels neglected or ignored by others.
11. Feels unable to meet own performance expectations.
12. Lack of personal care behaviors.
13. Engages in self-defeating behavior (e.g., sexual acting out, substance abuse, antisocial practices, negative attention seeking) in order to gain recognition or acceptance.

__. _____
   _____
__. _____
   _____
__. _____
   _____

LONG-TERM GOALS

1. Believe in self as being lovable and capable.
2. Accept love and recognition from significant others.
3. Identify and internalize areas of personal strength, and develop a positive self-image.
4. Establish appropriate interpersonal skills, assertiveness, confidence in self, and reasonable risk taking.
5. Demonstrate persistence and confidence in various areas of functioning.
6. Solve problems alone and in a cooperative effort with appropriate others.

—. _____
   _____
   _____
—. _____
   _____
   _____
—. _____
   _____

SHORT-TERM GOALS

1. Cooperate with an assessment of self-esteem. (1, 2, 3, 4, 5)

THERAPEUTIC INTERVENTIONS

1. Administer a self-concept inventory to the student (e.g., the Piers-Harris Self-Concept Scale or the Coopersmith Self-Esteem Inventory) to determine specific areas of low self-esteem.

2. Give the student the Goals of Misbehavior Inventory (Manly) or another index to identify his/her current wrong assumptions, which motivate inappropriate behavior according to Dreikurs' theory of misbehavior. (See *Children: The Challenge* by Dreikurs and Stoltz.)

3. Have the student complete a personal profile

informational sheet that details pertinent personal data (or assign the "My Personal Profile" activity from the *School Counseling and School Social Work Homework Planner* by Knapp).

4. Ask the student to make a list of significant others in his/her life, including family members, friends, teachers, or mentors and role models, and to rate the degree of support given, closeness felt, or influence each person has.

5. Discuss questions and answers from the self-esteem inventory and the goals of misbehavior to begin the process of reframing and building a more positive self-image. Have the student explain responses in more detail to establish and clarify possible causes of low self-esteem.

2. Identify significant others who communicate love and care. (3, 4, 7, 9)

3. Have the student complete a personal profile informational sheet that details pertinent personal data (or assign the "My Personal Profile" activity from the *School Counseling and School Social Work Homework Planner* by Knapp).

4. Ask the student to make a list of significant others in his/her life, including family members, friends, teachers, or mentors and role models, and to rate the degree of

support given, closeness felt, or influence that person has.

7. Have the student select photographs or draw pictures to create a journal entry entitled "Who I Am." This can include pictures of the student with his/her family, engaged in activities, with friends, at school, and so forth.

9. Assist the student in writing a definition of unconditional love (e.g., complete and constant love given regardless of personal attributes, attitude, behavior, or performance) in a self-esteem journal and list significant others who can give unconditional love.

3. Acknowledge loveable/likeable personal qualities to self. (5, 6, 7, 8)

5. Discuss questions and answers from the self-esteem inventory and the goals of misbehavior to begin the process of reframing and building a more positive self-image. Have the student explain responses in more detail to establish and clarify possible causes of low self-esteem.

6. Create a self-esteem journal with the student that will contain his/her therapeutic worksheets and serve as a record of progress.

7. Have the student select photographs or draw pictures to create a journal entry entitled "Who I Am." This can include pictures of the student with his/her family, en-

gaged in activities, with friends, at school, and so forth.

8. Assist the student in developing a written list of his/her positive personal attributes; save the list in his/her self-esteem journal, and post the list prominently at home.

4. Define and list sources of unconditional love. (9)

9. Assist the student in writing a definition of unconditional love (e.g., complete and constant love given regardless of personal attributes, attitude, behavior, or performance) in a self-esteem journal and listing significant others who can give unconditional love.

5. Increase eye contact, smiles, and appropriate touch. (10, 11)

10. Use puppets or role-play having the student practice eye contact and smiles, first with the puppets, and then transfer this skill to the counselor.

11. Teach the student the importance of good eye contact, smiling, and appropriate physical touching in making friends, gaining acceptance, and building relationships; ask him/her to practice eye contact and smiles throughout the week with family and friends and during subsequent counseling sessions.

6. Identify situations or relationships that have contributed to low self-esteem. (3, 5, 12)

3. Have the student complete a personal profile informational sheet that details pertinent personal data (or assign the "My Personal Profile" activity from the

School Counseling and School Social Work Homework Planner by Knapp).

5. Discuss questions and answers from the self-esteem inventory and the goals of misbehavior to begin the process of reframing and building a more positive self-image. Have the student explain responses in more detail to establish and clarify possible causes of low self-esteem.

12. Explore with the student situations or relationships that have contributed to low self-esteem (e.g., failed efforts, critical parents, outstandingly successful older sibling, lack of social skills, peer rejection or teasing).

7. Identify strategies to overcome factors that have contributed to low self-esteem. (13)

13. Assist the student in identifying constructive strategies to overcome factors that have contributed to low self-esteem (e.g., family therapy with a critical parent or successful sibling, positive self-talk, social skills training, group therapy focused on self-esteem building).

8. Identify and verbalize personal feelings. (14, 15, 16, 17)

14. Teach the student the process of labeling personal emotions by reviewing an extensive list of adjectives that describe a variety of feelings. Assign the student to identify words that describe personal feelings and to record them in a daily journal.

15. Use a chart of faces depicting various emotions to assist the student in labeling and describing his/her own feelings.

16. Use a therapeutic game (e.g., the Talking, Feeling, Doing Game, available from Creative Therapeutics; Let's See about Me, available from Childswork/Childsplay, LLC; or The Ungame, available from The Ungame Company) to promote the student becoming more aware of himself/herself and his/her feelings.

17. Refer the student to group sessions that focus on building healthy self-esteem and expressing feelings.

9. Attend group sessions that are focused on increasing self-esteem and expressing feelings. (17)

17. Refer the student to group sessions that focus on building healthy self-esteem and expressing feelings.

10. Reframe negative self-talk into positive, realistic messages. (18, 19, 20)

18. Use a journal to reinforce the reframing process by having the student describe an event in his/her life and then rewrite the scenario to reflect a healthier interpretation.

19. Brainstorm positive statements of encouragement that could be applied by the student to himself/herself. Ask him/her to record these affirmations in a counseling journal, in addition to actual encouraging statements received from others during the course of the week.

20. Assist the student in identifying his/her propensity for negative self-talk by reviewing situations in which he/she felt anxious, inferior, or rejected; reframe his/her thinking into more positive, realistic self-talk.

11. Recognize and acknowledge encouraging comments from others. (19, 21)

19. Brainstorm positive statements of encouragement that could be applied by the student to himself/herself. Ask him/her to record these affirmations in a counseling journal, in addition to actual encouraging statements received from others during the course of the week.

21. Role-play social encounters in which the student receives compliments or encouragement from others; emphasize the need to accept rather than discount such praise, thank the giver, and integrate the message into his/her self-concept.

12. Express feelings directly and assertively. (17, 22, 23)

17. Refer the student to group sessions that focus on building healthy self-esteem and expressing feelings.

22. Help the student to prepare for a discussion with his/her parents and/or a teacher, describing a feeling or concern. Role-play how to deliver this message.

23. Teach the student about "I" messages and the Bug-Wish Technique ("It bugs me when you . . . I wish you would. . . ."). Role-play

these methods of responding to harassment or frustrating behavior from others.

13. Increase social interaction with classmates and friends. (10, 17, 24, 25, 26)

10. Use puppets or role-play having the student practice eye contact and smiles, first with the puppets, and then transfer this skill to the counselor.

17. Refer the student to group sessions that focus on building healthy self-esteem and expressing feelings.

24. Plan for an after-school or weekend activity with a friend. Record the event in a journal with a photo, paragraph, or drawing.

25. Plan with the student for a social interaction with a classmate. Record the plan and outcome in a journal.

26. Encourage the student to join a social group or club. Brainstorm options and help him/her to make a selection.

14. Identify strengths in areas of multiple intelligences. (9, 27, 28)

9. Assist the student in developing a written list of his/her positive personal attributes; save the list in his/her self-esteem journal, and post the list prominently at home.

27. Perform a skill assessment with the student listing skills that are currently mastered, skills that are being learned, and skills that will be needed in the

future in each area of multiple intelligences (see *Intelligence Reframed: Multiple Intelligences for the 21st Century* by Gardner). Discuss the concept that skill acquisition is a lifelong process that requires effort and persistence.

28. Ask the student to draw a picture of a skill he/she now has, one that is being learned, and one that will be necessary in the future; discuss the importance of these skills during the counseling session (or assign the "Skill Assessment" activity from *The School Counseling and School Social Work Homework Planner* by Knapp).

15. Increase daily participation in class, and assume responsibility for daily academic assignments. (29, 30, 31)

29. Identify methods of increasing classroom participation, and have the student create a graph in the self-esteem journal to chart daily progress.

30. Help the student to create a plan for completing all classroom assignments and homework. Have him/her record the plan and progress in a journal.

31. Reinforce the student's academic, family, and social successes by drawing or photographing a completed project that triggers personal pride. Begin a section

16. Perform daily self-care and several chores at home. (32)

17. Participate in exploring the acquisition of a new skill, hobby, or interest. (33)

18. Demonstrate persistence and systematic problem solving in resolving academic, social, and family challenges. (34)

19. Parents and teachers increase recognition and encouragement of the student and reinforce his/her active attempts to build positive self-esteem. (35, 36, 37)

in a journal entitled *Accomplishments I Am Proud Of.*

32. Help the student to assume responsibility for daily personal care and for completing chores at home by identifying tasks to be done and charting the daily rate of completion.

33. Explore with the student his/her acquisition of a new hobby or outside activity that requires the development of a skill. Record progress and feelings in a journal with a descriptive paragraph, drawing, or photo.

34. Assist the student in developing personal problem-solving skills by recording problems in his/her personal journal and completing the steps necessary for resolution (e.g., identify the problem, brainstorm solutions, list the pros and cons of each solution, select a solution, assess the outcome) (or assign the "Personal Problem-Solving Worksheet" activity from the *School Counseling and School Social Work Homework Planner* by Knapp).

35. Encourage the parents and the teacher(s) to recognize and affirm the student daily by noticing small personal attributes and verbalizing an awareness of daily efforts and activities.

36. Encourage the teacher(s) and the parents to teach responsibility and enhance the student's self-esteem using chores, recognition for task completion, and consequences with empathy to address irresponsible behavior.

37. Refer the parents to a class on positive parenting, and process the techniques learned as they apply to the student's self-esteem.

20. Parents attend a class or didactic series focusing on positive parenting. (37)

37. Refer the parents to a class on positive parenting, and process the techniques learned as they apply to the student's self-esteem.

21. Acknowledge personal progress toward the development of healthy self-esteem. (38, 39)

38. Discuss evidence that the student is becoming stronger and more capable by recording past and expected future personal behavior, thoughts, and accomplishments as a baby, kindergartner, elementary student, secondary student, and adult in a self-esteem journal. Guide him/her to define these personal stages in positive terms (or assign the "Growing and Changing" activity from the *School Counseling and School Social Work Homework Planner* by Knapp).

39. Instruct the student to summarize and acknowledge his/her progress toward developing a healthier self-esteem in a self-esteem journal.

—. _____   —. _____
      _____   _____
—. _____   —. _____
      _____   _____
—. _____   —. _____
      _____   _____

DIAGNOSTIC SUGGESTIONS:

Axis I: 300.4   Dysthymic Disorder
             314.01   Attention-Deficit/Hyperactivity Disorder
             300.23   Social Phobia
             296.xx   Major Depressive Disorder
             307.1   Anorexia Nervosa
             309.21   Separation Anxiety Disorder
             303.02   Generalized Anxiety Disorder

             _____   _____

             _____   _____

Axis II: 317   Mild Mental Retardation
             V62.89   Borderline Intellectual Functioning
             799.9   Diagnosis Deferred
             V71.09   No Diagnosis on Axis II

             _____   _____

             _____   _____

SEXUAL RESPONSIBILITY

BEHAVIORAL DEFINITIONS

1. Sexually active without the use of protection, resulting in the risk of pregnancies and contraction of sexually transmitted diseases (STDs).
2. Seductive dress, actions, and language.
3. Use of alcohol and drugs to promote risk-taking behavior and reduce natural inhibitions.
4. Perpetrator of unwanted sexual advances, date rape, sexual harassment, and/or sexual abuse.
5. Victim of unwanted sexual advances, date rape, sexual harassment, and/or sexual abuse.
6. Lack of knowledge of the facts of sexual development, pregnancy, and STDs.
7. Absence of a personal code of behavior that reflects integration of sexual behavior with moral values and personal responsibility.
8. Excessive interest in sex and sexuality at a prepuberty level of maturity.
9. Violation of curfew, household rules, and substance abuse laws.
10. Reluctance to discuss sexual ethics and values with trusted adults.

__. _____

_____

__. _____

_____

__. _____

_____

LONG-TERM GOALS

1. Learn the facts about sexual development and adolescent sexuality.
2. Parents share their sexual ethics and values and set clear standards for adolescent sexual behavior.
3. Maintain sexual abstinence as an expression of self-control guided by moral or religious values.
4. Choose abstinence because it is the safest, most effective method of dealing with adolescent sexuality and of preventing pregnancy and STDs.
5. If sexually active, choose safe and medically recommended methods of birth control and protection from STDs.
6. Demonstrate personal sexual responsibility and respect for own and others' sexual ethics and values.
7. Develop effective refusal skills to use when confronted with unwanted sexual advances.

—. _____

_____

—. _____

_____

—. _____

_____

SHORT-TERM OBJECTIVES

1. Enroll in a class focusing on adolescent sexuality offered by the school, a community agency, or a place of worship. (1, 2, 3)

THERAPEUTIC INTERVENTIONS

1. Refer the student to a class on adolescent sexuality [e.g., *Sexual Integrity for Teens* by Hansen (see also www.nnfr.org/adolsex)] to clarify sexual values, gather relevant information on human development, and view sexuality as a natural and healthy part of living.

2. Assist the student in exploring the human sexuality education opportunities available within his/her faith-based organization.

3. Involve the student in group counseling sessions that focus on psychosexual topics of concern to adolescents (e.g., teen dating, physical maturation, sexuality, sexual integrity, and responsible social interaction).

2. Discuss personal concerns about sexuality with a trusted adult. (4, 5)

4. Encourage the student to involve his/her parents and other trusted and knowledgeable adults in conversations about sexual responsibility; role-play typical conversations the student may have with a trusted adult (e.g., parent, relative, doctor, chaplain, teacher, or counselor), and assign the initiation of at least one student-adult discussion during the following week.

5. Brainstorm with the student appropriate questions to ask a parent, religious advisor, doctor, or teacher during a discussion of sexuality (e.g., What is love? When should kids start dating? When is it okay to have sex? What are your opinions about contraception and abstinence?).

3. Recognize sexual myths, and learn facts about sex and sexuality. (6, 7)

6. Ask the student to list some commonly repeated information about sex and sexuality and to identify whether the statement is fact or myth [e.g., all teens are having sex these days (myth), pregnancy cannot occur from the first sexual

experience (myth), HIV can affect both heterosexuals and homosexuals (fact)].

7. View with the student the video *Sex Myths and Facts (Revised)* (Alfred Higgins Productions), and follow up with a discussion of typical myths that create confusion and sexual problems for adolescents.

4. Parents express a willingness to discuss sexual ethics and values with their children on an ongoing basis while fostering an atmosphere of love and trust. (8, 9, 10)

8. Meet with the parents and teach them the importance of maintaining open lines of communication with their children about sexual responsibility; help the parents predict and prepare for typical questions that might arise during a discussion (e.g., What is happening to my body? How can I prevent pregnancy? What causes STDs and AIDS? What does sexual responsibility really mean?).

9. Teach the parents effective communication techniques by role-playing conversations using "I" statements, active listening, not interrupting, avoiding absolutes like *always* and *never,* not trying to solve all issues in one conversation, and leaving the door open for future discussions.

10. Inform the parents of the importance of using honesty, sincerity, and empathy with their teens while discussing sexuality; assign

them to initiate a conversation with their child and to record the positive results and areas to modify for the next discussion.

5. Parents verbalize clear expectations for adolescents in areas of curfew deadline, dress code, dating guidelines, substance abuse, and sexual activity. (11, 12)

11. Instruct the parents to set firm guidelines for their child (e.g., dress code, dating, substance abuse, sexual activity) as a primary method of establishing sexual responsibility and healthy self-esteem. Discuss reasonable limits, and indicate to the parents that parental monitoring decreases sexual activity in younger adolescents and decreases the odds that older teens will be high-risk takers. (See *Adolescent Sexuality and Childbearing* by Mercer.)

12. Support the parents' resolve to remain strong when resistance from the student occurs by informing them that firm limits and parental supervision are a major deterrent to teen pregnancies, STDs, and other dysfunctional adolescent behavior.

6. Write a personal sexuality responsibility code and a behavior plan for its implementation. (13, 14)

13. Show the video *Everyone Is Not Doing It: Parts I, II, and III* (M.L. Video Productions), and ask the student to brainstorm reasonable limits in the areas of substance abuse, dress code, curfew, and abstaining from sexual activity that can lead to pregnancy or STDs.

14. Instruct the student to complete the "My Personal Sexual Responsibility Code" activity from the *School Counseling and School Social Work Homework Planner* (Knapp) to express his/her positive intentions in the areas of adolescent sexuality. Ask the student to review the activity with his/her sex education teacher or counselor and to indicate his/her commitment by signing the code.

7. Communicate personal views about sexual responsibility and appropriate sexual behaviors with dating partner and peers. (15, 16)

15. Assign the student to discuss his/her ideas about sexual responsibility with his/her peers in a small-group setting in class or during a counseling group.

16. Instruct the student to communicate his/her sexual ethics and moral/religious standards with his/her dating partner, parents, and friends, and to record the reactions in a personal journal or share them in a counseling session.

8. Verbalize abstinence as a viable option for avoiding the dangers of adolescent sex. (17, 18, 19)

17. List with the student the many reasons for choosing abstinence as the preferred method of avoiding the pitfalls of adolescent sexual intercourse (e.g., preventing pregnancy, avoiding STDs, maintaining sexual responsibility, enhancing a healthy self-esteem, avoiding the emotional trauma of adolescent sex, maintaining

integrity with a personal moral/religious code).

18. Teach the student the primary indicators of not being ready for a sexual relationship (e.g., not ready for the responsibilities of parenthood, not sure about the relationship with his/her partner, afraid to ask a doctor for birth control, desire to avoid STDs, not emotionally ready to have sex, desire to wait until marriage, feelings of guilt), and ask him/her to add some of his/her own ideas.

19. Assign the student to rehearse or role-play techniques for maintaining his/her commitment to abstinence (e.g., avoid the use of alcohol and drugs; say, "No, I've made a commitment to wait"; say, "I care for you, but I won't change my mind"; say, "If you cared for me you wouldn't keep pressuring me to have sexual intercourse") to strengthen the resolve and prepare for situations when the decision for abstinence is tested.

9. Identify enjoyable sex-free alternatives that allow for the expression of affection and promote healthy adolescent relationships. (20, 21)

20. Brainstorm with the student loving ways to relate to his/her dates or partners without breaking his/her commitment to abstinence (e.g., hugging, talking, sending flowers, cooking together, taking walks, sending notes or cards, showing

mutual respect). (See *Sexual Integrity for Teens* by Hansen.)

21. Discuss with the student the value of being friends with members of the opposite sex without sexual involvement in order to expand his/her friendship circle, to clarify what personality characteristics are and are not appealing, and to reduce the chances of becoming sexually active resulting from overinvolvement with one person.

10. List the life-altering and life-threatening dangers of sexual risk taking. (22, 23)

22. Play the video *Teens At Risk: Breaking the Immortality Myth* (Alfred Higgins Productions), and follow up with a group or class discussion to clarify the potential consequences of sexual risk taking (e.g., pregnancy, STDs, emotional trauma, and compromised future goals) and its effects on current future lifestyle and well-being.

23. Instruct the student to list his/her goals for the future in the areas of marriage, family, health, education, career, and leisure-time activities, and then identify how adolescent sexual behavior can impact the achievement of these goals.

11. Develop a sexual action plan to prevent the negative consequences of engaging in

24. Assign the student to identify during a class or group discussion several options

unprotected sexual relations. (24, 25)

for guarding against the unwanted results of unprotected sexual intercourse (e.g., abstinence, condoms, birth control pills, morning-after pill). List the benefits and drawbacks of each birth control method (e.g., prevent pregnancy at a less than 100 percent rate, offer only partial protection against STDs, offer no protection against the guilt and anxiety of engaging in adolescent sex).

25. If the student is sexually active, discuss community medical facilities where information about birth control and protection from STDs can be acquired (e.g., Planned Parenthood, health department, physicians, hospital-sponsored clinics).

12. Verbalize the awareness that abstinence continues to remain an option, even after being sexually active. (26, 27)

26. Teach the student that abstinence is a choice that can be made at any time, even after he/she has been sexually active.

27. Inform the student that many adolescents do not have sex again for months or years after their first sexual experience. (See *Adolescent Sexuality and Childbearing* by Mercer.)

13. Verbalize an understanding that sex and sexuality are two separate issues, and define each in terms of adolescent maturation. (28, 29, 30)

28. Instruct the student to list the multiple aspects of sexuality and the full range of actions, feelings, and biological development that influence sexual attitudes and

behaviors throughout our lifetime (e.g., dating, kissing, physical attraction to another person, holding hands, intimate touching, physical maturation of the sex organs) and to differentiate these from sexual intercourse (i.e., the physical act of sex that can produce pregnancy).

29. View the video *Dear Diary* (Copperfield Films) to teach information about puberty, sex, and sexuality, and follow up with a class discussion about adolescent sexuality.

30. Assign the student to differentiate between the need to love and be loved and the desire for sex by listing examples and the long-term effects of each.

14. List the signs of potential violence in a dating partner. (31, 32)

31. Introduce information about relationship abuse by presenting an abuse prevention program (e.g., Peer Program, developed by Center for the Elimination of Violence in the Family).

32. Brainstorm with the student the indicators for potential violence in a dating partner or friend (e.g., victim of early childhood abuse, frequent loss of temper, substance abuse, controlling behavior). (See *Sexual Integrity for Teens* by Hansen.)

15. Initiate counseling to terminate an abusive relationship and to understand the underlying psychology of abuse. (33, 34, 35)

16. Confront sexual harassment by naming it and asking the offender to terminate the behavior. (36, 37)

33. Refer the student to individual or group counseling to explore the underlying psychology of abuse and to gain an understanding of the causes for violence, violent tendencies, and prevention of victimization.

34. Show the student the video *Matter of Choice: A Program Confronting Teenage Sexual Abuse* (United Learning) to help gain a deeper understanding of adolescent abuse and how it occurs.

35. Encourage the student to adapt a personal zero-tolerance policy for dating violence by writing his/her personal pledge, signing it, and reading it to the class or group.

36. Define sexual harassment for the student: "Unwanted verbal or physical behavior of a sexual nature that interferes with a person's school or work performance or that creates an environment that is hostile or intimidating" (from *Sexual Integrity for Teens* by Hansen). Ask him/her to identify several examples (e.g., physical intimidation, sexual jokes or remarks, patting or unwelcome touching, pressure to engage in sexual activity).

37. Encourage the student to address sexual harassment

by naming the offending behavior and emphatically asking the offending party to stop. Role-play this refusal skill by choosing a sexually objectionable behavior and demonstrating how to confront the harassment (e.g., "That's sexual harassment, it's illegal and I want you to stop!").

17. Report sexual abuse or harassment from an adult or peer to a teacher, counselor, administrator, or other trusted adult. (38, 39)

38. Review the school policy on sexual harassment and abuse with the student and give him/her information about reporting any incidents of concern (e.g., when to report, how to state the problem, whom to contact, verbally or in writing).

39. Counsel the student to seek help in developing the courage to confront a perpetrator of harassment and to seek assistance in the reporting process if the harassment continues.

18. Verbalize the connection between a healthy self-esteem and defined, positive future goals and the ability to refuse or delay sexual advances or relationships. (40, 41)

40. Instruct the student to complete the "Control of My Sexuality and Healthy Self-Esteem" activity from the *School Counseling and School Social Work Homework Planner* (Knapp) to identify areas where adolescents control sexual destiny and how this correlates with a healthy self-esteem.

41. Brainstorm with the student the areas where he/she can take control of his/her sexuality (e.g., confronting

harassment, refusing to allow sexual abuse, choosing abstinence, using adequate protection).

19. Practice sexual refusal skills with a parent, friend, teacher, or counselor. (42, 43)

42. Ask the student to record in a personal journal actual or anticipated situations that call for sexual refusal skills and develop a role play that addresses the circumstances. Have him/her present the role play to the class or group.

43. Instruct the student to seek information about sexual refusal skills from parents, teachers, peers, and counselors. Assign him/her to record the information and present it in written form or orally to the class or group.

—. _____

—. _____

—. _____

—. _____

—. _____

—. _____

DIAGNOSTIC SUGGESTIONS

Axis I:

300.4	Dysthymic Disorder	
314.01	Attention-Deficit/Hyperactivity Disorder, Predominantly Inattentive Type	
314.9	Attention-Deficit/Hyperactivity Disorder, NOS	
313.81	Oppositional Defiant Disorder	
312.30	Impulse Control Disorder, NOS	
301.6	Dependent Personality Disorder	
300.02	Generalized Anxiety Disorder	
309.21	Separation Anxiety Disorder	

	303.90	Alcohol Dependence
	305.00	Alcohol Abuse
	V71.02	Child Antisocial Behavior
	V61.20	Parent-Child Relational Problem
	_____	_____
	_____	_____
Axis II:	799.9	Diagnosis Deferred
	V71.09	No Diagnosis on Axis II
	_____	_____
	_____	_____

SIBLING RIVALRY

BEHAVIORAL DEFINITIONS

1. Verbal hostilities between siblings are a common occurrence and foster detachment between them.
2. Physical aggression frequently erupts between siblings, requiring adult intervention.
3. Antagonism between siblings present since early childhood.
4. Competition among siblings over limited family resources (e.g., time, attention, love, approval, privileges, material resources).
5. First-born child resents time and attention given to subsequent siblings.
6. Younger siblings resent status awarded to the older siblings.
7. Siblings vie for parents' love and desire to become the favored child.
8. Parents compare siblings and openly or privately express preferences.
9. Younger or less aggressive sibling develops protective defenses against older or more aggressive siblings.
10. Siblings develop a win/lose attitude, which influences their interactions and is often supported by the parents.

__. _____
    _____
__. _____
    _____
    _____
__. _____
    _____

LONG-TERM GOALS

1. Stop hurtful verbal and/or physical interactions between siblings.
2. Learn conflict management techniques and settle disputes with siblings using peacemaking strategies.
3. Siblings coexist peacefully within the family unit and develop a positive relationship with each other.
4. Parents refrain from expressing favoritism or comparing siblings with one another.
5. Parents view each sibling as a unique individual and focus on the strengths and abilities of each child.

—. _____
   _____
   _____

—. _____
   _____
   _____

—. _____
   _____
   _____

SHORT-TERM OBJECTIVES

1. Parents and the involved siblings identify the existing level of family conflict and the underlying causes of the interpersonal conflict. (1, 2)

2. Parents attend a parenting class or read literature on the topic of sibling rivalry, its causes, and cures. (3, 4)

THERAPEUTIC INTERVENTIONS

1. Meet with the parents to obtain the student's and his/her siblings' developmental histories and information about family harmony, sibling interaction, and discipline.

2. Meet with the student to address concerns about sibling problems and how this affects his/her adjustment and performance in other areas of functioning.

3. Refer the parents to a parenting group that teaches strategies of positive discipline and addresses the topic of sibling rivalry (e.g.,

Siblings without Rivalry by
Faber and Mazlish).

4. Assign the parents to read
*How to Talk So Kids Will
Listen and Listen So Kids
Will Talk* (Faber and Ma-
zlish) and *Siblings without
Rivalry* (Faber and Mazlish)
to develop additional positive communication skills
with their children and become aware of strategies to
promote positive sibling relationships.

3. Attend school counseling or
family therapy sessions to
address sibling hostility
and negative sibling interaction. (5, 6)

5. Schedule with the student
individual or group counseling sessions designed to
evaluate and reverse sibling
difficulties, using strategies
of open communication and
conflict management tech-
niques.

6. Refer the parents to a private therapist for family
counseling sessions that address the underlying
scripts, behaviors, thought
processes, and dysfunc-
tional interactions that are
contributing to the sibling
rivalry.

4. Verbalize thoughts and feelings regarding sibling(s),
and identify the issues that
precipitate conflict. (7, 8, 9)

7. Meet with the parents to
prepare them for actively
listening to the student's
feelings concerning his/her
siblings and to reinforce the
importance of providing
time for emotional expression and listening without
judgment.

8. Assign the student to complete the "I Statements"

activity from the *School Counseling and School Social Work Homework Planner* (Knapp) to assist in dealing with feelings of rejection, being discounted, jealousy, anger, or frustration, which may occur as the result of negative sibling interaction.

9. Ask the student to draw or write the name of each sibling on a large sheet of paper, list any frictions or problems that commonly occur with each sibling, as well as several strengths or positive characteristics for each, and to discuss these in a counseling session.

5. Share feelings of insecurity, fear of loss of attention and affection with the parent(s), and seek reassurance of the continuation of a strong, positive relationship between the parents and self. (10, 11)

10. Brainstorm with the student a list of fears, feelings, and concerns to share with his/her parents and the assurances from them that are being sought.

11. Help the student to write a note to his/her parent(s) requesting a meeting to discuss feelings regarding sibling-related difficulties; process the feelings that result from such a meeting.

6. List constructive ways to cope with an urge to demand parents' attention. (12)

12. Brainstorm with the student methods of resisting the desire to seek attention (e.g., complete homework, read a book, call a friend, read e-mail) when parents are interacting with a sibling.

7. Verbalize an understanding of the need of all family

13. Instruct the student to list the demands and

members to share the family's emotional, time, and financial resources. (13)

requirements that he/she places on the parents and other family members (e.g., parents' attention, love, time, and financial support) and create a similar list for each family member (or assign the "We Each Have Family Needs" activity from the *School Counseling and School Social Work Homework Planner* by Knapp) to develop an awareness of the demands that each family member places upon the family resources.

8. Family divides the household workload and discusses responsibilities and other family issues in a family forum. (14, 15)

14. Ask the family members to agree to hold weekly meetings during which family chores are delegated, family problems are discussed and resolved, allowance is distributed, and recognition is given for the efforts of each family member.

15. Assist the student in preparing for the family meeting by discussing concerns and ideas in the counseling session and then recording them in a personal journal.

9. Verbalize an understanding of empathy and how it can play a role in reducing conflict with siblings. (16, 17, 18)

16. Define empathy (e.g., understanding another's feelings and perceptions versus focusing only on our own thoughts and feelings) and discuss with him/her the role of empathy in the prevention and resolution of sibling conflicts.

17. Teach the student the importance of trying to predict the thoughts, feelings, and actions of others prior to the outbreak of a conflict.

18. Read a story involving sibling rivalry (e.g., *Pain and the Great One* by Blume and Trivas or *I'd Rather Have an Iguana* by Mario), and discuss with the student how empathy, communication, and awareness of another's point of view can prevent or reduce conflicts and jealousy.

10. List methods of resolving sibling conflict fairly and positively. (19, 20)

19. Teach a simple process for younger students to use in resolving conflicts with their siblings or peers: (1) state the problem; (2) listen to the other's point of view; (3) share feelings about the problem; (4) brainstorm ideas for solving the problem; (5) agree to a solution and implement it.

20. Teach a conflict resolution process for older elementary and secondary students to use in resolving sibling disputes: (1) find a private place to talk; (2) discuss the problem without judging; (3) brainstorm possible solutions; (4) agree on a solution that works for both; (5) try the solution and agree to renegotiate if it is not effective.

11. Parents diffuse sibling rivalry and strengthen bonds

21. Encourage the parents to reinforce positive behavior

between siblings through positive recognition, fair treatment, awareness of personal feelings, and inter-family activities. (21, 22)

from all siblings and administer discipline to each in an even-handed and logical manner, using consequences that fit the unique situation.

22. Assign the parents to use the concept of *unique* rather than *equal* to govern the distribution of love, attention, time, and physical needs (e.g., "I love you each uniquely." "You need my help with homework, your sister needs help with her piano lesson." "You need new pajamas, your brother needs some new jeans").

12. Use dramatization or drawing to identify ways to arrive at a peaceful resolution of conflict with siblings. (23, 24)

23. Role-play with the student a problematic situation involving a sibling, create several different outcomes or endings (e.g., physical fight, parents intervene, siblings work it out peacefully), and discuss which result works best in the long run.

24. Use cartooning [see "Cartooning as a Counseling Approach to a Socially Isolated Child" by Sonntag in *The School Counselor* (1985, vol. 32, pp. 307–312)] to illustrate a sibling dispute that has a peaceful or acceptable outcome, and assign the student to complete a similar cartoon at home with a sibling.

13. Participate in a social outlet or hobby to develop personal interests and diffuse sibling rivalry. (25, 26)

25. Explore with the student his/her acquisition of a new hobby or outside activity that reflects a personal interest; assign him/her to

record his/her progress and feelings in a journal with a descriptive paragraph, drawing, or photo.

26. Encourage the student to join a social or interest-related group in school or the community (e.g., Spanish club, choir, band, drama club, soccer) in which he/she can gain attention and be affirmed.

14. Parents establish a system of positive discipline that is balanced with love and designed to promote healthy self-esteem and responsible behavior. (27, 28, 29)

27. Ask the parents to read a book on parent-child interaction (e.g., *Parent Talk* by Moorman) and to discuss with a counselor how the proposed strategies can help in managing parent-child issues and sibling disharmony.

28. Suggest that the parents use disciplinary interventions that require cooperation between the siblings (e.g., disputing siblings work together on a 1000-piece jigsaw puzzle until a conflict is settled or complete a family chore together instead of fighting).

29. Assign the parents to use the Rewind Game when siblings engage in a verbal exchange that involves disparaging remarks and put-downs (or assign the "Rewind Game" from the *School Counseling and School Social Work Homework Planner* by Knapp).

15. Parents recognize each child in the family for his/her individual personality, goals, and aspirations, and work to reduce comparisons and competition between the siblings. (30, 31)

30. Instruct the parents to use descriptive rather than comparative words when addressing either a positive or negative behavior or characteristic in their children (e.g., "I see you're almost finished with you're homework," or "Your room needs some serious attention," versus "You've almost finished your homework and your brother hasn't even started," or "Your brother's room is spotless and yours is a disaster").

31. Teach the parents to affirm the efforts and progress of each child based on individual merit or personal best and never in comparison with the accomplishments or failure of a sibling.

16. List the benefits of close family relationships and ways to achieve such harmony. (32)

32. Ask the student to list the benefits of developing a close relationship with all family members (e.g., gaining help and support, reduction of personal stress, and family harmony) in a personal journal and then to brainstorm methods of improving interactions with his/her parents and siblings (e.g., stop put-downs, don't interrupt, share, use "I" statements).

17. Verbalize the awareness that parental love and recognition is an abundant resource that can be shared by all of the siblings with-

32. Ask the student to list the benefits of developing a close relationship with all family members (e.g., gaining help and support,

out any child being deprived. (32, 33)

reduction of personal stress, and family harmony) in a personal journal and then to brainstorm methods of improving his/her interactions with his/her parents and siblings (e.g., stop put-downs, don't interrupt, share, use "I" statements).

33. Assist the student in completing the "Many Rooms in My Heart" exercise from the *School Counseling and School Social Work Homework Planner* (Knapp) or assign him/her to draw a heart and fill in the name of each family member to illustrate that the heart's capacity to love is great.

18. Write about wishes for a positive sibling relationship as a goal for the future. (34, 35)

34. Assign the student to write a story entitled "A Day with My Sister and/or My Brother" defining the relationship as it is now and again as he/she would like the relationship to be in 10 years; encourage the use of as many feeling words as possible. Process the story during a future counseling session.

35. Ask the student to describe or imagine his/her relationship with siblings in the past, present, and future (or assign the "Sibling Relationships, An Amazing Evolution" activity from the *School Counseling and School Social Work Homework Planner* by Knapp).

19. Participate in positive activities that involve both total family and one-to-one interaction among family members. (36, 37)

36. Help the student to plan for doing a personal favor that expresses love and caring for each parent and sibling (e.g., cooking a meal, playing with a younger sibling, or helping an older sibling complete a chore).

37. Assign the student to play The Ungame (Zakich, Western Psychological Services) with all members of his/her family to facilitate family cooperation and sharing.

20. Identify demonstrations of love shown to self by other family members. (38)

38. Ask the student to identify several supportive and caring gestures made on his/her behalf by parents and siblings in an attempt to build a positive relationship.

21. Parents use sibling conflict as a means of teaching techniques of problem solving. (39)

39. Assign the parents to read *Help! The Kids Are at It Again* (Crary and Katayama) for an understanding of how to use sibling disputes to teach problem solving.

22. Participate in group counseling focused on sibling rivalry. (40, 41)

40. Refer the student to a school- or agency-sponsored group for children dealing with sibling rivalry, and discuss information and reactions during individual counseling sessions.

41. Help the student to understand his/her feelings of confusion and frustration experienced as a result of sibling rivalry and refer to private therapy if symptoms appear entrenched or overwhelming.

23. Parents affirm the need to work together as a unified team in dealing with sibling issues. (42, 43)

42. Assign the parents to read *The Seven Habits of Highly Effective Families* (Covey) to learn strategies for attaining a positive family atmosphere through maintaining a couple-centered approach.

43. Identify with the parents, the student, and the siblings any triangulation or sabotaging that is occurring in the family, and make plans to end it through open discussions, mutual problem solving, and the parents presenting a united front and valuing the unique qualities of each sibling.

24. Parents and siblings verbalize an understanding of the dangers of locking family members into negative or rigid roles and work to value each person for their unique contribution to the family unit. (44, 45)

44. Discuss with the student and his/her parents and siblings the damage done to siblings' self-esteem, family relationships, and goal achievement caused by designating negative family roles (e.g., bully, aggressive, mean, untrustworthy, loser) or exclusively positive family roles (e.g., most gifted, musical, athletic, beautiful, personable).

45. Encourage the parents to teach, model, and affirm the positive behaviors they hope to bring out in each of their children (e.g., persistence, responsibility, pride, cooperation) rather than negative traits (e.g., giving up, shirking duties, lacking

interest, being self-centered).

25. Parents and siblings acknowledge progress made toward family peace and harmony. (46, 47)

46. Ask the student to record in a personal journal points of family pride and progress, as well as areas that could be improved to promote and enhance positive sibling relationships and harmony among all family members.

47. Discuss with the student and his/her parents cooperative efforts and group projects to achieve family harmony. Encourage positive efforts and offer guidance in areas of problematic or reluctant participation.

—. _____

—. _____

—. _____

—. _____

—. _____

—. _____

DIAGNOSTIC SUGGESTIONS

Axis I:	313.81	Oppositional Defiant Disorder
	312.8	Conduct Disorder
	312.9	Disruptive Behavior Disorder, NOS
	314.01	Attention-Deficit/Hyperactivity Disorder, Predominantly Hyperactive-Impulsive Type
	314.9	Attention-Deficit/Hyperactive Disorder, NOS
	309.0	Adjustment Disorder With Depressed Mood
	309.3	Adjustment Disorder With Disturbance of Conduct
	309.24	Adjustment Disorder With Anxiety
	309.81	Posttraumatic Stress Disorder

	300.4	Dysthymic Disorder
	V62.81	Relational Problem, NOS
	V71.02	Child or Adolescent Antisocial Behavior
	_____	_____
	_____	_____
Axis II:	799.9	Diagnosis Deferred
	V71.09	No Diagnosis on Axis II
	_____	_____
	_____	_____

SOCIAL MALADJUSTMENT/ CONDUCT DISORDER

BEHAVIORAL DEFINITIONS

1. Serious violation of school, family, and societal rules (e.g., running away, curfew violations, truancy, classroom disruption).
2. Repeated confrontations with authority figures at home, school, work, or in the community.
3. Poor academic progress and a lack of desire to achieve in school.
4. Repeated attempts to intimidate others through physical fights, verbal abuse, use of weapons, or bullying.
5. Cruelty to people and animals.
6. Pleasure seeking and egocentric with a lack of remorse and empathy for others' feelings, circumstances, and needs.
7. Unwilling to accept responsibility for antisocial behavior, blames mistakes and problems on others, and shows no remorse for misbehavior.
8. Excessive risk taking and impulsive behavior without regard to consequences.
9. Antisocial behaviors are admired and reinforced by peers who are members of an antisocial subculture or gang.
10. Criminal behavior that may include theft, vandalism, fire setting, substance abuse, or assault.

—. _____
_____

—. _____
_____

—. _____
_____

LONG-TERM GOALS

1. Comply with family and school rules, and eliminate all cruel, destructive, and antisocial behavior.
2. Attend school regularly and progress toward individualized or grade-level academic expectations and/or graduation.
3. Parents and teachers use highly structured discipline and firm limits to help establish self-control and develop responsible behavior.
4. Establish a positive relationship with a mainstream peer group, parents, teachers, mentors, and role models.
5. Develop age-appropriate impulse control and consideration for the consequences of personal behavior.
6. Eliminate aggressive and intimidating behavior toward others and use appropriate techniques of conflict management to gain recognition and resolve disputes.
7. Demonstrate a normal level of conscience development, empathy, and the ability to experience remorse.

—. _____
_____

—. _____
_____

—. _____
_____

SHORT-TERM OBJECTIVES	THERAPEUTIC INTERVENTIONS
1. Cooperate with a complete psychosocial evaluation. (1, 2)	1. Meet with the parents to gather a developmental history and review the school's concerns about academic progress and maladaptive behavior.
	2. Arrange for a complete psychosocial evaluation of the student by the school evaluation team or by a private therapist.

2. Identify underlying perceptions and assumptions that lead to feelings of hostility, and plan for appropriate resolution of these feelings. (3, 4)

3. Verbalize a plan for improved compliance with rules at home and school. (5, 6)

4. Coauthor behavior plans for school and home that focus on cooperative, successful participation in each environment. (7, 8, 9)

3. Assess academic, social/emotional, and behavioral functioning by asking the student and his/her parents and teachers to complete assessment inventories (e.g., the Achenbach System of Empirically Based Assessment by Achenbach); compare and process specific responses during subsequent counseling sessions with him/her.

4. Read with the student children's literature that explores feelings and resulting behavior and suggests management strategies (e.g., *Hands Are Not for Hitting* by Agassi or *The Teenagers Guide to School Outside the Box* by Greene).

5. Review family rules with the student, and identify areas of compliance and noncompliance; help him/her formulate a plan for improved compliance in challenging areas and chart his/her progress.

6. Discuss the school rules with the student in either individual or group counseling sessions, identify those that are difficult to follow, and work together to develop a plan for compliance.

7. Assist the student in formulating ideas for a behavior management plan at school or home using a plan sheet that outlines the problem

and a proposed solution (or assign the "Problem Solving Worksheet" activity from the *School Counseling and School Social Work Homework Planner* by Knapp).

8. Caution the student and his/her parents and teachers to be realistic in expectations expressed in behavior plans in order to increase the success level and avoid defeat (e.g., target specific behaviors, recognize incremental progress, revise the plan frequently to reflect progress and address remaining problems).

9. Advise the student and his/her parents and teachers that a behavior plan addressing an existing problem must be completed by the student and accepted by the parents or teacher before he/she is able to enjoy or participate in any nonessential family or school activities (e.g., recess, TV, computer, meals with the family or classmates, playing games, using supplies). If the plan is ineffective, privileges are again suspended until a workable plan is in place.

5. Maintain a level of competence in academic performance that is acceptable to parents and teachers. (10, 11)

10. Discuss with the student and his/her parents and teachers his/her academic potential, and determine a mutually agreed-upon level of academic performance

that must be maintained to earn privileges at home or school.

11. Arrange a meeting with teacher(s), the parents, and the student to determine accommodations that encourage successful academic performance (e.g., supervising the student closely during times of transition; sitting the student near the teacher's desk in an area of low distractions or near a good role model; involving him/her in lesson discussions; giving simple, clear instructions; arranging for remedial tutoring).

6. Participate in special programming at school that establishes firm limits and teaches self-control. (12, 13, 14)

12. Advise the teachers and administrators to establish a time-out area or student responsibility center where the student can go when he/she is disruptive or uncooperative to cool off and plan for more appropriate behavior before returning to routine classroom activities.

13. Assist the teachers in developing a learning center area in the classroom or school where students who are experiencing academic performance problems due to resistance or lack of motivation spend time catching up on academic work in lieu of attending regular classes.

14. Recommend special education or Section 504 accom-

modations to help the student to participate successfully in the academic environment (e.g., <u>smaller classroom, assistance from an instructional or behavioral paraprofessional, reduced school day, one-to-one instruction, social work services</u>).

7. Participate in family counseling sessions focusing on rebuilding relationships and establishing family harmony. (15, 16)

15. Meet with the parents on a monthly basis to discuss the challenges of socially maladjusted behavior for the student and the family, develop strategies to help him/her and the family adjust, or refer to a private therapist or agency for family counseling.

16. Suggest that the parents and the student meet weekly in a family meeting at a designated time to review progress, give encouragement, note continuing concerns, and keep a written progress report to share with the counselor or a private therapist.

8. Parents attend parenting classes and read parenting literature to learn new discipline techniques to use in the family. (17, 18)

17. Refer the parents to a parenting class (e.g., *Systematic Training for Effective Parenting* by Dinkmeyer and McKay, *Becoming a Love and Logic Parent* by Fay, Cline, and Fay, or *The Parent Talk System* by Moorman and Knapp) to acquire techniques of positive discipline to use with the student.

18. Meet with the parents to help them initiate parenting strategies of positive discipline learned in parenting classes or from recommended parenting books or tapes (e.g., *Your Defiant Child: Eight Steps to Better Behavior* by Barkley or *Children: The Challenge* by Dreikurs and Stoltz).

9. Increase compliance with completing household chores and demonstrate respect toward the parents' role as head of the household. (19, 20)

19. Assign the parents and the student to create a list of household chores and to designate an appropriate number to him/her, taking into consideration his/her age, maturity, and ability level.

20. Instruct the student in the use of a chore chart, which monitors his/her weekly chores, time spent on a task, and a grade given by both the parents and the student (or assign the "Chore Report Card" from the *School Counseling and School Social Work Homework Planner* by Knapp).

10. Teachers formulate a structured system of discipline that enables them to set firm limits on the student and promote his/her responsible behavior. (21, 22)

21. Encourage the teachers to attend workshops or seminars defining socially maladjusted behavior and teaching strategies for working with students demonstrating disruptive and antisocial behavior.

22. Discuss social maladjustment with the teacher and its implications for effective classroom discipline (e.g.,

establish a highly structured environment, all privileges must be earned, teacher in control at all times, trust is established slowly, <u>use encouragement rather than praise, unconditional positive regard despite extreme challenges, seek support for teacher burnout</u>).

11. Participate in an extracurricular club, team, or religious organization for a designated period of time and chart progress. (23, 24)

23. Explore with the student various interest groups (e.g., sports, hobby, religious, exercise), and select one to join; determine a reasonable time duration, and ask him/her to chart his/her participation and reaction.

24. Assist the student in identifying the positive aspects of sustained involvement in a friendship or activity group; ask him/her to record ideas in a personal journal in either written or picture form.

12. Increase the frequency of positive interactions with the parents and educators. (25, 26)

25. Direct the student to create self-monitoring charts, which are kept on his/her classroom desk or in a personal planner, to track emotional reactions, behaviors, and social interactions (or assign the use of the "Student Self-Report" activity from the *School Counseling and School Social Work Homework Planner* by Knapp).

26. Review the student's self-monitoring charts during <u>weekly counseling sessions,</u>

13. Attend a social skills development group.
(27, 28, 29, 30)

giving affirmations for progress made and guidance in areas of no or little progress.

27. Include the student in a school social skills development group or refer him/her to a similar group offered by a mental health agency or private therapist.

28. Use children's literature to explore the effects of behavior upon interpersonal relationships (e.g., *Don't Pop Your Cork on Mondays!* by Moser and Pilkey, *Don't Feed the Monster on Tuesdays!* by Moser and Thatch, or *Everything I Do You Blame on Me* by Aborn).

29. Have the student review an experience in which an impulsive choice created an interpersonal conflict, then select a more appropriate action and predict the probable result (or assign the "Rewind Game" activity from the *School Counseling and School Social Work Homework Planner* by Knapp).

30. Brainstorm with the student, in either an individual or in a group session, strategies for initiating friendships at school or in the community (e.g., invite someone to play at recess, share a game, invite a classmate home for after-school play), and ask him/her to list these in a personal journal.

Have the student choose one strategy to implement during the following week, and discuss the results during next counseling session.

14. Parents, teachers, and counselor verbally affirm the student for progress that he/she has made in behavior management, academic achievement, and appropriate social interaction. (31, 32, 33)

31. Discuss with teachers and the parents the importance of giving frequent affirmations to the student in a private, low-key manner for progress noted.

32. Review with the student in weekly sessions his/her strategic plans for achieving social/emotional, academic, and behavioral goals, and give him/her recognition for progress made and guidance in remaining areas of concern. Ask him/her to record both the successful and in-progress behavioral strategies in a personal journal.

33. Ask the parents and teachers to monitor the student's assignment planner daily and to give him/her encouragement and direction as needed.

15. Demonstrate the ability to predict the consequences of personal decisions and resulting behavior. (34, 35)

34. Introduce activities from the program I Can Problem-Solve (Shure, ADHD Warehouse) to teach problem solving and predicting the result of specific actions.

35. Assign the student to record several problematic experiences in a personal journal and analyze them in terms of A = antecedent or prior

circumstances, B = the student's behavior, and C = the resulting consequences; discuss the long- and short-term consequences of personal decisions.

16. Reduce the frequency of lying to the teacher, counselor, and parents. (36, 37)

36. Help the parents and teachers to understand that appropriate skepticism is essential when dealing with children experiencing a behavioral disorder and that chronic lying is often the norm. Advise them to remain skeptical when lying is suspected and to express appreciation when honesty is shown by the student.

37. Advise the parents and teachers to place the burden of proof on the student when lying, stealing, or personal dishonesty is in question and to require restitution for damages caused (e.g., additional tasks or chores, repayment in the form of personal possessions or money, personal time spent helping the injured party).

17. Identify triggers and targets for angry outbursts and antisocial behavior. (38, 39)

38. Ask the student to identify triggers and targets for emotional outbursts and to record them in a personal journal.

39. Brainstorm with the student appropriate, socially acceptable methods of dealing with the triggers and targets for angry or antisocial outbursts (e.g., use an

"I" statement, walk away, use humor, take a personal time-out); role-play the use of these prosocial methods of anger management.

18. Identify and verbalize destructive entitlement beliefs that lead to chronic or excessive anger and antisocial behavior. (40, 41)

40. Define entitlement beliefs for the student (e.g., "The world owes me," I deserve to get what I want," "Pay up or I will blow up"); instruct him/her to brainstorm some examples and to list five destructive entitlement beliefs in a personal journal.

41. Assign the student to rephrase several personal entitlement beliefs to reflect more realistic and productive thinking (e.g., "I will start saving for some new clothes," versus "I deserve new clothes").

19. Express remorse and empathy to the family, counselor, teacher, or friends when actions or words create distress, problems, or pain for others. (42, 43, 44)

42. Ask the student to select feelings from a feelings chart that describe emotions he/she commonly experiences. Encourage a follow-up discussion exploring situations when the teachers, family members, or peers may also experience these feelings.

43. Review with the student any poor decisions that may have caused distress for others, and brainstorm with him/her appropriate expressions of remorse (or assign the "Recipes for Restitution" activity from the *School Counseling and*

School Social Work Homework Planner by Knapp).

44. Play the Talking, Feeling and Doing Game (Gardner) during a group counseling session to help the student identify and express feelings related to empathy and remorse.

20. Identify positive goals for the future in the areas of occupation, family, friends, leisure activities, lifelong learning, and spiritual and character development. (45, 46)

45. Discuss with the student his/her personal plans for the future and methods of achieving these goals.

46. Assign the student to complete the "My Predictions for the Future" activity from the *School Counseling and School Social Work Homework Planner* (Knapp) to help him/her establish positive goals for the future.

__. _____
_____

__. _____
_____

__. _____
_____

__. _____
_____

__. _____
_____

__. _____
_____

DIAGNOSTIC SUGGESTIONS

Axis I:	313.81	Oppositional Defiant Disorder
	312.8	Conduct Disorder/Childhood-Onset Type
	312.9	Disruptive Behavior Disorder NOS
	314.01	Attention-Deficit/Hyperactivity Disorder Predominantly Hyperactive-Impulsive Type
	314.9	Attention-Deficit/Hyperactivity Disorder NOS
	V71.02	Child Antisocial Behavior

	V61.20	Parent-Child Relational Problem
	_____	_____
Axis II:	799.9	Diagnosis Deferred
	V71.09	No Diagnosis on Axis II
	_____	_____
	_____	_____

SOCIAL SKILLS/PEER RELATIONSHIPS

BEHAVIORAL DEFINITIONS

1. Refuses to initiate or maintain social relationships with peers in the school or community, resulting in isolation.
2. Reluctance to engage in social activities or assume a leadership role.
3. Low self-esteem and lack of confidence in ability to fit in or be socially successful.
4. Is scapegoated or picked on by peers.
5. Refuses to accept responsibility for socially inappropriate behavior, and tends to blame others for the resulting consequences.
6. Immature social skills and lack of polite, expected social behavior.
7. Difficulty expressing personal thoughts and feelings.
8. Lack of empathy for another person's situation or feelings.
9. Difficulty with anger management, quick to anger, and easily frustrated.
10. Attempts to resolve conflicts only through confrontational or aggressive strategies.
11. Tendency to negatively stereotype individuals perceived as being different.

__. _____
_____

__. _____
_____

__. _____
_____

LONG-TERM GOALS

1. Develop essential social skills that will enhance the quality of interpersonal relationships.
2. Establish and maintain long-term (i.e., six months) interpersonal or peer friendships outside of the immediate family.
3. Demonstrate appropriate social interaction, assertiveness, confidence in self, and initiation of social contact.
4. Believe in self as being likable, capable, and socially accepted.
5. Acquire techniques for appropriate self-expression and active listening.
6. Develop empathy and understanding for another person or group's point of view.
7. Develop conflict management skills to use at home, school, and in the community.
8. Actively work to build a sense of community within the school environment, and eliminate discrimination, prejudice, and hidden biases toward any group or individual.

—. _____

_____

—. _____

_____

—. _____

_____

SHORT-TERM OBJECTIVES	THERAPEUTIC INTERVENTIONS
1. Cooperate with an assessment of social, emotional, and behavioral adjustment. (1, 2)	1. Administer a normed, self-reporting assessment scale to the student (e.g., the Coopersmith Self-Esteem Inventory by Coopersmith, the Revised Children's Manifest Anxiety Scale by Reynolds and Richmond, the Youth Self-Report by Achenbach, or the Piers-Harris Self-Concept Scale by Piers and Harris) to

determine specific areas of social/emotional concern; provide feedback of the results to the student.

2. Ask the student to complete an information sheet that details pertinent personal data (or assign the "Personal Profile" activity from the *School Counseling and School Social Work Homework Planner* by Knapp).

2. Identify positive personal qualities that are important for successful social interaction. (3, 4)

3. Assist the student in developing a written list of his/her positive personal attributes; save this list in a social skills journal, and post the list prominently at home.

4. Process questions and answers from the personal information sheet and the self-reporting scales to begin the process of reframing and building a more positive self-image. Have the student explain his/her responses in more detail to establish and clarify possible causes of low self-esteem or relationship difficulties.

3. Identify existing positive relationships and significant others who offer acceptance and friendship. (5)

5. Ask the student to make a list of positive significant others in his/her life, including family members, friends, teachers, mentors, and role models, and to rate the degree of support given, closeness felt, or influence that person has (or assign the "Important People in

My Life" activity from the *School Counseling and School Social Work Homework Planner* by Knapp).

4. List methods of establishing friendships. (6, 7)

6. Assist the student in listing methods of establishing friendships (e.g., smiling, conversing, sharing common interests or activities, offering emotional support) in a social skills journal (or assign the "Art of Creating and Maintaining Friendships" activity from the *School Counseling and School Social Work Homework Planner* by Knapp).

7. Facilitate a social skills group for students having difficulty with interpersonal relationships, socially acceptable behavior, or resolving conflicts at school or in the community.

5. Participate in a counseling group focusing on teaching social skills and techniques for resolving conflicts. (7)

7. Facilitate a social skills group for students having difficulty with interpersonal relationships, socially acceptable behavior, or resolving conflicts at school or in the community.

6. List ways to reduce the frequency of aggressive interactions to resolve conflicts. (8)

8. Brainstorm with the student appropriate, socially acceptable methods of dealing with the triggers and targets of his/her aggressive or inappropriate social interactions (e.g., use an "I" statement, walk away, use humor, take a personal time-out).

7. Define and demonstrate empathy. (9, 10)

9. Define empathy during a group session (e.g., understanding another's feelings and perceptions versus focusing only on one's own thoughts and feelings); discuss with the student the role of empathy in understanding another person's attitude and behavior.

10. Use role playing to teach the student the technique of predicting the thoughts, feelings, and actions of himself/herself and others in various social situations; ask him/her to share anticipatory thoughts and feelings and to indicate how this process enhances empathy and promotes positive relationships.

8. Express feelings directly and assertively. (11, 12)

11. Teach the student about "I" messages (see *Teacher Effectiveness Training* by Gordon) and the Bug-Wish Technique (e.g., "It bugs me when you . . . I wish you would. . . ."); role-play the use of these techniques to respond to distressing behavior from others or to clarify personal feelings or concerns.

12. Ask the student to describe a recent problematic situation with friends and create a positive ending using a storytelling approach, which involves a beginning (situation), middle (behavior or choice), and end (result or consequence); in a

group session, instruct the students to take turns describing the three parts of the story in a round-robin fashion.

9. Verbalize an understanding of the importance of listening to another's point of view and understanding both sides of an issue. (13, 14, 15)

13. Define active listening (see *Teacher Effectiveness Training* by Gordon) for the student (e.g., listening without interruption, decoding the other person's message, and reflecting back both the perceived message and the underlying feelings to check for understanding); instruct him/her to practice this technique using a role playing format.

14. Introduce the concept of *point of view* (individual perception) versus *factual information* (concrete data). Brainstorm with the student various situations where differing points of view can lead to conflict (e.g., who won the game, the grass needs cutting, it's my turn).

15. List for the student the steps that are necessary for understanding both points of view in a difference of opinion or conflict (e.g., allow each person to state his/her point of view without interruption, repeat back each statement to check for understanding).

10. Verbalize an understanding of the impact of nonverbal communication on inciting

16. Define nonverbal communication for the student (e.g., facial expression, eye

or resolving personal anger and interpersonal conflict. (16, 17)

contact, body posture, hand use), and teach how facial expressions and body language can either encourage or discourage a peaceful solution to a conflict.

17. Brainstorm examples of encouraging nonverbal communication cues (e.g., smile, eye contact, leaning toward speaker, nodding head) versus discouraging cues (e.g., rolling the eyes, finger-pointing, eyebrows raised, arms folded); have the student demonstrate and react to both types of nonverbal cues (or assign the "Cases of Conflict" activity from the *School Counseling and School Social Work Homework Planner* by Knapp).

11. Engage in daily activities that promote a sense of belonging in the classroom and community. (18, 19)

18. Encourage the teacher and other school personnel to involve the student in reciprocal activities that enhance a feeling of belonging and self-worth (e.g., one-to-one chats, high fives, daily greetings, reciprocal smiles, interactive tasks or activities, recognize and reinforce good behavior or small accomplishments, low-key personal affirmations).

19. Support the student in joining an extracurricular social group sponsored by the school, church, or community.

12. Participate in special programming at school that

20. Advise the teachers and administrators to establish a

promotes cooperation and teaches self-control. (20, 21)

time-out area or student responsibility center where the student can go when he/she is disruptive or uncooperative to cool off and plan for more appropriate behavior before participating in routine classroom activities.

21. Recommend special education or Section 504 accommodations to help the student participate successfully in the school environment (e.g., smaller classroom, assistance from an instructional or behavioral paraprofessional, reduced school day, one-to-one instruction, social work services).

13. Self-monitor personal behavior and interactions with adults and peers using a chart to record improvement in ability to remain appropriate. (22, 23)

22. Assist the student in creating self-monitoring charts, which are kept on his/her classroom desk or in a personal planner, to track emotional reactions, behaviors, and social interactions (or assign the "Student Self-Report" activity from the *School Counseling and School Social Work Homework Planner* by Knapp).

23. Review the student's self-monitoring charts, giving affirmations for progress made and guidance in areas of little or no progress.

14. List the underlying causes of interpersonal conflict. (24, 25)

24. Assist the student in developing a list of some preexisting conditions that contribute to conflict (e.g.,

friendship cliques; feelings of exclusion; excessive competition; lack of cooperation; blaming problems on others; failure to emphasize a harmonious classroom, school, or family atmosphere).

25. Read *The Cybil War* (Byars) and discuss the underlying causes of the conflict between friends and what could have prevented it.

15. List the benefits of using conflict resolution versus power struggles, anger, aggression, and arguments to solve disputes. (26, 27)

26. Read *Mop, Moondance, and the Nagasaki Knights* (Meyers) to illustrate how consensus problem solving (win/win) helps to unite people, whereas making decisions without communication and consensus (win/lose) creates conflict.

27. Brainstorm with the student the benefits of peaceful negotiations and problem solving (e.g., respect and dignity is maintained, problems are resolved rather than intensified, friendships continue or develop, social skills are learned) versus the results of conflict and power struggles (e.g., broken friendships, hostile school environment, suspicion, aggression).

16. List methods of resolving personal conflict fairly and positively. (28, 29)

28. Teach the student the Rules for Fighting Fair (see *Mediation: Getting to Win/Win* by Schmidt): identify the problem; focus on the problem; attack the problem, not

the person; listen with an open mind; treat the person's feelings with respect; take responsibility for your actions.

29. Assist the student in creating a conflict resolution chart, which lists various ways to solve a dispute (e.g., share, take turns, listen, talk it over, apologize, get help, use humor, start over, flip a coin) on different segments of the chart. Instruct him/her to use this chart when trying to determine options to using anger to problem-solve.

17. Demonstrate the ability to work toward a mutually acceptable, or win/win, solution. (30, 31, 32, 33)

30. Brainstorm with the student a list of win/lose scenarios (e.g., Jimmy gets to go first and Janice doesn't, Jamaul gets to play with the ball and Derrick doesn't, Cynthia invites Shirley to play and ignores Latricia) and win/win scenarios (e.g., Jimmy and Janice take turns, Jamaul and Derrick play ball together, Cynthia asks both Shirley and Latricia to play). Ask him/her to identify feelings resulting from a win/lose outcome versus feelings resulting from a win/win solution.

31. Assign the "Win/Win versus Win/Lose" activity from the *School Counseling and School Social Work Homework Planner* (Knapp) to

teach the long- and short-term interpersonal effects of each approach to problem solving.

32. Teach a simple process for younger students to use in resolving conflicts in their lives: (1) state the problem; (2) listen to the other's point of view; (3) share feelings about the problem; (4) brainstorm ideas for solving the problem; (5) agree to a solution and implement it.

33. Teach a conflict resolution process for secondary students to use in resolving personal disputes and in mediating the disputes of their peers: (1) find a private place to talk; (2) discuss the problem without judging; (3) brainstorm possible solutions; (4) agree on a solution that works for both; (5) try the solution and agree to renegotiate if it is not effective.

18. Initiate action that shows leadership in the classroom and at home. (34)

34. Meet with the student and his/her parents and teachers to brainstorm areas where he/she could practice leadership and responsibility (e.g., babysitting, teaching a lesson, caring for the class pet or a pet at home, getting a job); ask him/her to select an area for participation and enlist the parents' and teachers' support.

19. Report success in initiating social contact with peers. (35, 36, 37)

35. Assign the student to initiate one new social interaction each week (e.g.,

sit with a group of friends at lunch, share a playground game, phone a friend to chat, join an after-school activity), record the progress in a counseling journal, and share with a counselor in either individual or group sessions.

36. Encourage the student to join a social group or club; brainstorm options and help him/her to make a selection.

37. Ask the student to review an experience in which an inappropriate action created a negative interpersonal problem, then select a more appropriate action and predict the probable result (or assign the "Rewind Game" activity from the *School Counseling and School Social Work Homework Planner* by Knapp).

20. Participate in activities that require cooperation with others. (38, 39)

38. Engage the student during a group counseling session to participate in activities that require cooperation and shared responsibility (e.g., mutual storytelling, putting together a puzzle, creating a structure using Tinkertoys, planning a community project); analyze and discuss his/her cooperative efforts.

39. Assign the student to participate in a volunteer effort designed to help others that requires cooperation and team playing (e.g., school

food drive, tutoring a younger student, becoming a conflict manager, working with Habitat for Humanity).

21. Verbalize acceptance of responsibility for own behavior and develop positive alternatives to socially inappropriate behavior. (40, 41)

40. Instruct the student to role-play the process of making amends, which involves stating the damage caused by inappropriate personal actions, apologizing, and pledging to correct the hurtful behavior (or assign the "Problem Solving Worksheet" activity from the *School Counseling and School Social Work Homework Planner* by Knapp).

41. Read *Everything I Do You Blame on Me* (Aborn) during an individual or group session to help the student understand the importance of taking responsibility for his/her personal actions.

22. Verbalize how stereotypes and personal biases interfere with just treatment of others and positive social interaction. (42, 43)

42. Encourage the student to seek information about stereotypical thinking or personal biases from teachers, family, and friends that interfere with positive social interaction and to record his/her findings in a social skills journal.

43. Instruct the student to list personal strengths and weaknesses that influence his/her ability to accept differences in others (e.g., self-confidence, popularity, enjoys a variety of people versus low self-esteem,

23. List methods for promoting social harmony within the school. (44, 45)

difficulty meeting people, entitlement beliefs), and assign him/her to select one intolerant behavior or perception to eliminate each week.

44. Assign the student to solicit suggestions from diverse groups of classmates for creating cohesion and tolerance in the school or community. List the ideas in a personal journal or discuss them during a social skills group session.

45. Brainstorm with the student roadblocks to social harmony in the school and community, and list methods of building bridges between diverse groups (e.g., share an ethnic meal, learn ethnic words and phrases, attend a multicultural festival, explore different cultural customs, view videos exploring various world cultures).

__. _____   __. _____
    _____   _____
__. _____   __. _____
    _____   _____
__. _____   __. _____
    _____   _____

DIAGNOSTIC SUGGESTIONS

Axis I: 300.4   Dysthymic Disorder
              300.23   Social Phobia

	300.00	Anxiety Disorder NOS
	314.01	Attention-Deficit/Hyperactivity Disorder, Combined Type
	300.02	Generalized Anxiety Disorder
	309.21	Separation Anxiety Disorder
	312.30	Impulse Control Disorder, NOS
	312.9	Disruptive Behavior Disorder, NOS
	312.8	Conduct Disorder
	V62.81	Relational Problem, NOS
	V71.02	Child Antisocial Behavior
	_____	_____
	_____	_____
Axis II:	799.0	Diagnosis Deferred
	V71.09	No Diagnosis on Axis II
	_____	_____
	_____	_____

SUBSTANCE ABUSE

BEHAVIORAL DEFINITIONS

1. Use of alcohol or drugs to become intoxicated or high at least three times per week.
2. Physical evidence of alcohol or drug use found on the student's person or in personal areas at home or school.
3. Significant shift in peer group, interests, or activities toward those with a chemical dependence orientation.
4. Oppositional defiance at home or school, drop in grades, truancy, and/or lawbreaking.
5. Mood swings, irritability, emotional distancing, isolation, and depression.
6. Suicidal thoughts or attempts.
7. Deterioration in physical appearance and health (e.g., bloodshot eyes, runny nose, sore throats, cough, weight loss).
8. Lies or is evasive about plans, activities, friends, and whereabouts.
9. Changes in eating or sleeping patterns.
10. Increased risk-taking behavior (e.g., sexual promiscuity, driving while under the influence, stealing, curfew violation, defiance of authority).
11. Frequently talks about getting drunk or high, and pressures others to drink alcohol or use drugs.

—. _____
   _____
—. _____
   _____
—. _____
   _____

LONG-TERM GOALS

1. Establish a healthy, drug-free lifestyle.
2. Cooperate with a treatment program designed to achieve and maintain recovery from all mood-altering addictions.
3. Connect or reconnect with a supportive drug-free peer group.
4. Family members reduce codependency and establish ongoing encouragement for the student's abstinence.
5. Develop a personal plan to avoid relapse and deal with the temptations of substance abuse.
6. Acquire social skills and coping techniques that encourage feelings of empowerment and healthy self-esteem.

___. _____
   _____

___. _____
   _____

___. _____
   _____

SHORT-TERM OBJECTIVES

1. Parents, teacher(s), and other concerned parties meet with the counselor/social worker to discuss their concerns about the student's symptoms of substance abuse. (1, 2, 3)

THERAPEUTIC INTERVENTIONS

1. Meet with the parents and teacher(s) to discuss concerns about the student's substance abuse; offer support and gather background information about his/her social/emotional functioning, symptoms of chemical dependency, and behavior problems at home or school.

2. Collaborate with the parents and teacher(s) to develop a short-term intervention plan to address potential chemical dependency with the student; enlist the assistance of a drug intervention specialist, if necessary.

3. Provide the student and his/her family with community resources that deal with adolescent substance abuse (e.g., Alcoholics Anonymous, Narcotics Anonymous, Alateen, residential treatment centers, private therapists, rehabilitation clinics).

2. Describe current patterns of use of alcohol, drugs, or other mood-altering substances. (4, 5, 6)

4. Meet with the student to gather personal data and to assess current level of social/emotional functioning and any evidence of substance use or abuse.

5. Ask the student to disclose his/her current level of substance abuse, including the type and amount of substance used, as well as frequency, history, and circumstances of use.

6. Elicit a signed commitment from the student to submit to a drug screening test, or ask him/her to complete the questions in a *Message to Teenagers* (see the Alcoholics Anonymous website at www.aa.org) to address drug or alcohol dependency issues.

3. Participate in a complete chemical dependence evaluation to determine treatment recommendations necessary to address any abuse of substances. (7, 8)

7. Refer the student and his/her family for a complete chemical dependence evaluation performed by qualified professionals to assess the student's current level of involvement with mood-altering substances and to develop treatment recommendations.

8. Support the family and the student in accepting all treatment recommendations deemed appropriate to prevent his/her self-destructive behavior and return him/her to a lifestyle free from substance abuse.

4. Participate in individual and family counseling to address the underlying causes of substance dependency. (9, 10, 11)

9. Review the results of the substance abuse evaluation with the student and the parents, and discuss treatment options (e.g., inpatient treatment, outpatient therapy, family therapy, substance abuse rehabilitation groups, Alcoholics Anonymous). Enlist from the student a firm commitment to a course of treatment, and review his/her progress in regular follow-up sessions.

10. Refer the student and his/her family to a certified substance abuse therapist who will address both the presenting chemical dependence and any underlying causes.

11. Strongly encourage the family to seek counseling and rehabilitation for any family members who have problems with substance abuse that are contributing to the student's oppositional behavior, feelings of despair, and attempts to escape through chemical dependence.

5. Family and concerned

12. Help the parents to compile a list of community

others agree to participate in a group intervention to confront the student's substance abuse. (12, 13, 14)

resources, friends, and family who will participate in a chemical dependence intervention.

13. Teach the parents and other close associates (e.g., drug-free friends, teachers, clergy, relatives, or coaches) about the nature and process of a chemical dependence intervention technique in which the group confronts the student with their concerns and insist upon him/her entering treatment.

14. Record a list of goals for the intervention technique and role-play how each person will present their concerns; have a treatment facility available to work with the student immediately after the intervention.

6. Participate in an intervention in which family and other concerned relatives and friends confront the substance abuse and urge appropriate treatment. (15, 16)

15. Warn the parents and other intervention participants that lies, stories, excuses, resistance, and challenges from the student are to be expected during the intervention technique and recovery process. Help them to prepare for maintaining a loving, yet strong and determined approach in the face of his/her anger and denial.

16. Conduct or arrange for a substance abuse counselor to conduct a chemical dependence group intervention; facilitate the student's immediate entry into substance abuse treatment on

7. Seek medical intervention to determine the need for medication to treat the addiction and assist in the recovery. (17, 18)

8. Identify significant others who have been negatively affected by the substance abuse and who will support recovery. (19)

9. Explore feelings that are related to the chemical dependency, and identify appropriate methods for expressing these feelings. (20, 21)

a residential or outpatient basis.

17. Advise the student and/or his/her parents to consult with a physician to determine the need for antidepressant medication or other medical interventions to treat the chemical dependence.

18. Cooperate with the physician to monitor the effects of antidepressant medication upon the student's attitude and social/emotional adjustment.

19. Ask the student to make a list of significant others in his/her life, including family members, friends, teachers, mentors, and role models, and to rate the degree of support given, closeness felt, or influence that person has (or assign the "Important People in My Life" activity from *The School Counseling and School Social Work Homework Planner* by Knapp). Brainstorm with him/her how his/her substance abuse affects each of these significant others and how each might support a drug-free lifestyle.

20. Explore the student's personal feelings related to his/her substance abuse and its effect on himself/herself and others.

21. Encourage the student to draw pictures, write songs or poems, play music, or use sculpting or sand play to describe his/her personal feelings of sadness, anger, or despair. Assign him/her to share these artistic expressions of personal feelings in a therapy group or during an individual counseling session.

10. Reframe situations that have triggered feelings of despair, anger, or frustration concerning self, parents, family, school, friends, and others. (22, 23)

22. Use rational emotive techniques (or assign the "Reframing Your Worries" activity from the *School Counseling and School Social Work Homework Planner* by Knapp) to help the student to identify situations that have contributed to feelings of anger, frustration, and loss of control and to reevaluate these events in a more realistic and positive manner. (See *A New Guide to Rational Living* by Ellis.)

23. Council the parents to help the student reframe situations that trigger feelings of fear, anger, loss of control, or despair by discussing events rationally and logically with their child.

11. Demonstrate persistence and implement systematic problem solving in resolving academic, social, and family challenges. (24, 25)

24. Assign the student to keep a personal journal detailing daily interactions and challenges that could potentially trigger substance abuse; discuss the journal entries during weekly counseling sessions, and analyze

his/her coping skills, giving redirection and guidance where indicated.

25. Assist the student in developing personal problem-solving skills by recording problems in a personal journal and completing the steps that are necessary for resolution (e.g., identify the problem; brainstorm solutions; list the pros and cons of each solution; select a solution; assess the outcome) (or assign the "Personal Problem-Solving Worksheet" activity from the *School Counseling and School Social Work Homework Planner* by Knapp).

12. Participate in an aerobic exercise on a regular basis to reduce tension and enhance energy level. (26, 27)

26. Encourage the student to participate in an aerobic exercise for one-half hour, three to four times per week.

27. Assign the student to enroll in a physical education class or sports activity to increase his/her energy level and reduce tension.

13. Renew interest in former healthy activities or acquire a new skill, hobby, or interest. (28, 29)

28. Explore with the student the acquisition of a new hobby or developing a renewed interest in a former activity; ask him/her to record his/her progress and feelings in a journal with a descriptive paragraph, drawing, or photo.

29. Brainstorm with the student the interests that he/she now has, that he/she

had in the past, and that he/she will have in the future. Compare the number of interests and activities listed in each developmental stage, and determine how the use of mood-altering substances is correlated to a reduced interest level; discuss how increasing his/her personal level of involvement can help to reduce his/her anger and despair.

14. Increase social interaction with a substance-free peer group. (30, 31)

30. Assist the student in planning for an after-school or weekend activity with a substance-free friend; record the event in a personal journal with a photo, paragraph, or drawing.

31. Assign the student to join a group of substance-free friends for lunch daily and discuss the experience during the next counseling session.

15. Participate in at least two organized or informal extracurricular events or activities per week that are substance-free. (32, 33)

32. Support the student in joining an extracurricular group sponsored by a school, religious group, or community.

33. Assign the student to attend at least two school-sponsored functions per month with a substance-free friend or group of friends. Use a personal journal to plan for the event (or assign the "Planning for Fun" activity in the *School Counseling and*

School Social Work Homework Planner by Knapp).

16. Increase daily participation in class and assume responsibility for completing at least 90 percent of daily academic assignments. (34, 35)

34. Help the student to create a plan for completing all classroom assignments and homework. Assign the student to record the plan and progress made in a journal (or assign the "Assignment Completion Worksheet" activity from the *School Counseling and School Social Work Homework Planner* by Knapp).

35. Reinforce the student's academic, family, and social successes by drawing or photographing a completed project that triggers personal pride (or assign the "Accomplishments I Am Proud Of" activity from the *School Counseling and School Social Work Homework Planner* by Knapp).

17. Attend group sessions focused on increasing self-esteem, expressing feelings, and developing social and assertiveness skills. (36, 37)

36. Refer the student to group counseling sessions that focus on building social skills, healthy self-esteem, and expressing feelings.

37. Assign the student to participate in a conflict management or assertiveness training program to develop interpersonal skills, appropriate assertiveness, and conflict resolution abilities.

18. List the devastating effects of substance abuse upon behavior, relationships, health, and future goals. (38, 39, 40)

38. Ask the student to list the negative effects of substance abuse upon his/her life (e.g., loss of former friends, drop in grades,

family problems, loss of job, lack of substance-free interests, health problems, memory loss, legal problems).

39. Instruct the student to define the process of addiction or chemical dependency in personal terms, by describing his/her initial exposure to mood-altering substances, his/her gradual process of dependency, his/her awareness of the negative effects of addiction, and his/her ongoing recovery process.

40. Assign the student to describe his/her future life as a substance abuser versus a recovered lifestyle and to write or draw the description in a personal journal; process the description during subsequent counseling sessions, adding to the list as his/her personal awareness increases.

19. Parents and other family members gain a deeper understanding of the student's self-destructive behavior, its causes, and treatment strategies by attending counseling sessions, joining a support group, reading recommended literature, and viewing tapes about substance abuse. (40, 41, 42)

40. Assign the student to describe his/her future life as a substance abuser versus a recovered lifestyle and to write or draw the description in a personal journal; process the description during subsequent counseling sessions, adding to the list as his/her personal awareness increases.

41. Direct the student and his/her family to informational resources offering interventions and treatments

for preventing and treating adolescent chemical dependence [e.g., Partnership for a Drug-Free America (www.drugfreeamerica.org); Talking with Kids about Tough Issues (www.talking-withkids.org); Teen Drug Use and Abuse Prevention (www.parentingteens.com); Parents Resource Institute for Drug Education, Inc. (800-677-7433); or National Council on Alcoholism and Drug Dependence, Inc. (800-622-2255)].

42. Assign the student and his/her family to read literature that describes adolescent substance abuse, its causes, and coping strategies (e.g., *Street Wise Drug Prevention* by Jalil or *Field Guide to the American Teenager: A Parent's Companion* by DiPrisco).

20. Parents and teachers increase recognition and encouragement of the student and reinforce his/her active attempts to effectively cope with chemical dependency. (43, 44)

43. Teach the parents and the teacher(s) to recognize and affirm the student daily by noticing small personal attributes and verbalizing an awareness of daily efforts and activities that promote recovery.

44. Meet with the parents, family members, and teachers to prepare them for actively listening to the student's feelings and to reinforce the importance of providing time for emotional expression on an ongoing basis (or assign the "Heart-to-Heart

Smart Talks" activity from the *School Counseling and School Social Work Homework Planner* by Knapp).

21. Define the threats to recovery and maintaining a substance-free lifestyle. (45, 46)

45. Brainstorm with the student the many factors that influenced his/her substance abuse and gradually led to his/her dependency; list the positive factors that can combat these threats to recovery, and discuss how to implement these factors to maintain a drug-free lifestyle.

46. Assign the student to complete the "Antidotes to Relapse" activity in the *School Counseling and School Social Work Homework Planner* (Knapp) to define healthy activities that support recovery.

22. Create a plan for long-term abstinence from all mind-altering substances. (47, 48)

47. Assist the student in developing and signing a contract for both long- and short-term substance-free living. Include long- and short-term goals, support people, and the consequences of recovery versus dependency.

48. Assign the student to complete the "My Contract for a Substance-Free Lifestyle" activity in the *School Counseling and School Social Work Homework Planner* (Knapp) to reinforce his/her commitment to total recovery.

23. Set personal goals, describe personal hopes and dreams, and express optimism for the future. (49, 50)

49. Ask the student to define a vision of his/her life five years in the future, focusing on possible relationships, family, career goals, and personal aspirations, and to record these in a personal journal (or assign the "My Predictions for the Future" activity from the *School Counseling and School Social Work Homework Planner* by Knapp) to reinforce the importance of life's experiences in gaining coping skills and wisdom.

50. Assign the student to interview three classmates or acquaintances who have overcome chemical dependence and list the strategies that contributed to their successfully coping with this condition.

—. _____

—. _____

—. _____

DIAGNOSTIC SUGGESTIONS

Axis I: 305.00   Alcohol Abuse
303.90   Alcohol Dependence
305.20   Cannabis Abuse
304.30   Cannabis Dependence
304.20   Cocaine Dependence
304.50   Hallucinogen Dependence

	305.30	Hallucinogen Abuse
	313.81	Oppositional Defiant Disorder
	312.8	Conduct Disorder
	300.4	Dysthymic Disorder
	309.28	Adjustment Disorder With Mixed Anxiety and Depressed Mood
	309.4	Adjustment Disorder With Mixed Disturbance of Emotions and Conduct

_____   _____

_____   _____

Axis II:	799.0	Diagnosis Deferred
	V71.09	No Diagnosis on Axis II

_____   _____

_____   _____

SUICIDAL IDEATION/ATTEMPT

BEHAVIORAL DEFINITIONS

1. Verbalization of suicide threats.
2. Previous suicide attempts.
3. Overwhelming feelings of depression, pessimism, helplessness, hopelessness, and anger at self or the world.
4. Recurrent themes of death, dying, and morbidity evident in conversations, writing, artwork, music, and selection of reading or viewing materials.
5. Expressed feelings of being better off dead or expecting to not be missed by friends and family.
6. Marked changes in habits (e.g., eating, sleeping, somatic complaints, self-care, grooming).
7. Self-mutilation or other self-destructive acts.
8. Extreme changes in personality (e.g., withdrawal, increased aggressiveness, sudden lifting of depression, high-risk behavior).
9. Abuse of mood-altering substances.
10. Lack of interest in or giving away of personal possessions.
11. Inability to cope with recent personal loss or rejection (e.g., parents' divorce; romantic breakup; death of a parent, friend, pet).
12. Lack of problem-solving skills or the inability to seek support and assistance in dealing with personal dilemmas.
13. Deterioration of academic performance.

—. _____
   _____

—. _____
   _____

—. _____
   _____

LONG-TERM GOALS

1. Alleviate suicidal ideation and eliminate the eminent danger of suicide.
2. Identify feelings of anger, fear, sadness, helplessness, and hopelessness, and work to resolve the underlying causes of the suicidal ideation.
3. Participate in crisis counseling, hospitalization, or other recommended care to manage the current suicidal crisis.
4. Develop life skills, coping mechanisms, and problem-solving abilities that lead to a sense of hope for the future.
5. Develop a support network of family and friends.
6. Stabilize mood swings, eliminate self-destructive behavior and somatic complaints, and establish normalized eating and sleeping patterns.
7. Resume interest in daily experiences, and develop feelings of optimism toward present circumstances and the future.

—. _____
 _____

—. _____
 _____

—. _____
 _____

SHORT-TERM OBJECTIVES	THERAPEUTIC INTERVENTIONS
1. Discuss thoughts and plans of suicide with the school counselor/social worker or other trained professional. (1, 2)	1. Meet with the student to gather personal data and assess the current level of social/emotional functioning by administering a depression inventory [e.g., the Children's Depression Inventory (CDI), the Beck Depression Inventory (BDI), or the Center for Epidemiological Studies Depression Scale (CES-D)] to screen for symptoms and level of depression. Provide feedback

to him/her regarding the test results.

2. Sign a contract to not engage in self-destructive behavior and to contact a counselor or other concerned adult if the urge to die becomes overwhelming. (3, 4)

2. Ask the student to describe any thoughts of suicide, including specific plans, availability of lethal materials, written suicide note, and previous attempts.

3. Elicit a signed commitment from the student to control suicidal urges and to contact the counselor, social worker, other trained professional, or a suicide prevention hotline if the desire to commit suicide becomes overpowering.

4. Provide the student and his/her family with a 24-hour suicide prevention hotline and other emergency access numbers, and insist that these numbers be carried at all times by the student and responsible family members.

3. Parents, teacher(s), and other concerned parties share their concerns about the student's symptoms of depression and self-destructive behavior. (4, 5, 6)

4. Provide the student and his/her family with a 24-hour suicide prevention hotline and other emergency access numbers, and insist that these numbers be carried at all times by the student and responsible family members.

5. Meet with the parents, teacher(s), and other concerned parties to advise them of the student's suicidal thinking, to offer support, and to gather background information

about his/her social/emotional functioning, symptoms of depression or acting out, and previous suicidal thinking or attempts.

6. Collaborate with the parents and teacher(s) to develop a short-term intervention plan to thwart any suicide attempts (e.g., seeking immediate psychiatric intervention, remove all lethal weapons from the student's access, form a 24-hour suicide watch during the crisis).

4. Participate in an evaluation at a psychiatric hospital or clinic to determine if hospitalization is needed to thwart a suicide attempt. (7, 8)

7. Refer the student for a complete psychiatric evaluation to assess the critical level of current suicidal thinking and to develop treatment recommendations.

8. Support the family and the student in accepting hospitalization, if necessary, to prevent self-destructive behavior and return him/her to a safe level of emotional functioning.

5. Seek medical intervention to determine the need for antidepressant medication. (9, 10)

9. Advise the student and/or his/her parents to consult with a physician to determine the need for antidepressant medication or other medical intervention to treat the depression.

10. Coordinate with the physician to monitor the effects of the antidepressant medication upon the student's attitude and social/emotional adjustment.

6. List significant people and the degree of closeness felt to them. (11)

11. Ask the student to make a list of significant others in his/her life, including family members, friends, teachers, mentors, and role models, and to rate the degree of support given, closeness felt, or influence that person has (or assign the "Important People in My Life" activity from the *School Counseling and School Social Work Homework Planner* by Knapp). Brainstorm with the student how his/her suicide would affect each of these significant others.

7. Explore feelings related to suicide, hopelessness, and helplessness, and identify appropriate methods for expressing these feelings. (12, 13)

12. Discuss the student's answers from the depression scales or the personal interview, and begin the process of reframing to build a positive self-image and a greater sense of empowerment; ask the student to explain his/her responses in more detail to establish and clarify possible causes of despair, depression, or melancholy.

13. Encourage the student to draw pictures, write songs or poems, play music, or use sculpting or sand play to describe his/her personal feelings of sadness, anger, or despair. Assign him/her to share these artistic expressions of personal feelings in a therapy group or during an individual counseling session.

8. Reframe situations that have triggered feelings of despair concerning self, parents, family, school, friends, and so forth. (14, 15)

9. Demonstrate persistence and systematic problem solving in resolving academic, social, and family challenges. (16, 17)

14. Counsel the parents to help the student to reframe situations that trigger feelings of fear, anger, abandonment, or sadness by discussing events rationally and logically with their child.

15. Use rational emotive techniques (see *A New Guide to Rational Living* by Ellis) to help the student to identify situations that have contributed to fearful feelings and to reevaluate these events in a more realistic and positive manner (or assign the "Reframing Your Worries" activity from the *School Counseling and School Social Work Homework Planner* by Knapp).

16. Assign the student to keep a personal journal detailing daily thoughts, emotions, personal interactions, and reactions. Discuss the journal entries during weekly counseling sessions, and analyze his/her coping skills, giving redirection and guidance where indicated.

17. Assist the student in developing personal problem-solving skills by recording problems in a personal journal and completing the steps that are necessary for resolution (e.g., identify the problem; brainstorm solutions; list the pros and cons of each solution; select a

solution; assess the outcome) (or assign the "Personal Problem-Solving Worksheet" activity from the *School Counseling and School Social Work Homework Planner* by Knapp).

10. Describe the history and current use pattern of mood-altering substances. (18)

18. Explore with the student his/her history, frequency, and nature of substance abuse.

11. Attend drug rehabilitation or substance abuse classes or group sessions. (19, 20)

19. Refer the student to Alcoholics Anonymous, Al-Anon, a community drug rehabilitation program, or a school-sponsored class to deal with his/her problems with substance abuse.

20. Strongly encourage the family to seek counseling and rehabilitation for any family problems with substance abuse that are contributing to the student's feelings of despair and suicidal thinking.

12. Attend group sessions focused on increasing self-esteem, expressing feelings, and developing social skills and problem-solving abilities. (21, 22)

21. Refer the student to group counseling sessions that focus on building social skills, healthy self-esteem, and expressing feelings.

22. Assign the student to participate in a conflict management or assertiveness training program to develop interpersonal skills, appropriate assertiveness, and conflict resolution abilities.

13. The parents and other family members verbalize a deeper understanding of the

23. Refer the student and his/her parents to a mental health professional, clinic,

student's self-destructive behavior, its causes, and treatment strategies. (23, 24, 25, 26)

or agency for ongoing individual and family counseling to assist in coping with the suicide attempt or ideation.

24. Encourage the student and his/her family to participate in a suicide support group sponsored by the school, a mental health clinic, hospital, or religious group.

25. Direct the student and his/her family to informational resources offering interventions and treatments for preventing adolescent suicide [e.g., American Foundation for Suicide Prevention (AFSP) (888-333 AFSP, www.afsp.org), Suicide Prevention Advocacy Network (SPAN), (888-649-1366, www.spanusa.org), or the American Academy of Child and Adolescent Psychiatry (800-333-7636, www.aacap.org)].

26. Assign the student and his/her family to read literature that describes adolescent suicide, its causes, and coping strategies (e.g., *Out of the Nightmare* by Conroy, *Suicide: The Forever Decision* by Quinnett or *Choosing to Live* by Ellis and Newman).

14. Teachers, parents, and other family members reassure the student about his/her personal security, express an awareness and

27. Meet with the parents, family members, and teachers to prepare them for actively listening to the student's feelings and to reinforce the

empathy for his/her fears or despair, and affirm that they will maintain a supportive and loving relationship with him/her. (27, 28, 29)

importance of providing time for emotional expression on an ongoing basis (or assign the "Heart-to-Heart Smart Talks" activity from the *School Counseling and School Social Work Homework Planner* by Knapp).

28. Assign the parents to read books on the topic of developing additional positive communication skills for use with the student (e.g., *How to Talk So Kids Will Listen and Listen So Kids Will Talk* by Faber and Mazlish or *Parent Talk* by Moorman).

29. Teach the parents or other family members to plan for a time and method of reassuring the student about personal security and expressing awareness and empathy for his/her fears and feelings of helplessness and hopelessness.

15. Reduce excessive daytime sleep, and develop a regular nighttime sleep routine. (30, 31)

30. Assist the student in developing a bedtime routine that reduces anxiety and encourages sleep (e.g., taking a bath or shower, playing soft music, reading a story, repeating a positive self-talk phrase, or counting backward until sleep occurs).

31. Plan with the student and/or his/her parents to develop a daily routine in order to reduce daytime

16. Participate in an aerobic exercise three or more times per week to reduce tension and enhance energy level. (32, 33)

17. Renew interest in former healthy activities or acquire a new skill, hobby, or interest. (34, 35)

18. Increase the frequency of social interaction with classmates and friends to at least once per day. (36, 37, 38, 39)

sleep and promote normal nighttime sleep.

32. Encourage the student to participate in an aerobic exercise for one-half hour, three to four times per week.

33. Assign the student to enroll in a physical education class or sports activity to increase his/her energy level and reduce tension.

34. Explore with the student the acquisition of a new hobby or developing a renewed interest in a former activity. Ask him/her to record his/her progress and feelings in a journal with a descriptive paragraph, drawing, or photo.

35. Brainstorm with the student the interests that he/she now has, had in the past, and will have in the future, comparing the number of interests and activities listed in each developmental stage and determining how depression or suicidal thinking is correlated to a reduced interest level. Discuss how increasing one's personal level of involvement can help to reduce apathy and despair.

36. Assist the student in planning for an after-school or weekend activity with a friend. Ask him/her to record the event in a

personal journal with a photo, paragraph, or drawing.

37. Assign the student to join a group of friends for lunch daily, and discuss the experience during the next counseling session.

38. Support the student in joining an extracurricular group sponsored by a school, religious group, or community.

39. Assign the student to attend at least two school-sponsored functions per month with a friend or group of friends. Use a personal journal to plan for the event (or assign the "Planning for Fun" activity in the *School Counseling and School Social Work Homework Planner* by Knapp).

19. Increase daily participation in class and assume responsibility for daily academic assignments. (40, 41, 42)

40. Encourage the student's teacher(s) to involve him/her in compatible cooperative learning groups.

41. Help the student to create a plan for completing all classroom assignments and homework. Ask the student to record the plan and progress in a journal (or assign the "Assignment Completion Worksheet" activity from the *School Counseling and School Social Work Homework Planner* by Knapp).

42. Reinforce the student's academic, family, and social successes by drawing or photographing a completed project that triggers personal pride (or assign the "Accomplishments I Am Proud Of" activity from the *School Counseling and School Social Work Homework Planner* by Knapp).

20. Parents and teachers increase recognition and encouragement of the student and reinforce his/her active attempts to effectively cope with depression and/or suicide. (43)

43. Teach the parents and the teacher(s) to recognize and affirm the student daily by noticing small personal attributes and verbalizing an awareness of daily efforts and activities.

21. Set personal goals, describe personal hopes and dreams, and express optimism for the future. (44, 45)

44. Ask the student to define a vision of his/her life five years in the future, focusing on possible relationships, family, career goals, and personal aspirations, and to record these in a personal journal (or assign the "My Predictions for the Future" activity from the *School Counseling and School Social Work Homework Planner* by Knapp) to reinforce the importance of life's experiences in gaining coping skills and wisdom.

45. Assign the student to interview three classmates or schoolmates who have overcome feelings of despair and thoughts of suicide and to list the strategies that contributed

22. Describe any experiences of rejection, abandonment, or abuse. (46, 47)

23. Verbalize a sense of personal worth and improved self-esteem. (48, 49)

to their successfully coping with this condition.

46. Explore the student's background for experiences of rejection, abandonment, or abuse.

47. Report any instances of abuse to the proper child protection authorities, as required by law.

48. Facilitate the student in expressing feelings of hurt and alienation that stem from experiences of rejection or abuse.

49. Reassure the student regarding his/her inherent worth, and focus on his/her talents, positive traits, value to others, and God.

___. _____
_____

___. _____
_____

___. _____
_____

___. _____
_____

___. _____
_____

___. _____
_____

DIAGNOSTIC SUGGESTIONS

Axis I: 300.4   Dysthymic Disorder
296.2x   Major Depressive Disorder, Single Episode
296.3x   Major Depressive Disorder, Recurrent
298.89   Bipolar II Disorder
296.xx   Bipolar I Disorder
301.13   Cyclothymic Disorder
309.0   Adjustment Disorder With Depressed Mood
311   Depressive Disorder NOS

	309.81	Posttraumatic Disorder
	V62.82	Bereavement
	_____	_____
	_____	_____
Axis II:	301.83	Borderline Personality Disorder
	799	Diagnosis Deferred
	V71.09	No Diagnosis on Axis II
	_____	_____
	_____	_____

TEEN PREGNANCY

BEHAVIORAL DEFINITIONS

1. Pregnancy is unplanned, the result of consensual sexual intercourse.
2. Fearful regarding the anger, disappointment, and/or rejection that may result from announcing pregnancy to parents and other family or friends.
3. Confused and anxious regarding the significant alteration of educational, employment, and lifestyle goals.
4. Feelings of helplessness, hopelessness, and lack of control of the future.
5. Teen parents are required to determine how to respond to the pregnancy (e.g., getting married, remaining single, releasing the baby for adoption, or choosing abortion).
6. Self-defeating behavior in areas other than sexual activity (e.g., substance abuse, stealing, school attendance, job performance).
7. In need of prenatal medical care, counseling, and information about pregnancy and the birthing process.
8. Requiring financial and emotional support from parents and/or the father of the baby.
9. Victim of abuse, neglect, or maltreatment in the family of origin.
10. A strong desire to be emancipated or independent.
11. Longing to create a loving family or solidify a romantic relationship.

__. _____
   _____
__. _____
   _____
__. _____
   _____

LONG-TERM GOALS

1. Complete valid pregnancy testing and share the results with the child's father and both sets of parents.
2. Attend counseling sessions with the coparent (father of the baby) to assist in responsible decision making and planning for the pregnancy and birth.
3. Acquire prenatal medical care and follow recommendations for a healthy pregnancy.
4. Resolve immediate educational issues for both parents.
5. Involve the baby's father in planning and decision making during the pregnancy, the birth process, and postdelivery.
6. Plan for short- and long-term housing and financial needs.
7. Attend birthing and child development classes with the child's father or other supportive person.
8. Develop realistic personal and family goals, and plan for the future.

—. _____

_____

—. _____

_____

—. _____

_____

SHORT-TERM OBJECTIVES

1. Disclose concerns about pregnancy and get recommendations for a medical facility or private physician for a pregnancy test and health evaluation. (1, 2)

THERAPEUTIC INTERVENTIONS

1. Meet with the student and listen actively and nonjudgmentally to concerns about a suspected or confirmed pregnancy. Answer questions and offer support and the availability of ongoing counseling sessions to assist in coping with the pregnancy and related issues.

2. Recommend that the student see a private physician, hospital, or prenatal

clinic for a pregnancy test and health evaluation; give recommendations, literature, and phone numbers, if needed.

2. Plan how to share the results of a positive pregnancy test with the baby's father and own parents. (3, 4)

3. Assist the student in making a list of people who should be informed of the pregnancy. Discuss the importance of seeking support and involvement from the baby's father and both sets of parents, if possible.

4. Assign the student to record important thoughts, facts, and feelings about the pregnancy that she wants to communicate with the baby's father and other family members. Ask the student to read from her journal or role-play how to tell significant others about the pregnancy.

3. Coparents meet with a pregnancy counselor to learn options for addressing the pregnancy and the baby's birth. (5, 6)

5. Meet with the pregnant student, the baby's father, and their parents to explain the pregnancy counseling process and to encourage their participation and support in making the essential decisions regarding the pregnancy (e.g., adoption, abortion, single parenthood, marriage).

6. Refer the student and her coparent to a private therapist, agency, or pregnancy clinic for counseling, which will present options for dealing with the pregnancy, the baby's birth, and future

parenthood or releasing the baby for adoption [e.g., Parents Anonymous (800-421-0300), the Alan Guttmacher Institute (212-248-1111), or Planned Parenthood (800-230-7526)].

4. Coparents determine which pregnancy option best suits their current feelings, commitment, level of maturity, educational status, financial and family resources, their personal beliefs and values, and those of their families. (7, 8)

7. Encourage the teen parents and their families to record their thoughts and feelings in a personal journal during the decision-making process.

8. Support the coparents and their families during the decision-making period by listening to their feelings and reactions and encouraging them to continue with independent pregnancy counseling until appropriate decisions are made regarding pregnancy, birth, and postpregnancy arrangements.

5. Make an appointment with a clinic or physician for a prenatal examination, and schedule routine checkups as recommended by the doctor. (9, 10)

9. Review the importance of prenatal health care with the pregnant teen and her coparent, and ask if there are personal or family resources or insurance to cover private medical care.

10. Offer a list of medical facilities, private doctors, and community agencies offering medical assistance to pregnant teens (e.g., Planned Parenthood, the Salvation Army, the Pregnancy Crisis Hotline, Pregnancy Resource Center,

6. Keep a personal journal of the events, physical changes, and emotional reactions during the pregnancy. (11, 12)

7. Follow recommended healthy habits, nutritional guidelines, and cooperate with appropriate medical tests during the gestation period. (9, 13, 14)

religious organizations, hospitals).

11. Encourage both future parents to keep a journal of all the experiences of the pregnancy, including physical changes, emotional reactions, problems encountered, solutions, support people, resources, and thoughts and feelings about the pregnancy.

12. Assign the prospective mother to record information acquired from her regular medical checkups (e.g., weight changes; blood pressure; baby's measurements; size, location, and position of the fetus; fetal heart rate) and to share this information during the counseling session and with the baby's father and her own parents. Record any questions to ask the physician at the next appointment.

9. Review the importance of prenatal health care with the pregnant teen and her coparent, and ask if there are personal or family resources or insurance to cover private medical care.

13. Encourage the student to make and keep appointments with a medical practitioner according to the recommended schedule for prenatal care (e.g., weeks 1 through 20: one visit every 4 weeks; weeks 20 through

36: one visit every 2 weeks; weeks 36 through birth: one visit per week).

14. Review with the student nutritional guidelines to follow during the pregnancy, and help her to plan well-balanced meals and snacks that promote a healthy pregnancy; discuss cravings and normal weight gain (approximately 25 to 35 pounds for a single fetus).

8. Read literature or review audio- or videotapes explaining the stages of pregnancy and healthy prenatal care. (15, 16)

15. View a video with the prospective parents to help them understand the process of pregnancy and birth, including fetal development, physical changes of the mother, and ways the father can be involved and supportive (e.g., *The Baby System* by Lifestart Multimedia Corp.).

16. Review the changes in the pregnancy with the coparents by referring to literature describing the stages of pregnancy (e.g., *Your Pregnancy Week by Week* by Curtis and Schuler and *What to Expect When You're Expecting* by Eisenberg, Murkoff, and Hathaway).

9. Verbalize an understanding of the options for completing high school. (17, 18)

17. Outline educational options that are available for the student (e.g., staying in the current school, transferring to an alternative setting that includes day care,

enrolling in a program designed to meet the specific needs of pregnant teens or parents and their children, acquiring a GED, home-schooling).

18. Assign the student to list educational priorities and resources that are available to help attain her educational goals during and after the pregnancy (e.g., transportation, baby-sitters, day care centers, supportive family members, help from the baby's father).

10. Visit available educational programs for pregnant teens, and decide upon the best option. (19, 20)

19. Visit with the student and her coparent community programs that provide an education and other support services for pregnant teens and their babies, and assist them in determining which program is best suited for themselves and their unique circumstances.

20. Assist the student in the enrollment procedures, and support her in the adjustment to a new school setting; complete in-house paperwork to allow her to transfer to a different school.

11. Enroll in and attend prenatal counseling and educational sessions with the coparent. (21, 22, 23)

21. Provide a list of classes (provided by local hospitals or clinics that explore prenatal development, care of the pregnant mother, role of the father, maintaining a healthy lifestyle, and preparing for the birth of

the baby) that are available to pregnant teens.

22. Assist the prospective teen mother in choosing a prenatal and birthing class that is consistent with her preferred type of delivery (e.g., natural, at-home, Lamaze, with or without anesthetic and medical intervention), and encourage her to attend with the baby's father or another supportive and reliable birthing coach.

23. Strongly encourage the pregnant teen and the father to continue with counseling from a private therapist or agency to help them adjust to their changing relationship, responsibilities, and their future as parents of an infant.

12. Develop a plan for coparenting, custody, support, visitation, and other parenting issues. (24, 25)

24. Direct the prospective parents to consider the legal aspects of future parenting (e.g., paternity, custody, child support, visitation, health care), and refer them to a legal aide clinic, if necessary.

25. Assign the expectant parents to prepare a list of legal questions before they seek advice from a lawyer, legal clinic, or family law mediator (or assign the "Legal Aspects of Teen Parenting" activity from the *School Counseling and School Social Work*

Homework Planner by Knapp).

13. Determine appropriate living arrangements and available financial support. (26, 27)

26. Meet with the expectant parents and their families to determine appropriate living arrangements during the pregnancy and after the birth. Assign the coparents to record their available resources and estimate whether there will be sufficient support for themselves and the baby or whether additional resources will be needed.

27. Ask the families of the expectant parents what resources and financial support they are able to contribute during the pregnancy and after the birth of the baby; brainstorm potential solutions for such issues as housing, medical care, living expenses, education, and employment of the expectant parents.

14. Apply for public assistance and other resources designed to support pregnant parents and their families in need. (28, 29)

28. Assist the student in obtaining needed financial resources by applying for such help as public assistance, Medicaid, or food stamps by providing directions to the intake center, helping with the application process, and locating necessary documentation.

29. Help the student to compile a list of community resources (e.g., Catholic Social Services, Lutheran Family Services, Women's Resource

Centers, clinics for women, pregnancy resource centers), which offer help for needed services (e.g., pregnancy and or adoption counseling, day care, pregnancy clothing, baby items), and determine which agencies are most likely to assist.

15. Enroll in and attend child development classes to prepare for caring for and nurturing the infant after the birth. (30, 31)

30. Enroll the student in child development and family living classes provided by the high school or alternative education program.

31. Assign the student to contact community hospitals and family resource centers and to enroll in a child development class along with her coparent.

16. Verbalize an understanding of the underlying emotional reasons the pregnancy occurred. (32, 33)

32. Brainstorm with the student the many reasons teens may become pregnant before they are ready (e.g., family, personal or relationship problems, wanting to become emancipated, friends who are pregnant), and ask her to select the ones that apply to her.

33. Assign the student to complete the "Given Another Chance, I'd Make a Different Choice" activity from the *School Counseling and School Social Work Homework Planner* (Knapp) to identify possible personal reasons behind the pregnancy and to recognize that alternative solutions were and are available.

17. Identify how low self-esteem contributed to becoming pregnant. (34, 35, 36)

34. Administer a self-concept inventory to the student (e.g., the Piers-Harris Self-Concept Scale or the Coopersmith Self-Esteem Inventory) to determine specific areas of low self-esteem.

35. Help the student to verbalize how specific areas of low self-esteem may have contributed to poor choices that led to the teen pregnancy.

36. Encourage the coparents to discuss their relationship stresses and problems during counseling sessions in school, or advise them to continue with their independent pregnancy and family counselor.

18. Develop personal educational, career, and lifestyle goals, and plan for their achievement. (37, 38)

37. Ask the student or coparents to develop a wish list of future educational, career, family, and lifestyle goals; organize these goals on a time line, and develop a plan for attaining the near-term goals.

38. Strongly encourage the coparents to continue their education through high school and college or technical school, if possible. Develop a list of resources needed to enable the continuing education (e.g., day care, transportation, housing, financial assistance).

19. Create a plan for preventing future accidental and/or

39. Assign the student to identify the several options for

unwanted pregnancies.
(39, 40, 41)

guarding against the unwanted results of unprotected sexual intercourse (e.g., condoms, birth control pills, morning-after pill); list the benefits and drawbacks of each birth control method (e.g., offer protection against pregnancy and STDs but at a less than 100 percent rate, need to remember to use during each sexual experience, expensive, need a prescription). (See the Sexual Responsibility chapter in this Planner.)

40. Discuss community medical facilities where information about birth control and protection from STDs can be acquired (e.g., Planned Parenthood, health department, physicians, hospital-sponsored clinics).

41. Remind the coparents that abstinence is a choice that can be made at any time, even after they have been sexually active.

20. Prepare for raising a happy, well-adjusted child and making a life as a teen parent. (42, 43, 44)

42. View the video *Expect More Than a Baby!* (Churchill Films) with the expectant couple to develop an awareness of issues that concern new parents of infants (e.g., sleep deprivation, shift in family dynamics, volatile emotions and postpartum depression, time management).

43. Assign the student or coparents to access websites that give helpful information to young parents and their infants [e.g., the Gerber website (www.geber.com), the Similac formula website (www.welcomeaddtion.com), or the Enfamil formula website (www.herhealth care.com)]. Ask the student to make a list of her preferred websites and to briefly describe them in her pregnancy journal to share with other pregnant teens.

44. Refer the students to a group for teen parents in the school or community for continued support and guidance and for social interaction with teens in similar situations.

—. _____   —. _____
   _____   _____
—. _____   —. _____
   _____   _____
—. _____   —. _____
   _____   _____

DIAGNOSTIC SUGGESTIONS

Axis I: 300.4   Dysthymic Disorder
             314.01   Attention-Deficit/Hyperactivity Disorder,
                        Predominantly Hyperactive-Impulsive Type
             314.9   Attention-Deficit/Hyperactivity Disorder, NOS
             313.81   Oppositional Defiant Disorder
             312.30   Impulse Control Disorder, NOS
             301.6   Dependent Personality Disorder

	300.02	Generalized Anxiety Disorder
	309.21	Separation Anxiety Disorder
	303.90	Alcohol Dependence
	305.00	Alcohol Abuse
	V71.02	Child Antisocial Behavior
	V61.20	Parent-Child Relational Problem
	_____	_____
	_____	_____
Axis II:	799.9	Diagnosis Deferred
	V71.09	No Diagnosis on Axis II
	_____	_____
	_____	_____

Appendix A

BIBLIOTHERAPY SUGGESTIONS

ACADEMIC MOTIVATION/STUDY AND ORGANIZATIONAL SKILLS

Brown-Miller, A. (1994). *Learning to Learn: Ways to Nurture Your Child's Intelligence.* New York: Plenum Press.

Clark, L. (1996). *SOS: Help for Parents* (2nd ed.). Bowling Green, KY: Parent's Press.

Galbraith, J. (1996). *The Gifted Kid Survival Guide: A Teen Handbook.* Minneapolis, MN: Free Spirit Publishing.

Galbraith, J. (1998). *The Gifted Kid Survival Guide: Ages 10 and Under.* Minneapolis, MN: Free Spirit Publishing.

Gordon, T. (1989). *Teaching Children Self-Discipline.* New York: Random House.

Martin, M., and C. Waltman-Greenwood. (eds.) (1995). *Solving Your Child's School-Related Problems.* New York: Harper Perennial.

Rimm, S. (1989). *Underachievement Syndrome, Causes and Cures.* Watertown, WI: Apple Publishing.

Rimm, S. (1990). *How to Parent So Children Will Learn.* Watertown, WI: Apple Publishing.

Rimm, S. (1996). *Smart Parenting: How to Raise a Happy, Achieving Child.* New York: Crown Publishers.

Schmidt, C., A. Friedman, E. Brunt, and T. Solotoff. (1996). *Peacemaking Skills for Little Kids.* Miami, FL: Peace Education Foundation.

Silverman, S. (1998). *13 Steps to Better Grades.* Plainview, NY: Childswork/Childsplay.

ANGER MANAGEMENT/AGGRESSION

Byars, B. (1981). *The Cybil War.* New York: Viking.

Crumbley, J., J. Aarons, and W. Fraser. (1994). *Anger Management Developing Options to Anger.* Eugene, OR: C.A.F. Associates.

DeClement, B. (1981). *Nothing's Fair in Fifth Grade.* New York: Viking.

Meyers, W. (1992). *Mop, Moondance, and the Nagasaki Knights.* New York: Delacorte Press.

Moser, A., and D. Melton. (1994). *Don't Rant and Rave on Wednesdays!: The Children's Anger-Control Book.* Kansas City, MO: Landmark Editions.

Schmidt, F. (1994). *Mediation: Getting to Win/Win.* Pleasantville, NY: Sunburst Communications.

ANXIETY REDUCTION

Brett, D., and S. Chess. (1998). *Annie Stories.* New York: Workman Publishing.

Cary, E. (1996). *Mommy, Don't Go: Children's Problem Solving Book.* Seattle, WA: Parenting Press.

Darcey, J. S., L. Fiore, and G. Ladd. (2000). *Your Anxious Child: How Parents and Teachers Can Relieve Anxiety in Children.* San Francisco: Jossey-Bass.

Davis, M., M. McKay, and E. Robbins Eshelman. (1988). *The Relaxation and Stress Reduction Workbook.* Oakland, CA: New Harbinger Publications.

Ellis, A., and M. Powers. (1998). *A Guide to Rational Living.* North Hollywood, CA: Wilshire.

Fowler, S. L. (1994). *I'll See You When the Moon Is Full.* New York: Greenwillow.

Gordon, T. (1989). *Teaching Children Self-Discipline.* New York: Random House.

Hines, A. (1996). *Keys to Parenting Your Anxious Child.* Happauge, NY: Barrons Educational Series.

Schaefer, C., and J. Friedman. (1992). *Cat's Got Your Tongue?* New York: Magination.

Schmidt, F., A. Friedman, E. Brunt, and T. Solotoff. (1996). *Peacemaking Skills for Little Kids.* Miami, FL: Peace Education Foundation.

Talkington, B., and J. Kurtz. (1997). *Disney Pooh's Grand Adventure: The Search for Christopher Robin.* New York: Disney Press.

Viorst, J., and K. Chorao. (1988). *The Good-Bye Book.* Nesset, Vinterbro, Norway: Atheneum.

ATTACHMENT/BONDING DEFICITS

The Attachment Center at Evergreen, P.O. Box 2764, Evergreen, CO 80437-2764. 303-674-1910. (www.attachmentcenter.org)

Aborn, A. (1994). *Everything I Do You Blame on Me.* Plainview, NY: Childswork/Childsplay, LLC.

Barkley, R. (1998). *Your Defiant Child: Eight Steps to Better Behavior.* New York: Guilford.

Cline, F. (1991). *Hope for High Risk and Rage Filled Children.* Evergreen, CO: EC Publications.

Cline, F., and J. Fay. (1992). *Parenting Teens with Love and Logic.* Colorado Springs, CO: NavPress.

Fay, J., F. Cline, and C. Fay. (2000). *Becoming a Love and Logic Parent.* Golden, CO: The Love and Logic Press.

Keck, G., and R. Kupecky. (1998). *Adopting the Hurt Child.* Colorado Springs, CO: NavPress.

Koplewicz, H. (1996). *It's Nobody's Fault: New Hope and Help for Difficult Children.* New York: Random House.

Moorman, C. (1998). *Parent Talk: Words That Empower, Words That Wound.* Merrill, MI: Personal Power Press.

Moorman, C., and S. Knapp. (2001). *The Parent Talk System: The Language of Responsible Parenting.* Merrill, MI: Personal Power Press.

Moser, A. (1988). *Don't Pop Your Cork on Mondays.* Kansas City, MO: Landmark Editions.

Moser, A. (1991). *Don't Feed the Monster on Tuesdays.* Kansas City, MO: Landmark Editions.

Pickle, P. (1997) *Life in the Trenches: Survival Tactics.* Evergreen, CO: The Attachment Center at Evergreen.

Schooler, J. (1993). *The Whole Life Adoption Book.* Colorado Springs, CO: Pinon Press.

Thomas, N. (1997). *When Love Is Not Enough.* Glenwood Springs, CO: Families by Design.

Welch, M. (1988). *Holding Time.* New York: Simon and Schuster.

ATTENTION-DEFICIT/HYPERACTIVITY DISORDER (ADHD)

Alexander-Roberts, C. (1994). *The ADHD Parenting Handbook: Practical Advice for Parents from Parents.* Dallas, TX: Taylor.

Anonymous. (1991). *About Attention Deficit Disorder.* South Deerfield, MA: Channing L. Bete.

Barkley, R. (1998). *Attention-Deficit Hyperactivity Disorder: A Handbook for Diagnosis and Treatment.* New York: Guilford Press.

Brazelton, B. (1992). *Touch Points: Your Child's Emotional and Behavioral Development.* Reading, MA: Addison-Wesley.

Flick, G., and H. Parker. (1996). *Power Parenting for Children with ADD/ADHD: A Practical Parent's Guide for Managing Difficult Behaviors.* Center for Applied Research in Education.

Gordon, M. (1991). *Jumpin' Johnnie Get Back to Work!* DeWitt, NY: Gsi Publications.

Greenberg, S., and W. Horn. (1991). *Attention Deficit Hyperactivity Disorder: Questions and Answers for Parents.* Champaign, IL: Research Press.

Moser, A., and D. Pilkey. (1988). *Don't Pop Your Cork on Mondays.* Kansas City, MO: Landmark Editions.

Moser, A., and N. Thatch. (1991). *Don't Feed the Monster on Tuesdays!: The Children's Self-Esteem Book.* Kansas City, MO: Landmark Editions.

Parker, H. (1992). *The ADHD Hyperactivity Handbook for Schools.* Plantation, FL: Specialty Press.

Quinn, P., and J. Stern. (1993). *Putting on the Brakes: Young People's Guide to Understanding Attention Deficit Hyperactivity Disorder (ADHD).* New York: Magination Press.

Shure, M. (2001). *I Can Problem-Solve*. Champaign, IL: Research Press.

Stevens, L., and W. Crook. (2000). *12 Effective Ways to Help Your ADD/ADHD Child: Drug-Free Alternatives for Attention Deficit Disorder*. New York: Avery Penguin Putman.

Ullmann, R., E. Sleator, and R. Sprague. (1996). *Conners' Teacher and Parent Rating Scales, ACTeRS*. Plantation, FL: ADD Warehouse.

Wender, P. (1987). *The Hyperactive Child, Adolescent, and Adult*. New York: Oxford University Press.

ATTENTION-SEEKING BEHAVIOR

Aborn, A. (1994). *Everything I Do You Blame on Me*. Plainview, NY: Childswork/ Childsplay, LLC.

Cline, F., and J. Fay. (1990). *Parenting with Love and Logic*. Colorado Springs, CO: Navpress.

Darcey, J. S., L. Fiore, and G. Ladd. (2000). *Your Anxious Child: How Parents and Teachers Can Relieve Anxiety in Children*. San Francisco: Jossey-Bass.

Dinkmeyer, D., and G. McKay. (1989). *Systematic Training for Effective Parenting (STEP)*. Circle Pines, MN: American Guidance Service.

Dreikurs, R., and V. Soltz. (1964). *Children: The Challenge*. New York: Plume Printing.

Fay, J., and D. Funk. (1995). *Teaching with Love and Logic*. Golden, CO: The Love and Logic Press.

Fay, J., F. Cline, and C. Fay. (2000). *Becoming a Love and Logic Parent*. Golden, CO: The Love and Logic Press.

Gardner, H. (1993). *Intelligence Reframed: Multiple Intelligences for the 21st Century*. New York: Simon & Schuster.

Gibbs, J. (1994). *TRIBES: A New Way of Learning and Being Together*. Windsor, CA: Center Source Systems.

Gordon, T. (1974). *Teacher Effectiveness Training*. New York: Random House.

Hines, A. G. (1994). *Even If I Spill My Milk?* Clarion Books.

Knapp, S. (2001). "Positive Discipline, What Does and Does Not Work" (presentation). (asksarahnow@aol.com)

Manassis, K. (1996). *Keys to Parenting Your Anxious Child*. Happauge, NY: Barrons Educational Series.

Moorman, C. (1998). *Parent Talk: Words That Empower, Words That Wound*. Merrill, MI: Personal Power Press.

Moorman, C., and S. Knapp. (2001). *The Parent Talk System: The Language of Responsible Parenting*. Merrill, MI: Personal Power Press.

Moorman, C., and N. Moorman. (1989). *Teacher Talk*. Merrill, MI: Personal Power Press.

Rimm, S. (1989). *The Underachievement Syndrome*. Watertown, WI: Apple Publishing.

BLENDED FAMILY

Cline, F., and J. Fay. (1990). *Parenting with Love and Logic.* Colorado Springs, CO: Navpress.

Faber, A., and E. Mazlish. (1982). *How to Talk So Kids Will Listen and Listen So Kids Will Talk.* New York: Avon Books.

Gordon, T. (2000). *Parent Effectiveness Training.* New York: Three Rivers Press.

MacLachlan, P. (1987). *Sarah Plain and Tall.* New York: Harper Trophy.

Marsolini, M. (2000). *Blended Families: Creating Harmony as You Build a New Home Life.* Chicago, IL: Moody Press.

Monroe, R. (1998). *I Have a New Family Now: Understanding Blended Families (Comforting Little Hearts Series).* St. Louis, MO: Concordia Publishing House.

Moorman, C. (1998). *Parent Talk: Words That Empower, Words That Wound.* Merrill, MI: Personal Power Press.

Moorman, C., and S. Knapp. (2001). *The Parent Talk System: The Language of Responsible Parenting.* Merrill, MI: Personal Power Press.

Roosevelt, R., and J. Lofas. (1976). *Living in Step.* Blue Ridge Summit, PA: McGraw-Hill.

Sargent, J. (1993). *Sarah Plain and Tall Trilogy.* New York: Hallmark Home Entertainment.

Visher, E., and J. Visher. (1982). *How to Win as a Stepfamily.* New York: Brunner/Mazel.

CAREER PLANNING

American Society of Civil Engineers. (1986). *Dream Your Own Dream.* St. Louis, MO: Lindhorst, Keim, and Wilson Advertising/Public Relations. (Video)

Austin, S. (2000). *Focus on Your Future: High School Planning for Career / College Choice.* Lakewood, CO: Focus on Your Future.

Fiske, E. (2001). *The Fiske Guide to Colleges 2002.* Naperville, IL: Sourcebooks.

Gale, L. (1998). *Discover What You're Best At.* New York: Fireside.

Holland, J. (2001). The Career Interest Game. Tampa Bay, FL: Psychological Assessment Resources. (http://career.missouri.edu/holland/)

Hutton, D. (1998). *Guide to Military Careers: Air Force, Army, Coast Guard, Marines, Navy.* Happauge, NY: Barrons Educational Series.

Kennedy, J. (2000). *Job Interviews for Dummies.* New York: Hungry Minds.

Messmer, M. (1999). *Job Hunting for Dummies.* New York: Hungry Minds.

Michigan Occupational Information System (MOIS). (2001). Mason, MI: Ingham Intermediate School District. (www.mois.org).

Nemko, M., P. Edwards, and S. Edwards. (2001). *Cool Careers for Dummies.* New York: Hungry Minds.

Robbins, J., and J. Ellis. (1986). *Self-Image and Your Career.* Pleasantville, NY: Pleasantville Media. (Video)

CONFLICT MANAGEMENT

Byars, B. (1981). *The Cybil War.* New York: Viking.

DeClement, B. (1981). *Nothing's Fair in Fifth Grade.* New York: Viking.

Gibbs, J. (1994). *TRIBES: A New Way of Learning and Being Together.* Windsor, CA: Center Source Systems.

Gordon, T. (1974). *Teacher Effectiveness Training.* New York: Random House.

Meyers, W. (1992). *Mop, Moondance, and the Nagasaki Knights.* New York: Delacorte Press.

Rizzo, S., D. Berkell, and K. Kotzen. (1997). *Peacemaking Skills for Little Kids.* Miami, FL: Peace Education Foundation.

Schmidt, F. (1994). *Mediation: Getting to Win-Win!* Pleasantville, NY: Sunburst Communications.

Sunburst Communications. (1994). *Conflict Resolution Skills.* Pleasantville, NY: Sunburst Communications.

Sunburst Communications. (1994). *Solving Conflicts.* Pleasantville, NY: Sunburst Communications.

DEPRESSION

Clayton, J. (1997). *Lessons from Geese.* Kent, OH: Counseling for Loss and Life Changes. (www.counselingforloss.com)

Dubuque, S. (1996). *Survival Guide to Childhood Depression.* Secaucus, NJ: Childswork/Childsplay.

Faber, A., and E. Mazlish. (1982). *How to Talk So Kids Will Listen and Listen So Kids Will Talk.* New York: Avon Books.

Fay, J., F. Cline, and C. Fay. (2000). *Becoming a Love and Logic Parent.* Golden, CO: The Love and Logic Press.

Miller, J. (1999) *The Childhood Depression Sourcebook.* New York: McGraw-Hill.

DIVERSITY/TOLERANCE TRAINING

Alfred Higgins Productions. (1993). *Different and the Same: That's Us!* North Hollywood, CA: Alfred Higgins Productions. (Video)

Banks, J. (1994). *An Introduction to Multicultural Education.* Boston: Allyn and Bacon.

Delpit, L. (1995). *Other People's Children: Cultural Conflict in the Classroom.* New York: The New Press.

Film Ideas. (1995). *Valuing Diversity: Multi-Cultural Communication.* Wheeling, IL: Film Ideas. (Video)

Gibbs, J. (1994). *TRIBES: A New Way of Learning and Being Together.* Windsor, CA: Center Source Systems.

Knight, M., and T. Chan. (1992). *Talking Walls.* Gardiner, ME: Tilbury House.

Search Institute. (1997). *40 Developmental Assets.* Minneapolis, MN: Search Institute.

DIVORCE

Brown, M., and L. Brown. (1986). *Dinosaurs Divorce: A Guide for Changing Families.* Boston: Atlantic Monthly Press.

Cline, F., and J. Fay. (1990). *Parenting with Love and Logic.* Colorado Springs, CO: Navpress.

Coloroso, B. (1999). *Parenting with Wit and Wisdom in Times of Chaos and Loss.* Toronto, ON: Penguin Books.

Faber, A., and E. Mazlish. (1982). *How to Talk So Kids Will Listen and Listen So Kids Will Talk.* New York: Avon Books.

Gardner, R. (1985). *The Boys and Girls Book about Divorce.* New York: Bantam Young Reader.

Garrity, C., and M. Baris. (1997). *Caught in the Middle.* San Francisco: Jossey-Bass.

Gordon, T. (2000). *Parent Effectiveness Training.* New York: Three Rivers Press.

Lansky, V. (1998). *It's Not Your Fault, Koko Bear—A Read Together Book for Parents and Young Children During Divorce.* Minnetonka, MN: Book Peddlers.

Minnick, M. (1990). *Divorce Illustrated.* Lansing, MI: Pineapple Press.

Nightingale, L. (1997). *My Parents Still Love Me Even Though They're Getting a Divorce.* New York: Nightingale Rose Publishers.

Teyber, E. (1992). *Helping Children Cope with Divorce.* San Francisco: Jossey-Bass.

GRIEF/LOSS

Bissler, J. (1997). *The Way Children Grieve* (article 35). Kent, OH: Counseling For Loss & Life Changes. (www.counselingforloss.com)

Buscaglia, L. (1985). *The Fall of Freddie the Leaf.* Chatsworth, CA: AIMS Media.

Clayton, J. (1997). *Lessons from Geese.* Counseling For Loss & Life Changes. (www.counselingforloss.com)

Coloroso, B. (1999). *Parenting with Wit and Wisdom in Times of Chaos and Loss.* Toronto, ON: Penguin Group.

Faber, A., and E. Mazlish. (1982). *How to Talk So Kids Will Listen and Listen So Kids Will Talk.* New York: Avon Books.

Grollman, E. (1967). *Explaining Death to Children.* Boston: Beacon Press.

Metzgar, M. (1996). *Developmental Considerations Concerning Children's Grief.* Seattle, WA: SIDS Foundation of Washington. (www.kidsource.com)

Moser, A. (1996). *Don't Despair on Thursdays.* Kansas City, MO: Landmark Editions.

Overbeck, L. (1997). *Do a Loss History.* Kent, OH: Counseling For Loss & Life Changes. (www.counselingforloss.com)

LEARNING DIFFICULTIES

Alexander-Roberts, C. (1994). *The ADHD Parenting Handbook: Practical Advice for Parents from Parents.* Dallas, TX: Taylor Publishing.

Cronin, E. M. (1994). *Helping Your Dyslexic Child: A Step-By-Step Program for Helping Your Child Improve Reading, Writing, Spelling, Comprehension, and Self-Esteem.* Rocklin, CA: Prima.

Dwyer, K. (1991). *What Do You Mean, I Have a Learning Disability?* New York: Walker and Company.

Gehret, K. (1990). *The Don't-Give-Up Kid and Learning Differences.* Fairport, NY: Verbal Images Press.

Gordon, T. (1989). *Teaching Children Self-Discipline.* New York: Random House.

Markel, G., and J. Greenbaum. (1996). *Performance Breakthroughs for Adolescents with Learning Disabilities or ADD.* Champaign, IL: Research Press.

McMurchie, S. (1994). *Understanding LD Learning Differences.* Minneapolis, MN: Free Spirit Publishing.

Schmidt, F., A. Friedman, E. Brunt, and T. Solotoff. (1996). *Peacemaking Skills for Little Kids.* Miami, FL: Peace Education Foundation.

Shure, M. (2001). *I Can Problem-Solve.* Champaign, IL: Research Press.

Silver, L. (1991). *The Misunderstood Child: A Guide for Parents of Children with Learning Disabilities,* Second Edition. New York: McGraw-Hill.

Winebrenner, S. (1994). *Teaching Kids with Learning Difficulties in the Regular Classroom.* Minneapolis, MN: Free Spirit Publishing.

OPPOSITIONAL DEFIANT DISORDER (ODD)

Aborn, A. (1994). *Everything I Do You Blame on Me.* Plainview, NY: Childswork/ Childsplay, LLC.

Agassi, M. (1996). *Hands Are Not for Hitting.* Minneapolis, MN: Free Spirit Publishing.

Barkley, R. (1998). *Your Defiant Child: Eight Steps to Better Behavior.* New York: Guilford.

Cline, F., and J. Fay. (1997). *Discipline with Love and Logic Resource Guide.* Golden, CO: The Love and Logic Press.

Dinkmeyer, D., and G. McKay. (1989). *Systematic Training for Effective Parenting (STEP).* Circle Press, MN: American Guidance Service.

Greene, R. (2001). *The Teenagers Guide to School Outside the Box.* Minneapolis, MN: Free Spirit Publishing.

Koplewicz, H. (1996). *It's Nobody's Fault: New Hope and Help for Difficult Children.* New York: Random House.

Mannix, D. (1995). *Life Skills Activities for Secondary Students with Special Needs.* Des Moines, IA: The Center for Applied Research in Education.

Moorman, C. (1998). *Parent Talk: Words That Empower, Words That Wound.* Merrill, MI: Personal Power Press.

Moorman, C., and S. Knapp. (2001). *The Parent Talk System: The Language of Responsible Parenting*. Merrill, MI: Personal Power Press.

Moser, A., and D. Pilkey. (1988). *Don't Pop Your Cork on Mondays!* Kansas City, MO: Landmark Editions.

Moser, A., and N. Thatch. (1991). *Don't Feed the Monster on Tuesdays!: The Children's Self-Esteem Book*. Kansas City, MO: Landmark Editions.

PARENTING SKILLS/DISCIPLINE

Barkley, R. (1998). *Your Defiant Child: Eight Steps to Better Behavior*. New York: Guilford.

Cline, F., and J. Fay. (1990). *Parenting with Love and Logic*. Colorado Springs, CO: Navpress.

Coloroso, B. (1994). *Kids Are Worth It!* New York: William Morrow and Company.

Covey, S. (1997). *The Seven Habits of Highly Effective Families: Building a Beautiful Family Culture in a Turbulent World*. New York: Golden Books Publishing.

Dinkmeyer, D., and G. McKay. (1989). *Systematic Training for Effective Parenting (STEP)*. Circle Pines, MN: American Guidance Service.

Dreikurs, R., and V. Stoltz. (1964). *Children: The Challenge*. New York: Plume Printing.

Ezzo, G., and R. Buckman. (1998). *On Becoming Baby Wise: Book One*. Sisters, OR: Multnomah Publishers.

Fay, J. (1988). *Helicopters, Drill Sergeants and Consultants*. Golden, CO: Cline/Fay Institute. (Audio tape)

Fay, J., and F. Cline. (1994). *Grandparenting with Love and Logic*. Golden, CO: The Love and Logic Press.

Fay, J., F. Cline, and C. Fay. (2000). *Becoming a Love and Logic Parent*. Golden, CO: The Love and Logic Press.

Ford, E. (1994). *Discipline for Home and School*. Scottsdale, AZ: Brandt Publishing.

Gordon, T. (2000). *Parent Effectiveness Training*. New York: Three Rivers Press.

Manly, L. (1986). *Goals of Misbehavior Inventory: Elementary School Guidance and Counseling*, pp. 160–162. Birmingham, AL: American Counseling Association.

Markman, S., S. Stanley, and S. Blumberg. (2001). *Fighting For Your Marriage: Positive Steps for Preventing Divorce and Preserving a Lasting Love*, New and Revised. San Francisco: Fossey-Bass.

Moorman, C. (1996). *Where the Heart Is: Stories of Home and Family*. Merrill, MI: Personal Power Press.

Moorman, C. (1998). *Parent Talk: Words That Empower, Words That Wound*. Merrill, MI: Personal Power Press.

Moorman, C., and S. Knapp. (2001). *The Parent Talk System: The Language of Responsible Parenting*. Merrill, MI: Personal Power Press.

Moorman, C., and N. Moorman. (1989). *Teacher Talk: What It Really Means.* Merrill, MI: Personal Power Press.

Rimm, S. (1990). *How to Parent So Children Will Learn.* Watertown, WI: Apple Publishing.

PHYSICAL DISABILITIES/CHALLENGES

Abeel, S. (2001). *Reach for the Moon.* Duluth, MN: Pfeifer-Hamilton.

Anonymous. (1999). *Disability Awareness in the Classroom: A Resource Tool for Teachers and Students.* Springfield, IL: Charles C. Thomas.

Benton, H. (1996). *Whoa, Nellie!* Columbus, OH: Open Minds.

Carter, A. R., and C. S. Carter (Photographer). (2000). *Stretching Ourselves: Kids with Cerebral Palsy.* Morton Grove, IL: Albert Whitman.

Gardner, H. (1993). *Intelligence Reframed: Multiple Intelligences for the 21st Century.* New York: Simon & Schuster.

Gordon, T. (1989). *Teaching Children Self-Discipline.* New York: Random House.

Heelan, J. R. (1998). *Making of My Special Hand: Madison's Story.* Atlanta, GA: Peachtree.

Heelan, J. R. (2000). *Rolling Along: The Story of Taylor and His Wheelchair.* Atlanta, GA: Peachtree.

Holcomb, N. (1992). *Andy Finds a Turtle.* Hollidaysburg, PA: Jason & Nordic.

Holcomb, N. (1992). *Andy Opens Wide.* Hollidaysburg, PA: Jason & Nordic.

Holcomb, N. (1992). *Fair and Square.* Hollidaysburg, PA: Jason & Nordic.

Moran, G., and N. B. Westcott. (1994). *Imagine Me on a Sit-Ski.* Morton Grove, IL: Albert Whitman.

Schmidt, C., A. Friedman, E. Brunt, and T. Solotoff. (1996). *Peacemaking Skills for Little Kids.* Miami, FL: Peace Education Foundation.

Shure, M. (2001). *I Can Problem-Solve.* Champaign, IL: Research Press.

South Carolina Educational TV Network. (1995). *Just Look at Us Now.* Conway, SC: South Carolina Educational TV Network. (Video)

The Learning S.E.E.D. (1999). *Disability Awareness.* Lake Zurich, IL: The Learning S.E.E.D. (Video)

Uzee, P. (1995). *They Don't Come with Manuals: Parenting Children with Disabilities.* Boston: Fanlight Productions. (Video)

PHYSICAL/SEXUAL ABUSE

AIMS Media. (1993). *McGruff on Self-Protection: Preventing Child Abuse and Neglect.* Chatsworth, CA: AIMS Media. (Video)

Barkley, R. (1998). *Your Defiant Child: Eight Steps to Better Behavior.* New York: Guilford.

Canfield, J., and M. Hansen. (1993). *Chicken Soup for the Soul.* Deerfield Beach, FL: Health Communications.

Cline, F., and J. Fay. (1990). *Parenting with Love and Logic*. Colorado Springs, CO: Navpress.

Coloroso, B. (1994). *Kids Are Worth It!* New York: William Morrow and Company.

Covey, S. (1997). *The Seven Habits of Highly Effective Families: Building a Beautiful Family Culture in a Turbulent World*. New York: Golden Books Publishing.

Dinkmeyer, D., and G. McKay. (1989). *Systematic Training for Effective Parenting (STEP)*. Circle Pines, MN: American Guidance Service.

Dreikurs, R. and V. Stoltz. (1964). *Children: The Challenge*. New York: Plume Printing.

Ezzo, G., and R. Buckman. (1995). *On Becoming Baby Wise: Book Two*. Sisters, OR: Multnomah Publishers.

Fay, J. (1988). *Helicopters, Drill Sergeants, and Consultants*. Golden, CO: Cline/Fay Institute. (Audio tape)

Fay, J., and F. Cline. (1994). *Grandparenting with Love and Logic*. Golden, CO: The Love and Logic Press.

Fay, J., F. Cline, and C. Fay. (2000). *Becoming a Love and Logic Parent*. Golden, CO: The Love and Logic Press.

Ford, E. (1994). *Discipline for Home and School*. Scottsdale, AZ: Brandt Publishing.

Markman, S. (1990). *Being Safe Grades 4–6*. North Hollywood, CA: Filmfair. (Video)

Markman, H., S. Stanley, and S. Blumberg. (1994). *Fighting for Your Marriage: Positive Steps for Preventing Divorce and Preserving a Lasting Love*. San Francisco: Jossey-Bass.

Moorman, C. (1996). *Where the Heart Is: Stories of Home and Family*. Merrill, MI: Personal Power Press.

Moorman, C. (1998). *Parent Talk: Words That Empower, Words That Wound*. Merrill, MI: Personal Power Press.

Moorman, C., and S. Knapp. (2001). *The Parent Talk System: The Language of Responsible Parenting*. Merrill, MI: Personal Power Press.

National Clearinghouse on Child Abuse and Neglect Information. (www.calib.com/nccanch)

POVERTY/ECONOMIC CONCERNS

Alliance for Children and Families. (1998). *FAST: Families and Schools Together*. Milwaukee, WI: Alliance for Children and Families.

Cline, F., and J. Fay. (1990). *Parenting with Love and Logic*. Colorado Springs, CO: Navpress.

Dinkmeyer, D., and G. McKay. (1989). *Systematic Training for Effective Parenting (STEP)*. Circle Pines, MN: American Guidance Service.

Fay, J., F. Cline, and C. Fay. (2000). *Becoming a Love and Logic Parent*. Golden, CO: The Love and Logic Press.

McEwan, E. (1998). *When Kids Say No to School: Helping Children at Risk of Failure, Refusal, or Dropping Out.* Wheaton, IL: Harold Shaw Publishing.

Moorman, C. (1998). *Parent Talk: Words that Empower, Words That Wound.* Merrill, MI: Personal Power Press.

Moorman, C., and S. Knapp. (2001). *The Parent Talk System: The Language of Responsible Parenting.* Merrill, MI: Personal Power Press.

Payne, R. (1998). *A Framework for Understanding Poverty.* Highlands, TX: RFT Publishing.

Schmidt, F., A. Friedman, E. Brunt, and T. Solotoff. (1996). *Peacemaking Skills for Little Kids.* Miami, FL: Peace Education Foundation.

RESPONSIBLE BEHAVIOR TRAINING

Cline, F., and J. Fay. (1990). *Parenting with Love and Logic.* Colorado Springs, CO: Navpress.

Dinkmeyer, D., and G. McKay. (1989). *Systematic Training for Effective Parenting (STEP).* Circle Pines, MN: American Guidance Service.

Dreikurs, R., and V. Stoltz. (1964). *Children: The Challenge.* New York: Plume Printing.

Fay, J., and D. Funk. (1995). *Teaching with Love and Logic.* Golden, CO: The Love and Logic Press.

Fay, J., F. Cline, and C. Fay. (2000). *Becoming a Love and Logic Parent.* Golden, CO: The Love and Logic Press.

Gardner, H. (1993). *Intelligence Reframed: Multiple Intelligences for the 21st Century.* New York: Simon & Schuster.

Knapp, S. (2001). "Positive Discipline, What Does and Does Not Work" (presentation). (asksarahnow@aol.com)

Moorman, C. (1998). *Parent Talk: Words That Empower, Words That Wound.* Merrill, MI: Personal Power Press.

Moorman, C., and S. Knapp. (2001). *The Parent Talk System: The Language of Responsible Parenting.* Merrill, MI: Personal Power Press.

Moorman, C., and N. Moorman. (1989). *Teacher Talk.* Merrill, MI: Personal Power Press.

Rhonke, K. (1984). *Silver Bullets.* Edina, MN: Project Adventure.

Rhonke, K., and J. Grout. (1998). *Back Pocket Adventure.* Edina, MN: Pearson Custom Publishing.

Rimm, S. (1989). *The Underachievement Syndrome.* Watertown, WI: Apple Publishing.

Shure, M. (2001). *I Can Problem-Solve.* Champaign, IL: Research Press.

SCHOOL REFUSAL/PHOBIA

Cline, F., and J. Fay. (1990). *Parenting with Love and Logic.* Colorado Springs, CO: Navpress.

Darcey, J., L. Fiore, and G. Ladd. (2000). *Your Anxious Child: How Parents and Teachers Can Relieve Anxiety in Children.* San Francisco: Jossey-Bass.

Dinkmeyer, D., and G. McKay. (1989). *Systematic Training for Effective Parenting (STEP).* Circle Pines, MN: American Guidance Service.

Ellis, A., and M. Powers. (1998). *A Guide to Rational Living.* North Hollywood, CA: Wilshire.

Fay, J. (1988). *Helicopters, Drill Sergeants and Consultants.* Golden, CO: Cline/Fay Institute. (Audio tape)

Fay, J., F. Cline, and C. Fay. (2000). *Becoming a Love and Logic Parent.* Golden, CO: The Love and Logic Press.

Gardner, H. (1993). *Intelligence Reframed: Multiple Intelligences for the 21st Century.* New York: Simon & Schuster.

McEwan, E. (1998). *When Kids Say No to School: Helping Children at Risk of Failure, Refusal or Dropping Out.* Wheaton, IL: Harold Shaw Publishing.

Moorman, C. (1998). *Parent Talk: Words That Empower, Words That Wound.* Merrill, MI: Personal Power Press.

Moorman, C., and S. Knapp. (2001). *The Parent Talk System: The Language of Responsible Parenting.* Merrill, MI: Personal Power Press.

Moorman, C., and N. Moorman. (1989). *Teacher Talk: What It Really Means.* Merrill, MI: Personal Power Press.

Moser, A., and D. Pilkey. (1988). *Don't Pop Your Cork on Mondays!* Kansas City, MO: Landmark Editions.

Moser, A., and N. Thatch. (1991). *Don't Feed the Monster on Tuesdays!: The Children's Self-Esteem Book.* Kansas City, MO: Landmark Editions.

Schmidt, F., A. Friedman, and T. Solotoff. (1996). *Peacemaking Skills for Little Kids.* Miami, FL: Peace Education Foundation.

SELF-ESTEEM BUILDING

Cline, F., and J. Fay. (1990). *Parenting with Love and Logic.* Colorado Springs, CO: Navpress.

Coloroso, B. (1994). *Kids Are Worth It: Giving Your Child the Gift of Inner Discipline.* New York: William Morrow and Company.

Dreikurs, R., and V. Stoltz. (1964). *Children: The Challenge.* New York: Plume Printing.

Gardner, H. (1993). *Intelligence Reframed: Multiple Intelligences for the 21st Century.* New York: Simon & Schuster.

Moorman, C. (1998). *Parent Talk: Words That Empower, Words That Wound.* Merrill, MI: Personal Power Press.

SEXUAL RESPONSIBILITY

AIMS Media. (1991). *Into Your Heart.* Chatsworth, CA: AIMS Media. (Video)

Alfred Higgins Productions. (1989). *Sex Myths and Facts (Revised).* Los Angeles: Alfred Higgins Productions. (Video)

Alfred Higgins Productions. (1995). *Teens at Risk: Breaking the Immortality Myth*. Los Angeles: Alfred Higgins Productions. (Video)

Center for the Elimination of Violence in the Family. (2000). Peer Program ("Pride + Equality = Respect"). Brooklyn, NY: Center for the Elimination of Violence in the Family.

Copperfield Films. (1981). *Dear Diary*. Boston: Copperfield Films. (Video)

Gordon, S., and J. Gordon. (1989). *Raising a Child Conservatively in a Sexually Permissive World*. New York: Fireside Books.

Hansen, G. (1996). *Sexual Integrity for Teens*. Lexington, KY: Kentucky Cooperative Extension Service. (www.nnfr.org/adolsex)

M.L. Video Productions. (1997). *Everyone Is Not Doing It*. Durham, NC: M.L. Video Productions. (Video)

Mercer, R. (2001). *Adolescent Sexuality and Childbearing*. Sunnyvale, CA: NurseWeek Publishing. (www.nurse.cyberchalk.com)

Scott, S. (1997). *How to Say No and Keep Your Friends*. Highland Ranch, CO: HRC Press.

Strasburger, V. (1993). *Getting Your Kids to Say No in the 90's When You Said Yes in the 60's*. New York: Fireside Books.

United Learning (1990). *Matter of Choice: A Program Confronting Teenage Sexual Abuse*. Niles, IL: United Learning. (Video)

SIBLING RIVALRY

Ames, L. (1989). *He Hit Me First: When Brothers and Sisters Fight*. New York: Warner Books.

Blume, J., and I. Trivas. (1984). *Pain and the Great One*. New York: Simon and Schuster.

Covey, S. (1997). *The Seven Habits of Highly Effective Families: Building a Beautiful Family Culture in a Turbulent World*. New York: Golden Books Publishing.

Coville, B., and M. Moss (Illustrator). (1997). *The Lapsnatcher*. Bridgewater, VA: Bridgewater Books.

Crary, E., and M. Katayama (Illustrator). (1996). *Help! The Kids Are at It Again: Using Kids' Quarrels to Teach "People" Skills*. Seattle, WA: Parenting Press.

Dunn, J. (1995). *From One Child to Two: What to Expect, How to Cope, and How to Enjoy Your Growing Family*. Greenwich, CT: Faucett Books.

Faber, A., and E. Mazlish. (1982). *How to Talk So Kids Will Listen and Listen So Kids Will Talk*. New York: Avon Books.

Faber, A., and E. Mazlish. (1998). *Siblings without Rivalry: How to Help Your Children Live Together So You Can Live Too*. New York: Avon Books.

Goldenthal, P. (1999). *How to Help Your Children Become Cooperative, Caring and Compassionate*. New York: Henry Holt.

Mario, H. (1998). *I'd Rather Have an Iguana*. Watertown, MA: Charlesbridge Publishing.

Moorman, C. (1998). *Parent Talk: Words That Empower, Words That Wound*. Merrill, MI: Personal Power Press.

SOCIAL MALADJUSTMENT/CONDUCT DISORDER

Aborn, A. (1994). *Everything I Do You Blame on Me.* Plainview, NY: Childswork/ Childsplay, LLC.

Agassi, M. (1996). *Hands Are Not for Hitting.* Minneapolis, MN: Free Spirit Publishing.

Barkley, R. (1998). *Your Defiant Child: Eight Steps to Better Behavior.* New York: Guilford.

Cline, F., and J. Fay. (1990). *Parenting with Love and Logic.* Colorado Springs, CO: Navpress.

Dinkmeyer, D., and G. McKay. (1989). *Systematic Training for Effective Parenting (STEP).* Circle Pines, MN: American Guidance Service.

Dreikurs, R., and V. Stoltz. (1964). *Children: The Challenge.* New York: Plume Printing.

Fay, J., F. Cline, and C. Fay. (2000). *Becoming a Love and Logic Parent.* Golden, CO: The Love and Logic Press.

Greene, R. (2001). *The Teenagers Guide to School Outside the Box.* Minneapolis, MN: Free Spirit Publishing.

Koplewicz, H. (1996). *It's Nobody's Fault: New Hope and Help for Difficult Children.* New York: Random House.

Mannix, D. (1996). *Life Skills Activities for Secondary Students with Special Needs.* The Center for Applied Research in Education.

Moorman, C. (1998). *Parent Talk: Words That Empower, Words That Wound.* Merrill, MI: Personal Power Press.

Moorman, C., and S. Knapp. (2001). *The Parent Talk System: The Language of Responsible Parenting.* Merrill, MI: Personal Power Press.

Moser, A., and Pilkey, D. (1988). *Don't Pop Your Cork on Mondays!* Kansas City, MO: Landmark Editions.

Moser, A., and N. Thatch. (1991). *Don't Feed the Monster on Tuesdays!: The Children's Self-Esteem Book.* Kansas City, MO: Landmark Editions.

Shure, M., and T. Digeronimo. (1996). *Raising a Thinking Child: Help Your Young Child Resolve Everyday Conflicts and Get Along with Others: The "I Can Problem-Solve" Program.* New York: Pocket Books.

Wachel, T., D. York, and P. York. (1982). *Toughlove.* Garden City, NJ: Doubleday.

SOCIAL SKILLS/PEER RELATIONSHIPS

Aborn, A. (1994). *Everything I Do You Blame on Me.* Plainview, NY: Childswork/ Childsplay, LLC.

Byars, B. (1981). *The Cybil War.* New York: Viking.

Giannetti, C., and M. Sagarese. (2001). *Cliques: Eight Steps to Help Your Child Survive the Social Jungle.* New York: Broadway Books.

Gordon, T. (1974). *Teacher Effectiveness Training.* New York: Random House.

Graham, S. (2000). *Teens Can Make It Happen.* New York: Simon & Schuster.

Meyers, W. (1992). *Mop, Moondance, and the Nagasaki Knights.* New York: Delacorte Press.

Schmidt, F. (1994). *Mediation: Getting to Win/Win*. Pleasantville, NY: Sunburst Communications.

Schmidt, F., A. Friedman, E. Brunt, and T. Solotoff. (1996). *Peacemaking Skills for Little Kids*. Miami, FL: Peace Education Foundation.

Thompson, M., C. O'Neill, and L. Cohen. (2001). *Best Friends, Worst Enemies: Understanding the Social Lives of Children*. New York: Ballantine Books.

SUBSTANCE ABUSE

Alcoholics Annonymous (1976). *Alcoholics Anonymous: The Big Book*. New York: AA World Service.

Anonymous (1982). *Narcotics Anonymous Big Book*. Van Nuys, CA: NA World Service. Independence Press.

DiPrisco, J. (2000). *Field Guide to the American Teenager: A Parent's Companion*. New York: Perseus Book Group.

Ellis, A., and M. Powers. (1998). *A Guide to Rational Living*. North Hollywood, CA: Wilshire.

Faber, A., and E. Mazlish. (1982). *How to Talk So Kids Will Listen and Listen So Kids Will Talk*. New York: Avon Books.

Jalil, G. (1996). *Street Wise Drug Prevention*. Reading, PA: No More Drugs.

Moorman, C. (1998). *Parent Talk: Words That Empower, Words That Wound*. Merrill, MI: Personal Power Press.

Quinett, P. (1989). *Suicide: The Forever Decision*. New York: Continuum.

Wachel, T., D. York, and P. York. (1982). *Toughlove*. Garden City, NJ: Doubleday.

SUICIDAL IDEATION/ATTEMPT

Conroy, D. (1991). *Out of the Nightmare: Recovery from Depression and Suicidal Pain*. New York: New Liberty Press.

Ellis, T., and C. Newman. (1996). *Choosing to Live: How to Defeat Suicide Through Cognitive Therapy*. Oakland, CA: New Harbinger Publications.

Ellis, A., and M. Powers. (1998). *A Guide to Rational Living*. North Hollywood, CA: Wilshire.

Faber, A., and E. Mazlish. (1982). *How to Talk So Kids Will Listen and Listen So Kids Will Talk*. New York: Avon Books.

Moorman, C. (1998). *Parent Talk: Words That Empower, Words That Wound*. Merrill, MI: Personal Power Press.

Quinett, P. (1989). *Suicide: The Forever Decision*. New York: Continuum.

TEEN PREGNANCY

Churchill Films. (1992). *Expect More Than a Baby!* Los Angeles, CA: Churchill Films. (Video)

Curtis, G., and J. Schuler. (2000). *Your Pregnancy Week by Week*. Cambridge, MA: Fisher.

Eisenberg, A., H. Murkoff, and S. Hathaway. (1996). *What to Expect When You're Expecting*. New York: Workman Publishing.

Holzman, G. (Ed.) (1991). *Planning for Pregnancy, Birth, and Beyond* (2nd ed.). Washington, D.C.: The American College of Obstetricians and Gynecologists.

Lifestart Multimedia Corp. (1997). *The Baby System: Pregnancy and Birth*. Salt Lake City, UT: Lifestart Multimedia Corp. (Video and book)

Spencer, P. (1998). *Parenting Guide to Pregnancy and Childbirth*. New York: Ballantine Books.

Sunburst Communications. (1996). *Real People: Teen Mothers and Fathers Speak Out*. Pleasantville, NY: Sunburst Communications. (Video)

Sunburst Communications. (1989). *Teenage Father*. Pleasantville, NY: Sunburst Communications (Video)

Appendix B

BIBLIOGRAPHY FOR PROFESSIONALS

Achenbach, T. (1991). *Achenbach System of Empirically-Based Assessment.* Burlington, VT: University of Vermont.

ACT, Inc. (1994). *ACT Career Planning Program.* Iowa City, IA: The American College Testing Program.

ACT, Inc. (2001). *Discover Career Guidance and Information Software System.* Iowa City, IA: The American College Testing Program.

Barkley, R. (1998). *Attention-Deficit Hyperactivity Disorder: A Handbook for Diagnosis and Treatment.* New York: Guilford Press.

Bavolek, S. (1990). *A Handbook for Understanding Child Abuse and Neglect.* Park City, UT: Family Development Resources.

Bennett, C. (1990). *Comprehensive Multicultural Education: Theory and Practice* (2nd ed.). Needham Heights, MA: Allyn and Bacon.

Charles C. Thomas Publishers. (1999). *Disability Awareness in the Classroom: A Resource Tool for Teachers and Students.* Springfield, IL: Charles C. Thomas Publishers.

Coopersmith, S. (1987). *Self-Esteem Inventories (CSEI).* Palo Alto, CA: Consulting Psychologists Press.

Cytryn, L., D. McKnew, and J. Wiener. (1998). *Growing up Sad: Childhood Depression and Its Treatment.* New York: W. W. Norton and Company.

Dinkmeyer, D., and G. McKay. (1989). *Systematic Training for Effective Parenting (STEP).* Circle Pines, MN: American Guidance Service.

Dreikurs, R., and V. Stoltz. (1964). *Children: The Challenge.* New York: Plume Printing.

Fassler, D., and L. Dumas. (1998). *"Help Me I'm Sad": Recognizing, Treating and Preventing Childhood and Adolescent Depression.* New York: Penguin USA.

Gardner, H. (1993). *Intelligence Reframed: Multiple Intelligences for the 21st Century.* New York: Simon & Schuster.

Gardner, H. (1983). *Frames of Mind: The Theory of Multiple Intelligences.* New York: Basic Books.

Gibbs, J. (1994). *TRIBES: A New Way of Learning and Being Together.* Windsor, CA: Center Source Systems.

Gordon, T. (2000) *Parent Effectiveness Training.* New York: Three Rivers Press.

Gordon, T. (1974). *Teacher Effectiveness Training.* New York: Random House.

Gysbers, N. (1991). *Missouri Comprehensive Guidance Model.* Jefferson City, MO: Missouri Department of Elementary and Secondary Education.

Hernandez, H. (1989). *Multicultural Education: A Teacher's Guide to Content and Process.* Columbus, OH: Merrill Publishing.

Johansson, C. (1996). *IDEAS Assessment.* Minnetonka, MN: NCS Pearson.

Knapp, S. (2002). *School Counseling and School Social Work Homework Planner.* New York: John Wiley & Sons.

Krup, J. (1995). *Self Esteem: Yours, Theirs, and Ours.* Audiotapes and Presenter's Notebook. ASCD #2-95017v29.

Manly, L. (1986). "Goals of Misbehavior Inventory." *Elementary School Guidance and Counseling,* 21(2): 160–162..

Markel, G., and J. Greenbaum. (1996). *Performance Breakthroughs for Adolescents with Learning Disabilities or ADD.* Champaign, IL: Research Press.

McCarney, S. (1995). *Attention Deficit Prereferral Checklist.* Columbia, MO: Hawthorne Educational Services.

Minnick, M. (1990) *Divorce Illustrated.* Lansing, MI: Pineapple Press.

Myers, I. (2000). *MBTI (Myers-Briggs Type Indicator).* Gainsville, FL: Consulting Psychologists Press.

Papolos, D., J. Papolos, and D. Papolos. (2002). *The Bipolar Child: The Definitive and Reassuring Guide to Childhood's Most Misunderstood Disorder.* New York: Broadway Books.

Piers, E., and D. Harris. (1996). *Piers-Harris Children's Self-Concept Scale (PHCSCS).* Point Roberts, WA: M. D. Angus and Associates Ltd.

Purkey, W. W. (1970). *Self-Concept and School Achievement.* Englewood Cliffs, NJ: Prentice-Hall.

Reynolds, C., and B. Richmond. (1994). *Revised Children's Manifest Anxiety Scale (RCMAS).* Los Angeles, CA: Western Psychological Services.

Rimm, S., M. Cornale, R. Manos, and J. Behrend. (1989). *Guidebook for Implementing the TRIFOCAL Underachievement Program for Schools.* Watertown, WI: Apple Publishing.

Shure, M. (2001). *I Can Problem-Solve.* Champaign, IL: Research Press.

Sonntag, N. (1985). "Cartooning as a Counseling Approach to a Socially Isolated Child." *The School Counselor, 32,* 307–312.

Wallerstein, J., and S. Blakeslee. (1990). *Second Chances.* New York: Ticknor and Fields.

Winebrenner, S. (1994). *Teaching Kids with Learning Difficulties in the Regular Classroom.* Minneapolis, MN: Free Spirit Publishing.

Appendix C

CATALOGUE DISTRIBUTORS OF
THERAPEUTIC PRODUCTS

ADD Warehouse
300 Northwest 70th Avenue,
Suite 102
Plantation, FL 33317
Phone: 800-233-9273
www.addwarehouse.com

Biodot Company
P.O. Box 1784
Indianapolis, IN 46206
Phone: 800-272-2370
Fax: 317-831-0488

Childswork/Childsplay, LLC
P.O. Box 1604
Secaucus, NJ 07096-1604
Phone: 800-962-1141
www.childswork.com

Courage to Change
P.O. Box 1268
Newburgh, NY 12551
Phone: 800-440-4003

Creative Therapeutics
P.O. Box 522
Cresskill, NJ 67626-0522
Phone: 800-544-6162
www.rgardner.com

Western Psychological Services
Division of Manson Western
Corporation
12031 Wilshire Boulevard
Los Angeles, CA 90025-1251
Phone: 800-648-8857
www.wpspublish.com

Appendix D

INDEX OF *DSM-IV*™ CODES ASSOCIATED WITH PRESENTING PROBLEMS

Asperger's Disorder   299.80
   Learning Difficulties
   Physical Disabilities/Challenges

**Attention-Deficit/
Hyperactivity Disorder**   314.01
   Responsible Behavior Training
   Self-Esteem Building

**Attention-Deficit/
Hyperactivity Disorder,
Combined Type**   314.01
   Academic Motivation
   Assessment for Special Services
   Attention-Deficit/Hyperactivity
      Disorder (ADHD)
   Attention-Seeking Behavior
   Social Skills/Peer Relationships

**Attention-Deficit/
Hyperactivity Disorder
Not Otherwise Specified**   314.9
   Anger Management/Aggression
   Assessment for Special Services
   Attachment/Bonding Deficits
   Attention-Deficit/Hyperactivity
      Disorder (ADHD)
   Conflict Management
   Oppositional Defiant Disorder (ODD)
   Parenting Skills/Discipline
   Sexual Responsibility
   Sibling Rivalry
   Social Maladjustment/Conduct
      Disorder
   Teen Pregnancy

**Attention-Deficit/Hyperactivity
Disorder, Predominantly
Hyperactive-Impulsive Type**   314.01
   Anger Management/Aggression
   Assessment for Special Services
   Attention-Deficit/Hyperactivity
      Disorder (ADHD)
   Conflict Management
   Oppositional Defiant Disorder (ODD)
   Parenting Skills/Discipline
   Sibling Rivalry
   Social Maladjustment/Conduct
      Disorder
   Teen Pregnancy

**Attention-Deficit/Hyperactivity
Disorder, Predominantly
Inattentive Type**   314.00
   Academic Motivation
   Assessment for Special Services
   Attention-Deficit/Hyperactivity
      Disorder (ADHD)
   Sexual Responsibility

Autistic Disorder   299.00
   Learning Difficulties
   Physical Disabilities/Challenges

Bereavement   V62.82
   Depression
   Grief/Loss
   Suicidal Ideation/Attempt

Bipolar I Disorder   296.xx
   Assessment for Special Services
   Attention-Deficit/Hyperactivity
      Disorder (ADHD)
   Depression
   Suicidal Ideation/Attempt

Bipolar II Disorder   296.89
   Depression
   Suicidal Ideation/Attempt

**Borderline Intellectual
Functioning**   V62.89
   Self-Esteem Building

**Borderline Personality
Disorder**   301.83
   Suicidal Ideation/Attempt

Cannabis Abuse   305.20
   Substance Abuse

Cannabis Dependence   304.30
   Substance Abuse

**Childhood Disintegrative
Disorder**   299.10
   Learning Difficulties
   Physical Disabilities/Challenges

**Child or Adolescent
Antisocial Behavior**   V71.02
   Anger Management/Aggression
   Diversity/Tolerance Training

Dissociative Disorder NOS   300.15
  Physical/Sexual Abuse

Dysthymic Disorder   300.4
  Academic Motivation
  Assessment for Special Services
  Attachment/Bonding Deficits
  Attention-Seeking Behavior
  Blended Family
  Depression
  Divorce
  Grief/Loss
  Parenting Skills/Discipline
  Physical/Sexual Abuse
  Responsible Behavior Training
  Self-Esteem Building
  Sexual Responsibility
  Sibling Rivalry
  Social Skills/Peer Relationships
  Substance Abuse
  Suicidal Ideation/Attempt
  Teen Pregnancy

**Expressive Language
Disorder**   315.31
  Physical Disabilities/Challenges

**Generalized Anxiety
Disorder**   300.02
  Anger Management/Aggression
  Assessment for Special Services
  Attention-Seeking Behavior
  Conflict Management
  Divorce
  Parenting Skills/Discipline
  Physical/Sexual Abuse
  Poverty/Economic Concerns
  Responsible Behavior Training
  School Refusal/Phobia
  Self-Esteem Building
  Sexual Responsibility
  Social Skills/Peer Relationships
  Teen Pregnancy

Hallucinogen Abuse   305.30
  Substance Abuse

Hallucinogen Dependence   304.50
  Substance Abuse

**Impulse-Control Disorder
Not Otherwise Specified**   312.30
  Anger Management/Aggression
  Parenting Skills/Discipline
  Sexual Responsibility
  Social Skills/Peer Relationships
  Teen Pregnancy

**Intermittent Explosive
Disorder**   312.34
  Anger Management/Aggression

Learning Disorder NOS   315.9
  Learning Difficulties

Major Depressive Disorder   296.xx
  Assessment for Special Services
  Physical/Sexual Abuse
  School Refusal/Phobia
  Self-Esteem Building

**Major Depressive Disorder,
Recurrent**   296.3x
  Attachment/Bonding Deficits
  Depression
  Grief/Loss
  Suicidal Ideation/Attempt

**Major Depressive Disorder,
Single Episode**   296.2x
  Depression
  Grief/Loss
  Suicidal Ideation/Attempt

Mathematics Disorder   315.1
  Academic Motivation
  Learning Difficulties

Mild Mental Retardation   317
  Learning Difficulties
  Self-Esteem Building

**Mixed Receptive-Expressive
Language Disorder**   315.32
  Physical Disabilities/Challenges

Moderate Mental Retardation 318.0
  Learning Difficulties

**Neglect of Child (if focus of clinical
attention is on the victim)**   995.52
  Attention-Seeking Behavior

Blended Family
Conflict Management
Diversity/Tolerance Training
Oppositional Defiant Disorder (ODD)
Sibling Rivalry
Social Skills/Peer Relationships

Rett's Disorder 299.80
Academic Difficulties
Physical Disabilities/Challenges

Separation Anxiety Disorder 309.21
Attention-Seeking Behavior
Divorce
Parenting Skills/Discipline
Physical/Sexual Abuse
Responsible Behavior Training
School Refusal/Phobia
Self-Esteem Building

Sexual Responsibility
Social Skills/Peer Relationships
Teen Pregnancy

**Sexual Abuse of Child
(if focus of clinical attention
is on the victim) 995.53**
Physical/Sexual Abuse

Social Phobia 300.23
Assessment for Special Services
Attention-Seeking Behavior
Self-Esteem Building
Social Skills/Peer Relationships

**Undifferentiated Somatoform
Disorder 300.82**
Divorce
School Refusal/Phobia